LIFE SAVINGS

NAVIGATE THE FINANCIAL COURSE

PI LUNA + EDWARD WORDEN

How To Use This Book ...

At the beginning of every section, there will be a transitional paragraph explaining how the previous section or chapter relates to the new one.

Section Topic

Section Topic

Section Topic

Section Topic

Blackboard Instruction

Throughout the book, you will see a blackboard explanation of how to perform math procedures. The math will be shown on the board and instructions will be shown in the word bubble next to the professor.

Vocabulary

Vocabulary is introduced throughout this course. Each term will be defined with a graphic illustration to accompany it.

Term
Definition ...

Term
Definition ...

Term
Definition ...

Now Do the Math ...

A key feature of this book is the opportunity to practice problems in class and record your work and answers in the book to use as a reference. Answers to these exercises are listed in the answer key starting on page 392.

What Do You Think?

After doing math, you will be asked to reflect on your answers and how they relate to your life and whether they make sense.

The Garcias

The homework for this book follows the story of the Garcias, a family living in Santa Fe, NM. Follow their journey as they make financial decisions and open their own businesses.

Homework

Homework problems will be assigned at the end of every section. The homework includes a combination of working with the Garcias' finances, working with your own finances, and reflecting on your own life experiences.

Chapter 1: Budgets

1A Saving Money

1B Managing Expenses

1C Setting Goals

1D Making a Budget

Section 1A: Saving Money

When you save a portion of the money you earn each month, you increase your financial stability. Saving helps you plan for long-term goals, helps you cover the costs of unexpected events, and reduces the possibility of going into debt. In this section, you will learn techniques for saving money.

Review Percentages

Calculate Monthly Savings

Calculate Long-Term Savings

Create Formulas in a Spreadsheet

WHY SAVE MONEY?

Unexpected car maintenance, house repairs, and medical bills can happen, and paying for them can be a challenge. Saving money prepares you better for life's unexpected events. It also means you are more likely to accomplish long-term financial goals, such as buying a car, a house, or another major purchase.

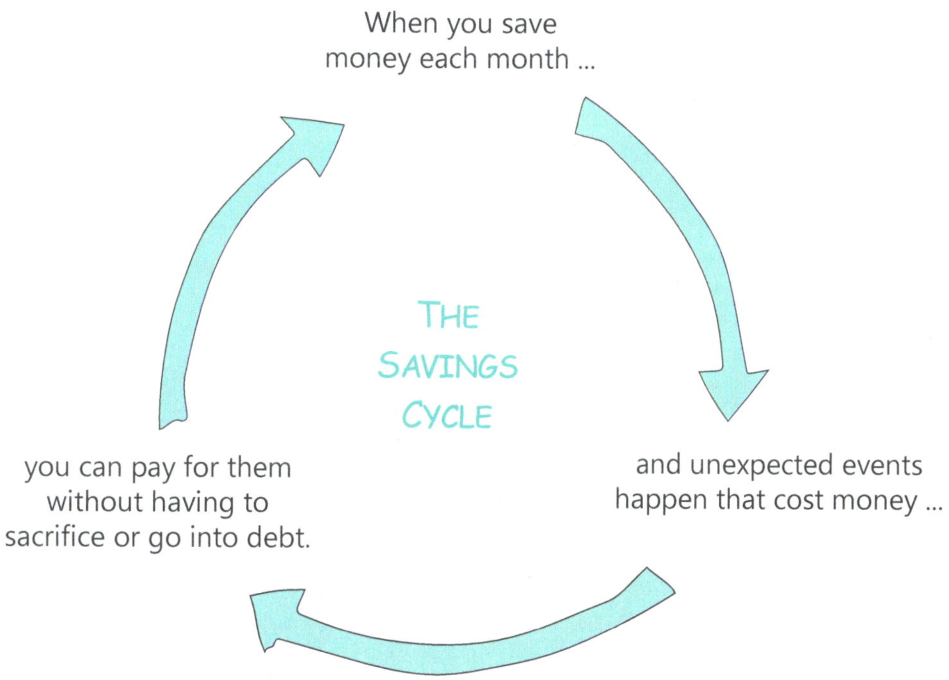

1. Class Discussion ...

A. What are some situations where savings would come in handy?

B. What are some challenges that get in the way of saving money?

C. Do you have any long-term goals you want to save for?

Review of Percentages

You will be using percentages to help you determine how much money to save each month. Percentages are always based on 100. The word percent has the word "cent" in it. Have a look at other words that contain "cent."

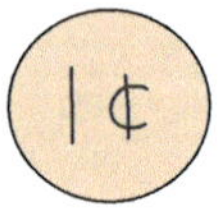

Cents
There are 100 pennies in a dollar.

Century
A period of time lasting 100 years.

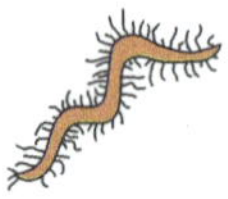

Centipede
A bug with 100 legs (not really, but they do have many legs).

%

Percent
Out of 100.

Percent of a Dollar

One way to explore percentages is to look at money, since there are 100 pennies in a dollar.

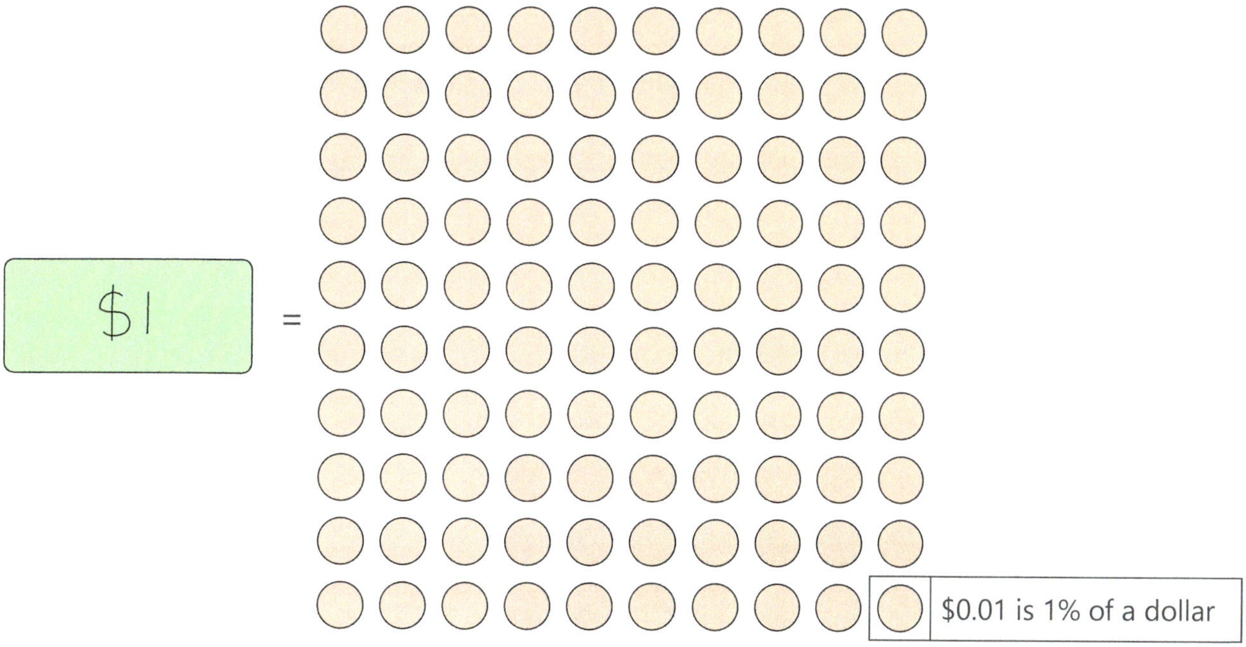

2. Now Do The Math ...

Based on your knowledge that a penny is 1% of a dollar, complete the following table.

Coin	Value	Percent of a Dollar
Penny	$0.01	1%
Nickel		
Dime		
Quarter		
Half-Dollar		
Dollar		

Creating a Savings Plan

The money you save is the money you get to keep. There are many ways to save money. In this section, you will explore a basic plan to get started. Every time you receive a paycheck, financial aid disbursement, or gift, place 10% of it in a savings account and don't spend it.

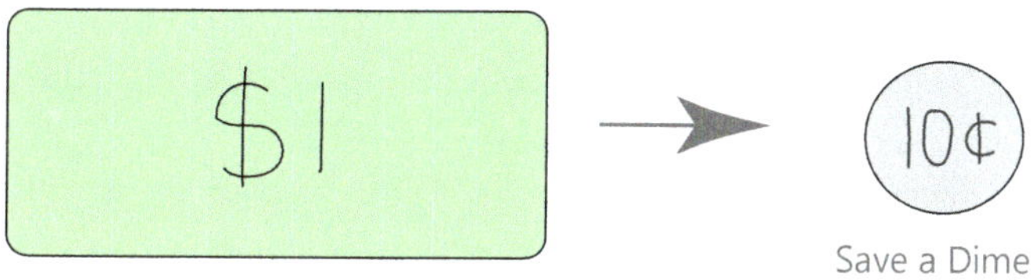

For every dollar you earn

Save a Dime
(10% of a dollar)

Percentages and Decimals

Percentages and decimals have a strong relationship. Being able to turn a percentage into a decimal allows you to make calculations. Since percentages are always based on 100, you can turn any percentage into its decimal equivalent by dividing the percentage by 100.

Calculating Monthly Savings

Now that you know how to turn a percentage into a decimal, you can find 10% of your income. For this example, assume you receive a paycheck of $856.00.

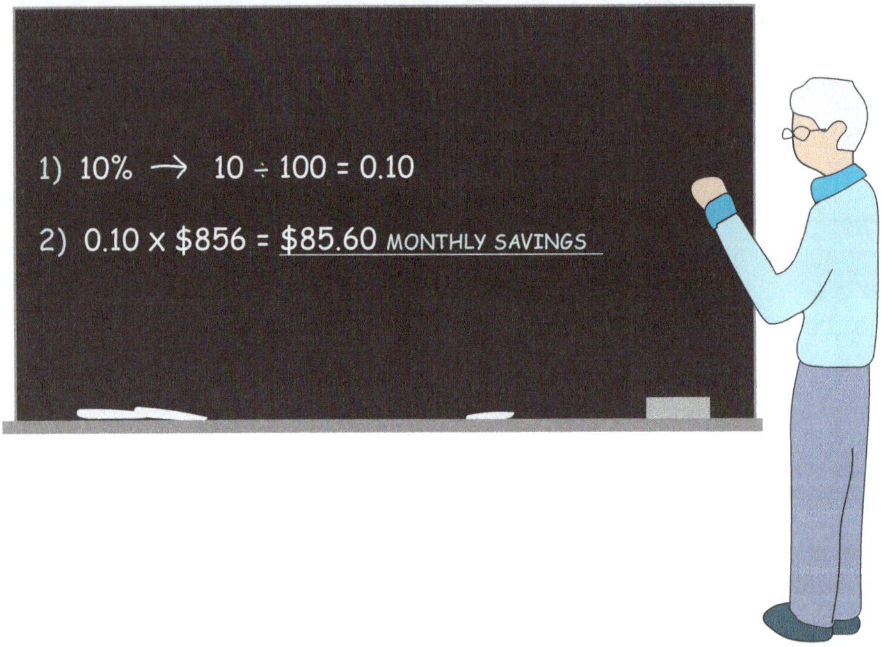

Step 1

Turn the percentage into a decimal: divide the percentage by 100 and remove the percent symbol (%).

Step 2

Multiply the decimal version of the percentage by the monthly income.

3. Now Do The Math ...

Complete the table below to find the 10% savings for each person. Be sure to show how you obtained your result. *Answers can be found in the answer key starting on page 392*

Name	Monthly Income	10% Savings
Sarah	$1,500.00	
Peter	$2,500.00	
Margaret	$1,175.00	
Gene	$3,245.00	

4. What Do You Think?

A. Based on your answers to the table on the previous page, who produced the largest amount of savings?

B. Who produced the smallest amount of savings?

C. What is different about these people's savings? What patterns do you notice?

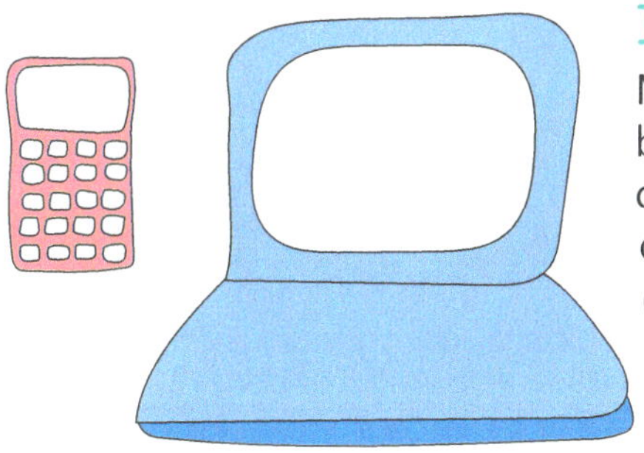

Introducing Spreadsheets

Making calculations by hand requires a lot of paper and brainpower. Using a calculator is convenient, but calculators only show one calculation at a time. Spreadsheets are computer-based calculators that allow you to perform elaborate calculations and save the information. The instructions in this book will work with any spreadsheet program, so become familiar with the one used at your school or work. Some examples of commonly used spreadsheet programs include Microsoft Excel®, Numbers®, Apache OpenOffice, and Google Sheets.

Spreadsheet Basics

Columns

Columns in a spreadsheet are labeled with the letters of the alphabet and run vertically.

	A	B	C	D
1				
2				

Rows

Rows in a spreadsheet are labeled with numbers and run horizontally.

	A	B	C	D
1				
2				

Cells

A cell is the intersection of a row and a column.

		B	C	D
2				

Cell Names

Sports teams wear numbered jerseys to help fans identify each player on the field, and it makes it easy to know who has the ball at a certain time. Spreadsheets are similar; each cell in a spreadsheet has a specific name so you can stay organized.

Naming a Cell

Select a Cell

To select a cell, click inside it. Once it is selected, you can type words and numbers into it.

	A	B	C	D
1				
2				
3				
4				

Cell Names

Each cell has a specific name. Once you select a cell, the column letter and the row number will be highlighted, telling you the name of that cell. In this case, B and 3 are highlighted, so the cell name is B3.

Note: The letter always goes first and the number second.

	A	B	C	D
1				
2				
3				
4				

Using a Spreadsheet to Calculate Monthly Savings

Spreadsheets act like calculators and can help you do math problems. In this example, you will calculate the 10% monthly savings for a person making $850.00 a month.

Step 1

When using a spreadsheet, it is important to stay organized. Start by opening a blank spreadsheet. At the bottom of the page, double-click on Sheet 1 to highlight it.

	A	B	C	D
1				
2				
3				
	Sheet 1	+		

Step 2

Rename it to Monthly Savings and then press the Enter key.

	A	B	C	D
1				
2				
3				
	Monthly Savings	+		

Step 3

Before making any calculations, it is helpful to create some headings to give meaning to your answers and get organized. In A1, type the word Income.

	A	B	C	D
1	Income			
2				
3				

Step 4

Select B1 and type the heading 10% Savings.

	A	B	C	D
1	Income	10% Savings		
2				
3				

Step 5

Once you set up your headings, you can fill in your information. In A2, type your income. In this example, it is $850.00.

	A	B	C	D
1	Income	10% Savings		
2	$850.00			
3				

Using a Spreadsheet to Calculate Monthly Savings

Step 6

Since you want to calculate the 10% savings, you can create a formula. To make any kind of calculation in a spreadsheet, always start with the equals = sign.

	A	B	C	D
1	Income	10% Savings		
2	$850.00	=		
3				

Step 7

Your goal is to find 10% of $850.00. Instead of typing in $850.00, you can simply click on its cell. The cell name, A2, will appear in your formula to represent the $850.00.

	A	B	C	D
1	Income	10% Savings		
2	$850.00	=A2		
3				

Step 8

In order to find the savings, you will need to multiply the income by 10%. Spreadsheets use the asterisk * symbol for multiplication. On your keyboard, press and hold the Shift key and press the 8 key.

Step 9

Then type 10% to complete the formula.

	A	B	C	D
1	Income	10% Savings		
2	$850.00	=A2*10%		
3				

Step 10

Press Enter and the spreadsheet will do the math showing that 10% of $850.00 is $85.00. Save your work as 1A Classwork.

	A	B	C	D
1	Income	10% Savings		
2	$850.00	$85.00		
3				

Conclusion

Spreadsheets can perform calculations and keep your information organized. In this example, you found that 10% of $850.00 is $85.00.

5. Now Do The Math in a Spreadsheet ...

Use a spreadsheet to calculate the 10% savings for each income amount listed. To help you take useful notes for future reference, write both the formula you used and the result in the space provided below. *Answers can be found in the answer key starting on page 392*

	A	B	C	D
1	Income	10% Savings		
2	$5,800.00	=A2*10% ← $580.00 ←	formula used result	
3	$975.00			
4	$1,350.55			
5	$2,249.20			

Savings Will Grow Over Time

In the beginning, your savings might seem small. At first, you might not have enough to go on a nice vacation or respond to an unexpected life event, but your savings will continue to grow over time. Within a few months, you'll start to have enough to feel good about.

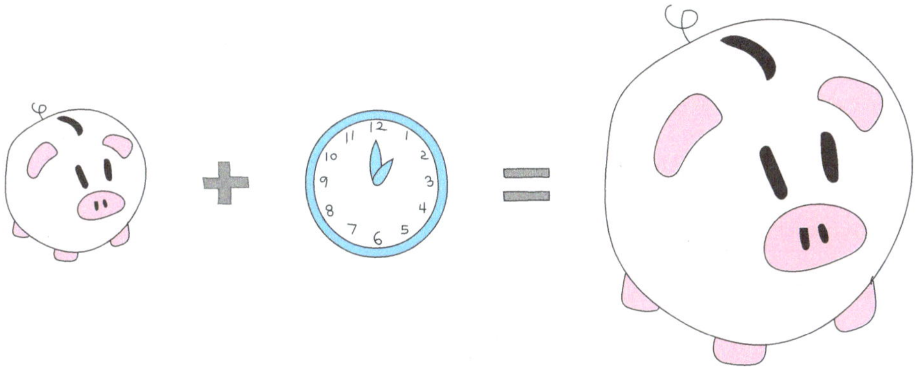

Finding Long-Term Savings

How much would you be able to save if you made $856.00 per month and saved 10% of it for 5 years?

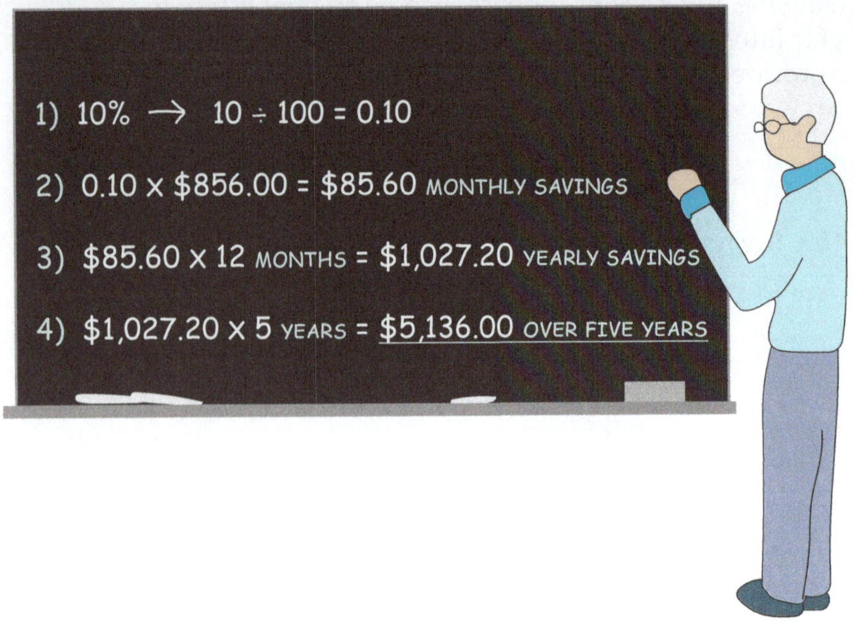

Step 1
Turn the percentage into a decimal by dividing it by 100.

Step 2
To find the monthly savings, multiply the decimal form of the percentage by the monthly income.

Step 3
To find the yearly savings, multiply the monthly savings by 12 since there are 12 months in a year.

Step 4
To find the long-term savings, multiply the yearly savings by the number of years. In this case, use 5 years.

6. Now Do The Math ...

A. Before making any calculations, how much do you think you would have if you saved $100 per month for 2 years? Now perform the calculation. How close were you to the actual amount of savings?

B. Sarah wants to buy a new car. She can save 10% of her income for the next 2 years. If she earns $2,600 a month, how much will she be able to save? Do you think that will be enough to get a new car? Why or why not?

C. What if Sarah decided to save 20% of her monthly income instead? How much would she be able to save after 2 years?

Using a Spreadsheet to Calculate Long-Term Savings

Spreadsheets allow you to make several calculations at the same time. In this example, calculate the 15% monthly savings over the next 10 years with a monthly income of $1,450.00

Step 1

Start by creating a new sheet. At the bottom of the page, click on the plus + symbol next to the sheet named Monthly Savings.

	A	B	C	D
1				
2				
	Monthly Savings	+		

Step 2

A new sheet will appear. Double-click on Sheet 2 to highlight it.

	A	B	C	D
1				
2				
	Monthly Savings	Sheet 2		

Step 3

Rename the new sheet to Long-Term Savings. This step will help you stay organized.

	A	B	C	D
1				
2				
	Monthly Savings	Long-Term Savings		

Step 4

Now select cell A1. Start by typing in only the word Monthly, since the heading Monthly Income is too large to fit in the cell.

	A	B	C	D
1	Monthly			
2				
3				

Step 5

Press and hold the Alt key on your keyboard, and then press the Enter key.
Note: If you have a Mac, press and hold the Option key on your keyboard and then press Enter.

Step 6

The cell will expand giving you more room. Type the word Income. Then press Enter.

	A	B	C	D
1	Monthly Income			
2				
3				

Using a Spreadsheet to Calculate Long-Term Savings

Step 7

Use the same process to create the following headings.

	A	B	C	D
1	Monthly Income	15% Monthly Savings	Yearly Savings	10-Year Savings
2				
3				

Step 8

After creating headings, type in the information you know. In A2, type the given monthly income.

	A	B	C	D
1	Monthly Income	15% Monthly Savings	Yearly Savings	10-Year Savings
2	$1,450.00			
3				

Step 9

To find the monthly savings for the first income amount, multiply it by the savings percentage. In B2, press =, click on the Monthly Income in A2, and multiply it by 15%. Then, press the Tab key.

	A	B	C	D
1	Monthly Income	15% Monthly Savings	Yearly Savings	10-Year Savings
2	$1,450.00	=A2*15%		
3				

Step 10

Your spreadsheet shows you will save $217.50 per month. To find the yearly savings, multiply the monthly savings by 12 months. In C2, press =, click on the Monthly Savings in B2, and multiply it by 12. Press Tab.

	A	B	C	D
1	Monthly Income	15% Monthly Savings	Yearly Savings	10-Year Savings
2	$1,450.00	$217.50	=B2*12	
3				

Step 11

Your spreadsheet shows that you will save $2,610.00 per year (cell C2). To find the savings after 10 years, multiply the yearly savings by 10. In D2 press =, click on cell C2 for the Yearly Savings, and multiply that by the number of years,10.

	A	B	C	D
1	Monthly Income	15% Monthly Savings	Yearly Savings	10-Year Savings
2	$1,450.00	$217.50	$2,610.00	=C2*10
3				

Using a Spreadsheet to Calculate Long-Term Savings

Step 12

Press Enter and the spreadsheet will do the math, showing that you can save $26,100.00 in 10 years. Be sure to save your work.

	A	B	C	D
1	Monthly Income	15% Monthly Savings	Yearly Savings	10-Year Savings
2	$1,450.00	$217.50	$2,610.00	$26,100.00
3				

Conclusion

This example shows how savings add up over time. If your take-home pay were $1,450.00 per month, you could save $26,100.00 over 10 years if you saved 15% of your income each month.

7. Now Do the Math ...

Use a spreadsheet to calculate 8% savings for 5 years for each monthly income amount listed. To help you take useful notes for future reference, write the formulas you use and the result in the space provided below.

	A	B	C	D
1	Monthly Income	8% Monthly Savings	Yearly Savings	5-Year Savings
2	$2,400.00	=A2*8% $192.00	=B2*12 $2,304.00	=C2*5 $11,520.00
3	$6,320.00			
4	$1,350.00			

8. What Do You Think?

A. Based on your results from the chart above, what is the largest amount of savings after 5 years?

B. If you had that much money today, what would you do with it?

C. Do you think it is worth waiting 5 years to have that much money? Why or why not?

Meet the Garcias

Susan and Carlos Garcia live in Santa Fe, NM with their five-year-old daughter, Penny. Carlos earned at degree in Culinary Arts at Santa Fe Community College and has been working as a shift manager at a restaurant downtown. Susan also attended SFCC and earned two degrees: one in Fashion Design and one in Business Administration. Soon after Penny was born, Susan got a job working in an office so she could support the family. Susan and Carlos have completely different schedules, which means they can trade off taking care of Penny while the other is at work, but it also means they don't get to spend much time together. Carlos would love to become a chef. Sometimes, Susan and Carlos feel they have put their career dreams on hold to do what's best for Penny and provide what she needs.

Section 1A: Homework

1. Penny's favorite birthday present this year was a piggy bank she got from Uncle Rob. Penny wants to add money to it and she searches the couch for spare change one afternoon and finds 2 nickels, 3 dimes, and a quarter.
    a. How much money did she find?
    b. What percent of a dollar did she find?

2. While Carlos and Susan were in the kitchen making dinner, they heard a load splash. Penny decided to plug up the upstairs bathtub so it would overflow and make a water slide down the stairs. She had fun, but the water damage will be expensive to fix. Uncle Rob agrees to pay 50% of the $1,864 repair bill. How much do the Garcias have to pay?

3. Carlos is used to being bailed out of situations like this, but Susan feels guilty about having to rely on Uncle Rob all the time. She is committed to paying him back and convinces Carlos to help her start a savings plan.
    a. Susan makes $2,104.16 per month and wants to save 15%. How much does she save each month? Round your answer to the nearest hundredth. *For a review of rounding, refer to appendix B.*
    b. Carlos makes $1,684.94 per month and agrees to save 5%. How much does he save each month? Round your answer to the nearest hundredth.
    c. How long will it take the two of them to pay Uncle Rob back? Round to the

nearest month.

4. Since paying Uncle Rob back didn't take that long, Carlos starts to see the value of saving. He and Susan commit to saving 10% of their combined monthly income regularly.
   a. How much do they save each month?
   b. How much will they have saved up after 6 months?
   c. If you saved up that much money, what would you do with it?

Problems 5-8 explore what the Garcia's could do with their savings. Use a spreadsheet and the instructions on page 28 to complete these problems.

5. One of Carlos and Susan's desires is to travel.
   a. If they continue to save 10% of their income, how much will they have for a vacation in 1 year?
   b. Carlos has always wanted to visit Brazil, but they will need to save more to travel abroad. If they save 15% of their income, how much more will they have after 1 year?

6. Carlos is also concerned about his truck. He thinks it will only last for 5 more years without costly repairs. Carlos proposes that they use their savings to get another car.
   a. How much will they have if they save 12% for 5 years?
   b. Susan suggests that they increase their savings to 18% for 3 years. How much will they have? Round your answer to the nearest hundredth.
   c. Which savings plan results in saving more money?
   d. What would you advise them to do?

7. If the Garcias only save 10% of their income toward the purchase of a new car and Carlos's truck does break down after 3 years, how much will they have saved up? Would they have enough to buy a new car?

8. Both Carlos and Susan had to take out student loans and work while they went to college. Penny is five years old now and they want to save money so Penny can go to college without the same stress.
   a. If they save 11% of their income, how much would they have saved after 13 years?
   b. How much more would they have if they chose to save 15% of their income for 13 years?
   c. Do you think that is enough for Penny to go to college?

In problems 9-10, reflect on your own life

9. What is your opinion about saving money? Write a list of what you believe to be 3 pros and 3 cons about saving money.

10. Think of a time in your life when an unexpected event happened that cost money. Describe the event and how you handled it. How could savings have made a difference? Write your response in 150-200 words.

Section 1B: Managing Expenses

In Section 1A, you learned how to calculate a percentage of your income and explored the benefits and challenges of saving. In order to save on a regular basis, you must spend less than you make. In this section, you will learn how to manage expenses.

- Identify Frequency of Expenses
- Calculate Yearly Costs
- Prorate Monthly Costs
- Understand Needs Versus Wants

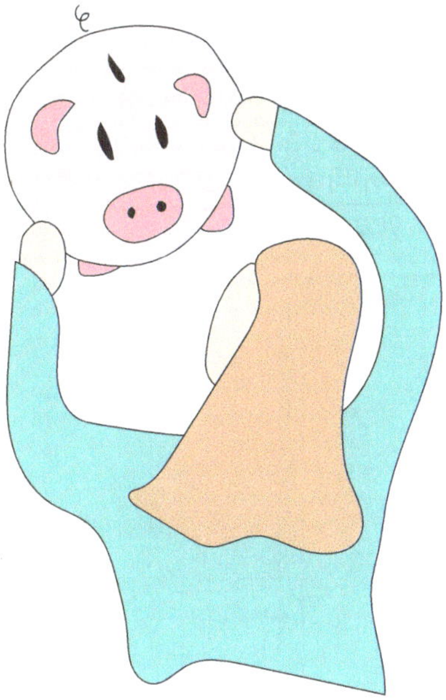

Is there enough money to save?

Income is only part of the wealth equation; expenses are also important. In other words, it's not just about how much you earn, it's about how much of that you can keep. Some spending you have control over, but some you don't. In this section, you will look at the expenses in your budget.

Frequency of Expenses

The frequency of an expense (how often it occurs) is an important part of creating your budget. Below are some common frequencies.

Annually
1 time per year

Semiannually
2 times per year

Quarterly
4 times per year

Monthly
12 times per year

Weekly
52 times per year

Daily
365 times per year

1. Class Discussion ...

In small groups or as a class, complete the chart below with 3 examples of expenses for each frequency category.

Annual Expenses • • •	Quarterly Expenses • • •	Weekly Expenses • • •
Semiannual Expenses • • •	Monthly Expenses • • •	Daily Expenses • • •

Time and Perception

When you see a small price like $3, it's easy to think an item at that price is a great deal. Whenever you look at the cost of an item, you need to also consider its frequency. If it's a daily cost, it will be paid 365 times per year, and that can really add up. The following advertisement for a smartphone explains that it costs "only" $3 per day, but that will add up to $1,095 per year.

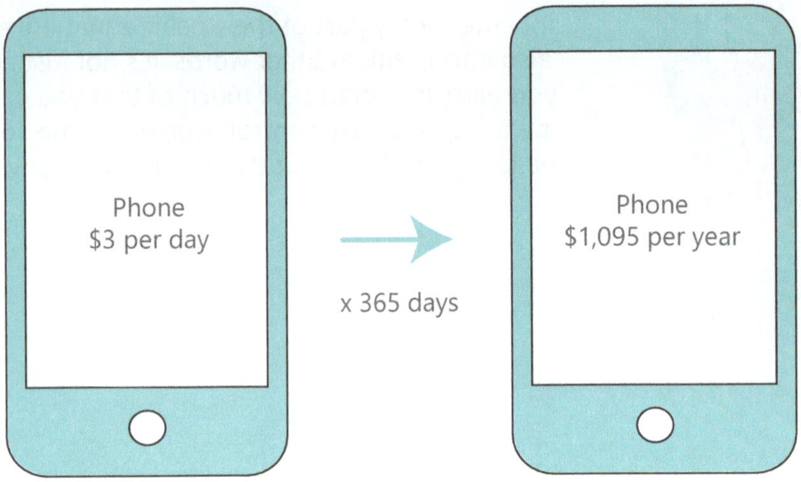

Find Annual (Yearly) Costs

In order to budget effectively, it's important to know how much you will spend in a year. To do this, multiply the expense by the number of times it occurs in a year. For example, let's find the annual cost of a $160 expense that happens quarterly.

2. Now Do the Math ...

A. Before making any calculations, look at the expenses listed in the chart below. Which one do you think will cost the most per year?

B. Complete the following table and write your answers below. Refer to page 27 for the list of frequencies.

Expense	Frequency	Cost	Annual Cost
Haircut	Quarterly	$22.00	4 x $22.00 = $88.00
Car Insurance	Monthly	$55.30	
Lunch	Daily	$5.50	
Holiday Gifts	Annually	$480.00	

3. What Do You Think?

A. Which expense costs the most per year? How does this compare to your answer to part A in the previous exercise?

B. Which expense had the largest difference between its cost and its annual cost? What was its frequency?

C. Why do you think there was such a big difference for this expense?

Use a Spreadsheet to Calculate Annual (Yearly) Costs

Use a spreadsheet to calculate the annual costs for the following expenses: groceries that cost $138.50 weekly, monthly rent of $975.00, and daily coffee that costs $3.25.

Step 1

Open a blank spreadsheet. At the bottom of the page, double-click on Sheet1 to highlight it.

	A	B	C	D
1				
2				
3				
	Sheet 1	+		

Step 2

Rename it to Calculate Annual Costs. Press Enter.

	A	B	C	D
1				
2				
3				
	Calculate Annual Costs	+		

Step 3

Before making any calculations, create some headings. Start in A1 and type in the following headings.

	A	B	C	D
1	Expense	Frequency	Cost	Annual Cost
2				
3				

Step 4

In column A, type in the name of each of your expenses.

	A	B	C	D
1	Expense	Frequency	Cost	Annual Cost
2	Groceries			
3	Rent			
4	Coffee			

Step 5

Next to each expense, type in the frequency for that expense. Refer to page 27 for the list of frequencies.

	A	B	C	D
1	Expense	Frequency	Cost	Annual Cost
2	Groceries	52		
3	Rent	12		
4	Coffee	365		

Step 6

Type in the cost for each expense.

	A	B	C	D
1	Expense	Frequency	Cost	Annual Cost
2	Groceries	52	$138.50	
3	Rent	12	$975.00	
4	Coffee	365	$3.25	

Use a Spreadsheet to Calculate Annual (Yearly) Costs

Step 7

Calculate the annual cost by multiplying the frequency of the expense by its cost. In D2 press equals (=), click on the Frequency in B2 and multiply it by the Cost in C2.

	A	B	C	D
1	Expense	Frequency	Cost	Annual Cost
2	Groceries	52	$138.50	=B2*C2
3	Rent	12	$975.00	
4	Coffee	365	$3.25	

Step 8

Press Enter and the spreadsheet will make the calculation, showing that you will pay $7,202.00 for groceries over the year.

	A	B	C	D
1	Expense	Frequency	Cost	Annual Cost
2	Groceries	52	$138.50	$7,202.00
3	Rent	12	$975.00	
4	Coffee	365	$3.25	

Step 9

Your spreadsheet can make the rest of the calculations for you. Start by selecting cell D2 and double-click on the fill handle.

	A	B	C	D
1	Expense	Frequency	Cost	Annual Cost
2	Groceries	52	$138.50	$7,202.00
3	Rent	12	$975.00	
4	Coffee	365	$3.25	DOUBLE-CLICK HERE

Step 10

Your spreadsheet will complete the calculations for the rest of the expenses. Save your file as 1B Classwork.

	A	B	C	D
1	Expense	Frequency	Cost	Annual Cost
2	Groceries	52	$138.50	$7,202.00
3	Rent	12	$975.00	$11,700.00
4	Coffee	365	$3.25	$1,186.25

Conclusion

When creating formulas, spreadsheets allow you to multiply different cells together. In this example, you found that groceries cost $7,202 per year, rent costs $11,700 per year, and daily coffee costs $1,186.25 per year.

4. Now Do the Math in a Spreadsheet ...

Use a spreadsheet to calculate the annual cost of the following expenses: weekly gas purchases of $33, a monthly phone bill of $89, and semiannual dental appointments that cost $120. To help you take useful notes for future reference, write both the formula you used and the result in the spaces provided below.

	A	B	C	D
1	Expense	Frequency	Amount	Annual cost
2	Gas	52	$33.00	=B2*C2 $1,716.00
3	Phone Bill			
4	Dentist			

Too Much Time

A year is often too long to keep track of a budget, so it's important to see how much money you need to set aside each month to cover your expenses without using your savings. Even though you don't pay your dentist monthly, you have to account for it in your budget so you have the money when the time comes. Figuring out how much you need to set aside each month for less frequent expenses is called prorating.

5. What Do You Think?

A. Would you rather pay for a house monthly or yearly? Explain why.

B. What are the advantages of thinking about expenses monthly rather than yearly?

Managing Expenses

In order to effectively manage expenses in your budget, you need to know the one-time cost of an expense, how frequently it occurs and its prorated cost. The most common budget to make is a monthly budget, so this section will focus on how expenses affect your monthly budget as you plan for them.

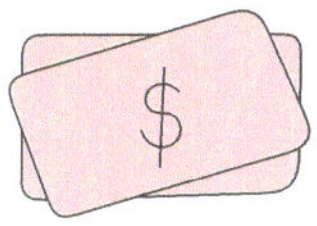

Cost

You can budget for an expense when you know its one-time cost. Knowing an expense's one-time cost will help you find its annual cost and budget accordingly.

Frequency

An expense's one-time cost only tells you part of how much it really costs in your monthly budget. Knowing the frequency of an expense allows you to plan for the expense in your monthly budget.

Prorating

Prorating allows you to see how much an expense costs over a certain period of time. In this section, you will focus on the monthly prorated cost in order to make a monthly budget, but you can prorate expenses for a week, a day, an hour, or any other time period.

Prorate Monthly Costs

You can prorate your expenses to see how much they cost you each month. To do this, you will divide the yearly expense by 12 because there are 12 months in a year. Let's prorate a dental expense of $115 that happens semiannually to see the average monthly cost.

Step 1

Determine the frequency of the expense.

Step 2

Find the annual cost by multiplying the frequency by the cost.

Step 3

Find the monthly cost by dividing the annual cost by 12.

Step 4

Since the answer did not come out evenly, round to the nearest hundredth. *For a review of rounding, refer to Appendix B.*

6. Now Do the Math ...

A. Carlos gets an oil change quarterly and pays $65 for the service. Prorate his monthly cost for oil changes. Round your answer to the nearest hundredth. *For a review of rounding, refer to Appendix B.*

B. Once each year, Susan has to renew her car registration, which costs $85. How much does she need to save each month to cover the cost? Round your answer to the nearest hundredth. *For a review of rounding, refer to Appendix B.*

Use a Spreadsheet to Prorate Monthly Costs

Since expenses happen at different times and intervals throughout the year, prorating your monthly expenses will help you create a budget. Use a spreadsheet to prorate the monthly cost for the expenses used in the previous spreadsheet example on page 30.

Step 1

Open the file named 1B Classwork in which you found your annual costs.

	A	B	C	D	E
1	Expense	Frequency	Cost	Annual Cost	
2	Groceries	52	$138.50	$7,202.00	
3	Rent	12	$975.00	$11,700.00	
4	Coffee	365	$3.25	$1,186.25	

Step 2

When you prorate your expenses, you find the average cost each month. In E1, create a new heading called Monthly Cost.

	A	B	C	D	E
1	Expense	Frequency	Cost	Annual Cost	Monthly Cost
2	Groceries	52	$138.50	$7,202.00	
3	Rent	12	$975.00	$11,700.00	
4	Coffee	365	$3.25	$1,186.25	

Step 3

To find the monthly cost, divide the annual cost by 12. In E2, press =, click on the Annual Cost in D2, and divide / it by 12.

	A	B	C	D	E
1	Expense	Frequency	Cost	Annual Cost	Monthly Cost
2	Groceries	52	$138.50	$7,202.00	=D2/12
3	Rent	12	$975.00	$11,700.00	
4	Coffee	365	$3.25	$1,186.25	

Use a Spreadsheet to Prorate Monthly Costs

Step 4

When you press Enter, the spreadsheet will make the calculation showing that the monthly cost of groceries is $600.17.

	A	B	C	D	E
1	Expense	Frequency	Cost	Annual Cost	Monthly Cost
2	Groceries	52	$138.50	$7,202.00	$600.17
3	Rent	12	$975	$11,700.00	
4	Coffee	365	$3.25	$1,186.25	

Step 5

To complete the rest of the calculations. Select E2 and double-click on the fill handle.

	A	B	C	D	E
1	Expense	Frequency	Cost	Annual Cost	Monthly Cost
2	Groceries	52	$138.50	$7,202.00	$600.17
3	Rent	12	$975.00	$11,700.00	
4	Coffee	365	$3.25	$1,186.25	

Double-click here

Step 6

Your spreadsheet will complete the rest of the calculations. Be sure to save your work.

	A	B	C	D	E
1	Expense	Frequency	Cost	Annual Cost	Monthly Cost
2	Groceries	52	$138.50	$7,202.00	$600.17
3	Rent	12	$975.00	$11,700.00	$975.00
4	Coffee	365	$3.25	$1,186.25	$98.85

Conclusion

In this example, groceries cost $600.17 per month, rent costs $975.00 per month, and daily coffee costs $98.85 per month.

7. Now Do the Math in a Spreadsheet ...

Use a spreadsheet to find the prorated monthly cost of the following expenses: monthly movie subscription that costs $16.95, annual birthday gifts that cost $350 and daily lunch in the cafeteria that costs $6 (assume 365 days each year). To help you take useful notes for future reference, write both the formula used and the result in the spaces provided below.

	A	B	C	D	E
1	Expense	Frequency	Cost	Annual Cost	Monthly Cost
2	Movie Subscription				
3	Birthday Gifts				
4	Lunch				

Needs Versus Wants: Finding the Balance

You can classify your expenses as two major kinds: needs and wants. Rent is usually considered a need since you need somewhere to live. Buying a new phone is usually considered a want, since you don't always need the newest phone. Deciding which expenses are needs and which are wants has a lot to do with personal preferences. Staying home instead of going out for dinner and a movie probably won't negatively affect your quality of life, but it could help you save for long-term financial goals and make you happier in the long run.

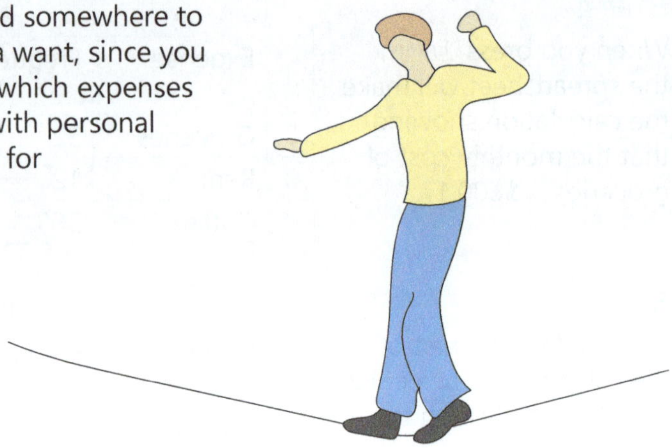

8. What Do You Think?

A. What would happen if you only paid for your needs and ignored your wants?

B. What would happen if you only paid for your wants and ignored your needs?

C. How are you able to maintain this balance in your own life?

9. Class Discussion ...

Decide whether each of the following expenses is a need or want. Choose a couple of your own for the last two options. Then explain why. Discuss your results as a class, or in small groups. *Note: there are no right or wrong answers to this exercise.*

Expense	Need	Want	Explain why
1. Rent/Mortgage	✓		If you do not pay rent, you will not have a place to live.
2. Car Payment			
3. Health Insurance			
4. Internet Access			
5. Childcare			
6. Eating Out			
7. Daily Coffee			
8. Gym Membership			
9. New Clothes			
10. Car Insurance			
11. Going to the Movies			
12. Cable TV			
13. Smartphone			
14. Music Downloads			
15. Dental Appointments			
16. Retirement Savings			
17.			
18.			

Is Food a Need or a Want?

You need to eat food to live, but how much you spend on food depends upon where you eat and the kind of food you're eating. Food is an expense that can vary dramatically and affect your ability to save for long-term financial goals.

10. Now Do the Math in a Spreadsheet ...

A. Before making any calculations, do you think it's cheaper to eat in the cafeteria, pack your lunch, or go out for fast food?

B. Use a spreadsheet to find the monthly cost for the following lunch options: eating in the cafeteria for $7.85 daily, packing your lunch for $20 weekly, or getting fast food for $4.35 daily. Record both the formula you used and your results below.

	A	B	C	D	E
1	Expense	Frequency	Amount	Annual cost	Monthly Cost
2	Cafeteria				
3	Packed Lunch				
4	Fast Food				

11. What Do You Think?

A. Based on your answers to the chart above, which lunch option costs the most each month?

B. Which costs the least?

Sales Tax

Sales tax is paid on certain goods and services. It varies by location based on state, county, and municipal tax rates. In 2015, in the city of Santa Fe, the total sales tax paid is 8.1875%, which includes the state's base rate of 5.125% and the additional county and city taxes. Items exempt from sales tax include unprepared food. Usually, sales tax is added to the price of an item at the point of purchase.

THE PRICE OF YOUR GOODS
$35.00

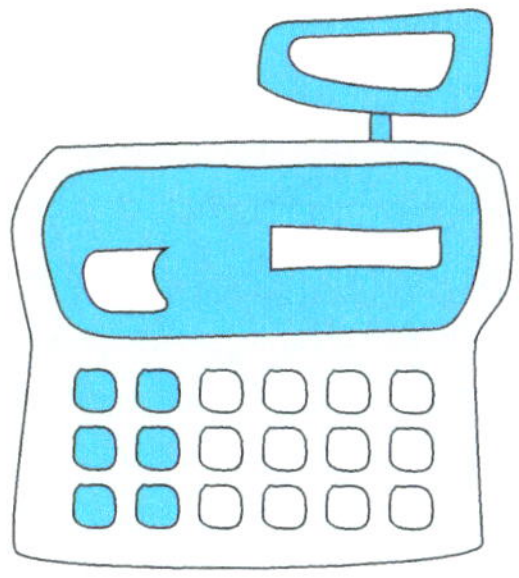

SALES TAX IS ADDED
8.1875%
0.081875 x $35.00
= $2.87

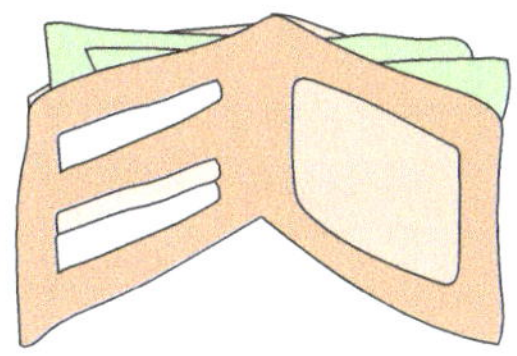

WHAT YOU PAY
$35.00 + $2.87
= $37.87

12. Now Do the Math ...

A. All prepared foods incur sales tax, but groceries do not. Calculate the sales tax on your monthly costs for the cafeteria and fast food purchases in the example on the previous page. Round your answers to the nearest hundredth. *For a review of rounding, refer to Appendix B.*

Cafeteria = ____________________

Fast Food = ____________________

B. How much will you pay for each lunch option when you include sales tax?

Cafeteria = ____________________

Packed Lunch = ________________

Fast Food = ____________________

Affording Daycare

An opening for a daytime sous chef has opened up at the restaurant where Carlos works and he wants to apply. This would mean that he would get back in the kitchen doing what he loves, but it also means the Garcias would have to afford daycare for Penny. They want to decide that the benefits of evening family time and Carlos pursuing his passion are worth it. Help the Garcias find a way to afford daycare for Penny!

Section 1B: Homework

1. Penny Garcia needs to go to daycare while her parents are at work. The daycare center charges $515 per month. How much will the Garcias spend on daycare in a year?

2. Carlos Garcia eats his lunches at the restaurant where he works. With his employee discount, he pays about $7.89 each day and he works 5 days a week. Given that there are 52 weeks in a year, how much does he spend each year?

3. If Carlos packed his own lunch every day, he would spend $14.00 a week on lunch.
    a. How much would he spend a year?
    b. How much would Carlos save by packing his lunch every day compared to buying lunch at his restaurant?

4. Susan loves to get coffee in the morning. She spends about $5.40 a day on her way to work. How much does she spend in a year?

5. If Susan made her own coffee in the morning, she would spend about $7.50 per week.
    a. How much would she spend in a year?
    b. How much would Susan save by making her own coffee each morning compared to buying her coffee at the coffee shop?

6. In order to afford daycare, Susan and Carlos will need to reduce their expenses. Based on your results from problems 1, 3 and 5, if Carlos packs his own lunch and Susan makes her own coffee, would they save enough to be able to afford Penny's daycare? If not, how much more will they need?

For problems 7 and 8, use a Spreadsheet to prorate the monthly costs

7. Susan and Carlos have the following expenses for their cars. Use a spreadsheet to prorate the monthly cost for each expense and record your answers in the chart below.

    . Monthly Car Payment for $120.00
    . Weekly Gas for $28.75
    . Quarterly Oil Changes for $52.00
    . Monthly Car Insurance for $105.00
    . Quarterly Car Washes for $10.99

	A	B	C	D	E
1	Expense	Frequency	Cost	Annual Cost	Monthly Cost
2					
3					
4					
5					
6					

For problems 9 and 10, reflect on your own life

8. Make a list of all of your expenses labeling which ones are needs and which ones are wants.

9. Everyone has an area where they tend to spend more money than they may want to spend.
    a. What is an area you would like to reduce your spending?
    b. How much do you spend on this expense each year?
    c. What would you like to do with that money instead?

Section 1C: Setting Goals

In Section 1B, you learned how to manage your expenses, which can help you save money each month. Extra savings can help you achieve larger goals such as buying a car or taking a vacation. In this section, you will explore your financial goals and create a plan to achieve them.

Calculate Disposable Income

Prioritize Financial Goals

Make Pie Charts in a Spreadsheet

Find the Time-line of a Goal

Achieve Goals with a Plan

You might desire many things in life, and some of your desires can only be realized if you plan for them and work toward them in a structured way. You've learned about saving and managing expenses in previous sections. In this section, you will explore your financial goals and how you can achieve them. Budgets tell you a tremendous amount of information about how your money is helping you accomplish your financial goals.

1. What Are Your Goals?

Think about some of the financial goals in your life. What are your top priorities when you consider creating your budget? What goals would you like to actively pursue? Pick your top 3 goals from the options below, or, if your goals aren't listed, write them in the space provided.

- ☐ Own your home
- ☐ Buy a car
- ☐ Retire securely
- ☐ Save for education (*for you or family*)
- ☐ Get out of debt
- ☐ Afford care for family member(s)
- ☐ Finance hobbies and recreation
- ☐ Donate to charity/religious organizations
- ☐ Afford material possessions
- ☐ Travel
- ☐ Invest money (*stocks, bonds, etc.*)
- ☐ Start your own business
- ☐ Create an Emergency Fund
- ☐ Other ______________________

2. What Do You Think?

List your goals below, along with how much you think each of them will cost and how long you think it will take to reach each goal.

Goal 1:

Goal 2:

Goal 3:

Types of Income

To find out how quickly you can accomplish your financial goals, you need to know how much money you have left over after you pay for your needs. The money you don't spend on needs or set aside for monthly savings is called disposable income.

Monthly Income

All the money you earn each month.

Monthly Savings

A percentage of your income that is set aside each month.

Fixed Expenses

The money you spend on needs that does not change from month to month, including rent, insurance, car payments, etc.

Disposable Income

The money left over after saving and paying for fixed expenses.

Calculating Disposable Income

Disposable income isn't money to throw away; it is the money that will fund your financial goals. Find the disposable income for someone with a monthly income of $1,480. Assume they save 10% of their income each month and have fixed expenses of $980.

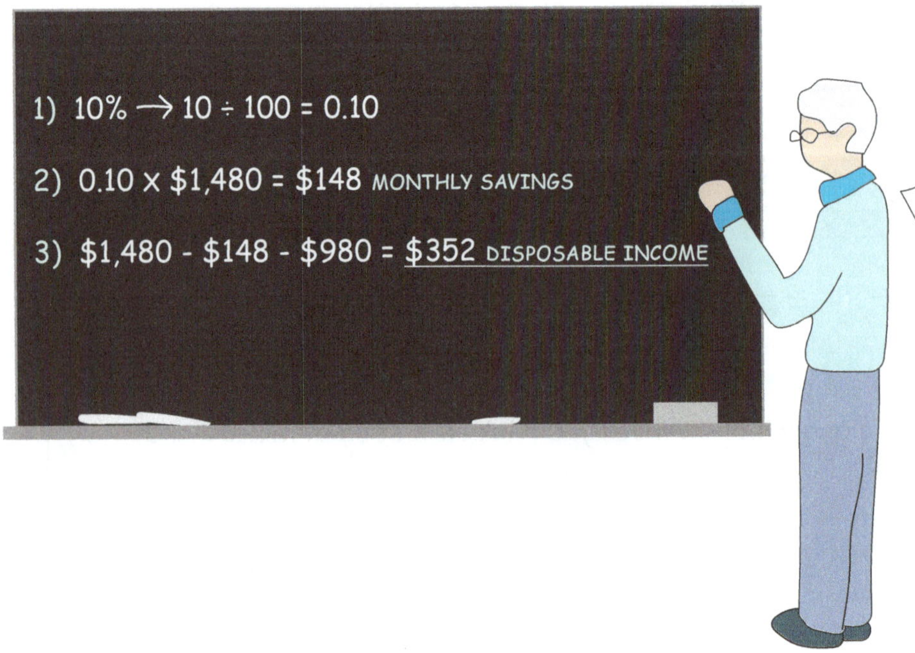

Step 1
Turn the percentage into a decimal by dividing it by 100.

Step 2
Find the monthly savings by multiplying the decimal form of the percentage by the monthly income.

Step 3
To find the disposable income, subtract the monthly savings and fixed expenses from the monthly income.

3. Now Do the Math ...

A. Before making any calculations, decide if you think you would have more disposable income by earning $30,000 per year with $15,000 in fixed expenses or by earning $60,000 per year with $55,000 in fixed expenses.

B. Nancy makes $3,500 per month. She saves 10% of her income and has fixed expenses of $2,700. What is Nancy's disposable income?

C. Fred earns $1,170 per month and saves 8% of it. His fixed expenses are $900. What is Fred's disposable income?

Using a Spreadsheet to Calculate Disposable Income

Calculate your disposable income if you earn $2,480 per month, save 10% of it and have fixed expenses of $1,730.

Step 1

Open a blank spreadsheet. At the bottom of the page, double-click on Sheet 1 to highlight it.

	A	B	C	D
1				
2				
	Sheet 1	+		

Step 2

Rename Sheet 1 as Disposable Income and press Enter.

	A	B	C	D
1				
2				
	Disposable Income	+		

Step 3

Before making calculations, create headings. Start in A1 and use the following headings.

	A	B	C	D
1	Monthly Income	10% Monthly Savings	Fixed Expenses	Disposable Income
2				

Using a Spreadsheet to Calculate Disposable Income

Step 4

Once you create headings, type in the information you know. In A2, type in the monthly income.

	A	B	C	D
1	Monthly Income	10% Monthly Savings	Fixed Expenses	Disposable Income
2	$2,480.00			

Step 5

To find the monthly savings, multiply the monthly income by 10%. In B2, press equals =, click on the Monthly Income in A2, and multiply * it by 10%. Then, press the Tab key.

	A	B	C	D
1	Monthly Income	10% Monthly Savings	Fixed Expenses	Disposable Income
2	$2,480.00	=A2*10%		

Step 6

Your spreadsheet shows that you will save $248.00 per month. In C2, type your fixed expenses of $1,730.00, in this example.

	A	B	C	D
1	Monthly Income	10% Monthly Savings	Fixed Expenses	Disposable Income
2	$2,480.00	$248.00	$1,730.00	

Step 7

Disposable Income is the amount of money you have after saving and paying your fixed expenses. In D2, press equals =, click on the Monthly Income in A2, subtract − the Monthly Savings in B2, and subtract − the Fixed Expenses in cell C2.

	A	B	C	D
1	Monthly Income	10% Monthly Savings	Fixed Expenses	Disposable Income
2	$2,480.00	$248.00	$1,730.00	=A2−B2−C2

Step 8

Press Enter and the spreadsheet will do the math, showing that your Disposable Income is $502 per month. Save your work as 1C Classwork.

	A	B	C	D
1	Monthly Income	10% Monthly Savings	Fixed Expenses	Disposable Income
2	$2,480.00	$248.00	$1,730.00	$502.00
3				

Using a Spreadsheet to Calculate Disposable Income

Conclusion

Based on monthly income of $2,480, you will have $502 left to put toward your financial goals if you save 10% and have fixed expenses of $1,730.

4. Now Do the Math in a Spreadsheet ...

A. Look at the table below. Peter, Nancy, and Bill all earn the same monthly income and save 10% of it, but they have different fixed expenses. Before making any calculations, decide who you think will have the most disposable income.

B. Use a spreadsheet to find the disposable income for Peter, Nancy and Bill. Write both the formula you used and your results below. How do your results compare to your answer from problem 1?

	A	B	C	D	E
1	Name	Monthly Income	10% Monthly Savings	Fixed Expenses	Disposable Income
2	Peter	$3,360.00		$1,500.00	
3	Nancy	$3,360.00		$1,950.00	
4	Bill	$3,360.00		$2,348.00	

5. What Do You Think?

A. Who has the most disposable income?

B. Who has the least disposable income?

C. Based on these results, how can a person increase disposable income without changing total income?

Prioritizing Your Goals

It's human nature to want more than is possible at any given moment – that's why people have dreams and ambitions for the future. A budget can protect your most important desires and goals from all the others. You will look at your top 3 financial goals as an example of how you can prioritize some of your goals over others.

6. What Do You Think?

What are your top three financial goals?

Goal 1:

Goal 2:

Goal 3:

The Role of a Pie Chart

Your financial goals might each have a different level of importance to you, so you can assign a percentage of disposable income toward accomplishing each goal. Pie charts are a great way to visualize this. Some goals require more money than others to accomplish, and a pie chart can help you determine which areas are receiving the greatest share of disposable income. The whole pie represents 100%. When you split the pie up into slices, all of the slices must total 100%.

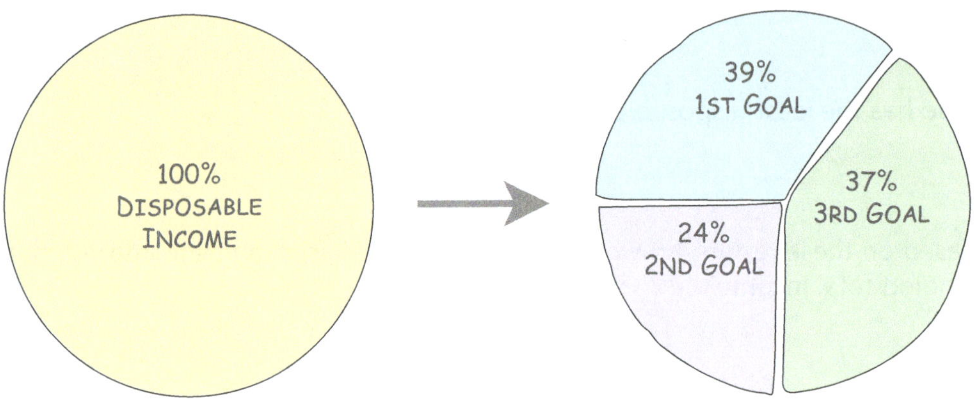

Making the Percentages in a Pie Chart Add Up to 100%

You will be asked to assign percentages to each of your financial goals and create a pie chart. Since all of the slices have to add up to 100%, picking a combination of percentages can be challenging. In this example, you assign 20% to your first goal and 44% to your second goal. How much is left to assign to your third goal?

Using a Spreadsheet to Create a Pie Chart

Use a spreadsheet to create a pie chart for the following financial goals: 30% toward retirement, 5% toward concert tickets, and 65% toward buying a house.

Step 1

At the bottom of your spreadsheet, click on the plus + symbol next to Disposable Income.

	A	B	C	D
1				
2				
	Disposable Income	+		

Step 2

A new sheet will appear. Double-click on Sheet 2 to highlight it.

	A	B	C	D
1				
2				
	Disposable Income	Sheet 2		

Step 3

Rename it as Pie Chart.

	A	B	C	D
1				
2				
	Disposable Income	Pie Chart		

Using a Spreadsheet to Create a Pie Chart

Step 4

Before making calculations, create headings. Start in A1 and type in the headings as shown.

	A	B	C	D
1	Financial Goals	Percentages		
2				

Step 5

Type in the name and percentages for each of your goals. Make sure the percentages add up to 100%.

	A	B	C	D
1	Financial Goals	Percentages		
2	Retirement	30%		
3	Concert Tickets	5%		
4	House	65%		

Step 6

Select your financial goals and their assigned percentages by clicking on cell A2, holding the mouse button down and dragging it to cell B4. Then let go of the mouse button.

	A	B	C	D
1	Financial Goals	Percentages		
2	Retirement	30%		
3	Concert Tickets	5%		
4	House	65%		

Step 7

Use your spreadsheet program to insert a pie chart.

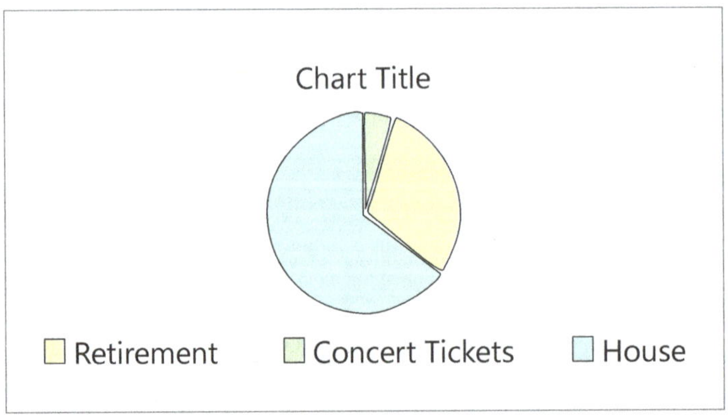

Step 8

Rename it to Financial Goals. Be sure to save your work.

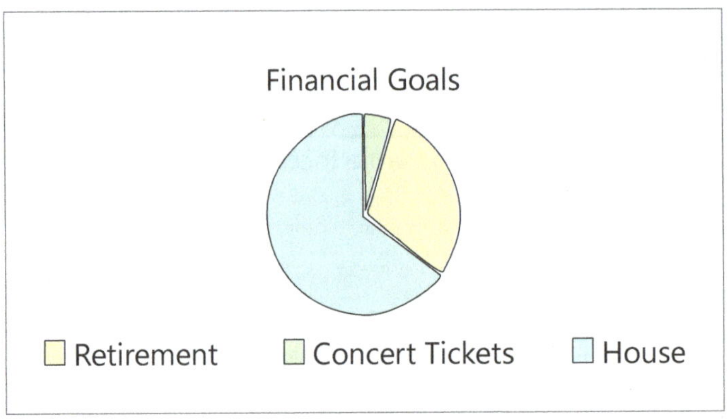

Using a Spreadsheet to Create a Pie Chart

Conclusion

Pie charts show the relationship between different percentages assigned to financial goals. This pie chart shows that most of the disposable income will go toward saving to buy a house.

7. Now Do the Math in a Spreadsheet ...

A. Create the following spreadsheet and fill in your top 3 financial goals. Assign a percentage to each goal. Make sure all of your percentages add up to 100%. Record your answers in the chart below.

	A	B	C	D
1	Financial Goal	Percentage		
2				
3				
4				

B. Use a spreadsheet program to create a pie chart. Draw a picture of your result below.

Show Me the Money

Percentages only tell you part of the story. Two people might have the same percentage of income set aside for a particular goal, but that could result in two different dollar amounts if they have different amounts of disposable income. In order to know how much money you are actually saving toward your financial goals, you need to make some calculations.

Finding the Dollar Amount for a Financial Goal

In the previous example, you assigned percentages to each of your financial goals and created a pie chart. To find the dollar amount going toward each of your goals, turn the assigned percentage into a decimal and multiply it by your disposable income. Find the dollar amount going toward a goal to go on a vacation if you have disposable income of $285 and assign 15% of it toward your vacation goal.

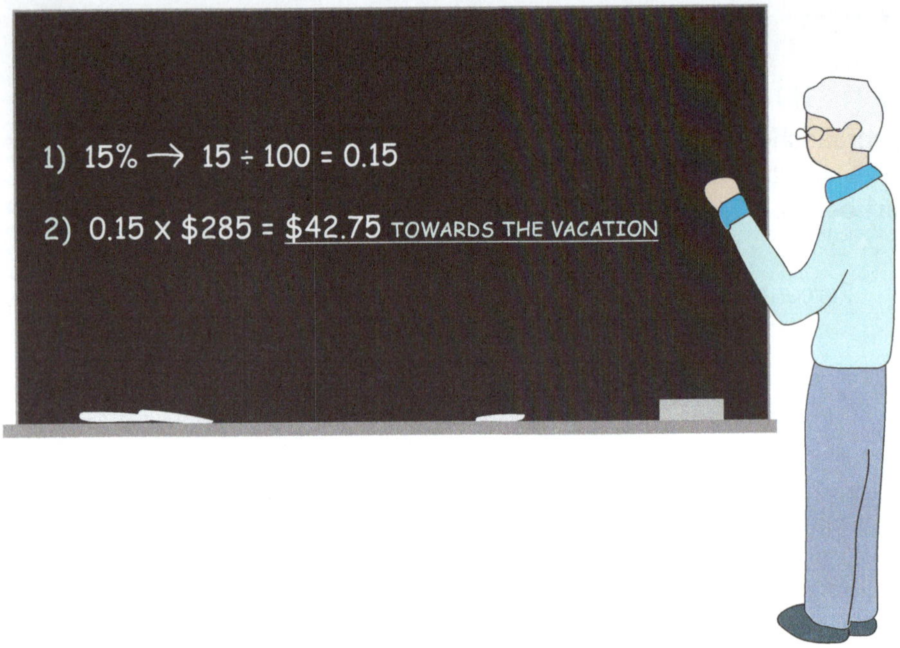

Step 1

Turn the percentage into a decimal by dividing it by 100.

Step 2

Multiply the decimal version of the percentage by your disposable income.

8. Now Do the Math ...

A. Carrie wants to buy a new car and sets aside 25% of her disposable income each month to go toward a down payment. What is the dollar amount she sets aside each month if her disposable income is $214?

B. Robert also wants to buy a new car and sets aside 25% of his disposable income toward a down payment. What is his dollar amount if his disposable income is $950?

9. What Do You Think?

On the previous page, both Carrie and Robert assigned the same percentage of disposable income to saving for a new car, so why does Robert save more money each month?

How Long Will it Take to Reach Your goal?

Some goals take only a few month to work toward, while other goals take much longer to accomplish. Knowing how long it will take to save for a goal can help with the planning and budgeting process.

Finding the Time-Line for a Goal

How long will it take to save $12,000 for a down payment on a house if you have $500 of disposable income each month and save 40% of it for the down payment?

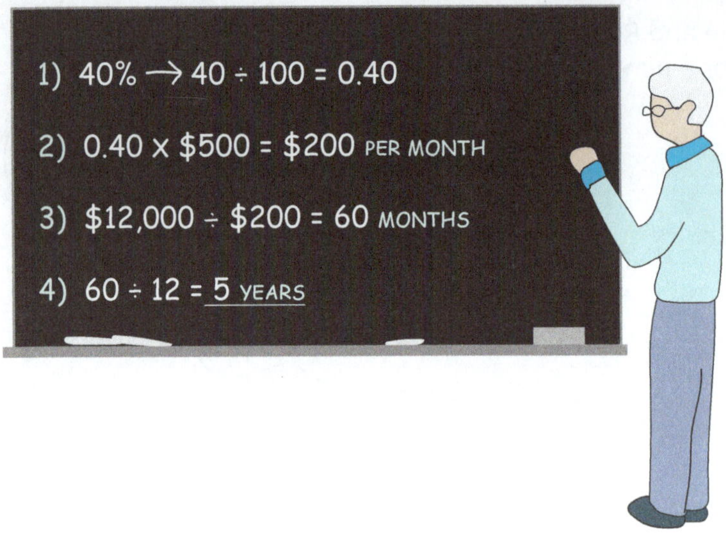

Step 1

Turn the percentage into a decimal by dividing it by 100.

Step 2

Multiply the decimal form of the percentage by the disposable income. This gives you the dollar amount that goes toward the goal each month.

Step 3

Divide the total amount needed for the goal by the monthly amount. This will tell you the number of months it takes to reach the goal.

Step 4

To find the number of years, divide the months by 12, since there are 12 months in a year.

10. Now Do the Math ...

A. Tim wants to go on a vacation. He will need $1,200 to cover his travel expenses. If he has $600 in disposable income each month and sets aside 20% of it for the vacation, how long will it take him to reach his goal? Give your answer in months.

B. Nicki wants to help pay for her daughter to go to college. She has $430 in disposable income each month and sets aside 40% of it for her daughter's education. If she wants to save $30,000, how long will it take? Round your answer to the nearest year. *For a review of rounding go to Appendix B.*

11. Now Do the Math With Your Goals ...

A. What percentage of your disposable income do you want to devote to each of your financial goals?

Goal 1:

Goal 2:

Goal 3:

B. How much money do you need to reach each goal?

Goal 1:

Goal 2:

Goal 3:

C. If your disposable income were $350 per month, how long would it take to reach each of your goals?

Goal 1:

Goal 2:

Goal 3:

Choosing Goals

In addition to affording daycare, the Garcias have other goals, such as going on a vacation, buying a new car, and buying a house. They are working hard and saving, but they don't know how much progress they are making toward their goals. Help the Garcias figure out how much they are saving toward their goals and how long it will take to accomplish them!

Section 1C: Homework

1. With Susan's promotion, the Garcias make $3,789.10 per month. They save 10% of their income.
   a. What is their monthly savings?
   b. What is their yearly savings?

2. Use the information from problem 1 to find the Garcias' disposable income if they have fixed expenses of $2,854.00 per month.

3. The Garcias' top 3 financial goals are to go on a vacation, buy a car and buy a house. If they put 15% of their disposable income toward the vacation and 25% to buying a car, what percent will go towards buying a house?

4. Create a pie chart to show the percentages for the Garcias' financial goals.

5. Use your answers from problems 1-3 to create a plan for each goal.
   a. Find the dollar amount that will go to each of the Garcias' financial goals each month.
   b. How much will each goal have after 1 year?
   c. How much will each goal have after 5 years?

6. How many months will it take to for the Garcias to buy a house if they need an $18,000 down payment? Round your answer to the nearest whole month.

7. What are your top 3 financial goals? How much money is needed to reach each goal?

8. Assign a percentage to each goal and use a spreadsheet to create a pie chart of your goals. Shade a picture of it below:

9. If your disposable income were $550 a month, how much would go to each goal each month?

10. How many months would it take to reach each of your goals?

Section 1D: Making a Budget

In Section 1C, you explored long-term financial goals and learned how to plan to achieve them. The next step is to create a budget to help you stick to your plan, continue to save money each month, and keep track of your spending. In this section, you will learn how to create and edit a budget.

Use a Spreadsheet to Create a Budget

Identify Projected versus Actual Spending

Analyze a Budget

Edit Your Budget

TAKE CONTROL OF YOUR FINANCES

If you don't have a plan, then achieving your goals is guesswork. Your budget is your plan to accomplish your financial goals and be in control of your finances. In this section, you will explore how to put together a complete budget and use it as a tool to work toward your financial goals.

PROJECTED VERSUS ACTUAL

Budgets start out as a plan of what you are going to spend. Life happens and sometimes you spend more than you thought you would. Sometimes you are able to save more than you thought you could. If you keep track of your actual expenses, your budget shows you the progress you are making toward your financial goals. After you make your budget you have to track your spending and see if you stayed within budget and what, if any, changes need to be made.

PROJECTED

The money you think you will earn and spend.

ACTUAL

The money you actually earn and spend.

Using a Spreadsheet to Make a Budget

Make a budget for the Garcias for the month of June. They take home $3,789.10 and plan to save 10% of it. They have calculated their total expenses to be $2,825. They want to use 15% of their disposable income to save for a vacation and 25% of it to save for a new car. Their remaining disposable income will go toward buying a house.

Step 1

Open a blank spreadsheet. At the bottom of the screen, double-click on Sheet1 to highlight it.

	A	B	C	D
1				
2				
	Sheet 1	+		

Step 2

Rename it Budget, and press enter.

	A	B	C	D
1				
2				
	Budget	+		

Step 3

You will make a new budget each month, so it's helpful to label it with the name of the current month. In A1, type the name of the month (in this example it's June) and Budget.

	A	B	C	D
1	June Budget			
2				
3				

Step 4

The first column of the budget needs to be wide enough for the names of the expenses. To make the column wider, place the cursor between columns A and B. Click, hold and drag your mouse until the column is wide enough.

	A	B	C
1	June Budget		
2			
3			
4			
5			
6			

PUT CURSOR HERE

Step 5

Every budget needs to include projected amounts (what you think you'll earn and spend) and actual amounts (what you actually earn and spend). Type Projected in B1 and Actual in C1.

	A	B	C
1	June Budget	Projected	Actual
2			
3			
4			
5			
6			

Using a Spreadsheet to Make a Budget

Step 6

In column A, fill in the income headings as they appear to the right.

	A	B	C
1	June Budget	Projected	Actual
2	Carlos' Income		
3	Susan's Income		
4	Total Income		
5			
6			

Step 7

In column B, fill in Carlos and Susan's projected income amounts.

	A	B	C
1	June Budget	Projected	Actual
2	Carlos' Income	$1,380.00	
3	Susan's Income	$2,104.16	
4	Total Income		

Step 8

To find total income, add Carlos' and Susan's income. In B4, press equals =, click on B2 (Carlos' Income) and add + B3 (Susan's Income). Press enter.

	A	B	C
1	June Budget	Projected	Actual
2	Carlos' Income	$1,380.00	
3	Susan's Income	$2,104.16	
4	Total Income	=B2+B3	

Step 9

From total income, determine monthly savings. To stay organized and find information easily, skip a row for each new section of the budget. In A6, type Monthly Savings.

	A	B	C
1	June Budget	Projected	Actual
2	Carlos' Income	$1,380.00	
3	Susan's Income	$2,104.16	
4	Total Income	$3,484.16	
5			
6	10% Monthly Savings		

Step 10

To calculate Monthly Savings, multiply * total income by the percentage of savings. In this case the Garcias want to save 10% of their monthly income. In cell B6, press =, click on total income (B4) and multiply * by 10%. Press enter.

	A	B	C
1	June Budget	Projected	Actual
2	Carlos' Income	$1,380.00	
3	Susan's Income	$2,104.16	
4	Total Income	$3,484.16	
5			
6	10% Monthly Savings	=B4*10%	

Step 11

Press enter and it shows their monthly saving is $348.42.

	A	B	C
6	10% Monthly Savings	$348.42	

Using a Spreadsheet to Make a Budget

Step 12

One of the benefits of using a spreadsheet is that it gives you the ability to edit budgets easily. Carlos gets a raise, which increases his monthly income to $1,684.94. To make the change, click on his income in B2 and type the new amount.

	A	B	C
1	June Budget	Projected	Actual
2	Carlos' Income	$1,684.94	
3	Susan's Income	$2,104.16	
4	Total Income	$3,484.16	
5			
6	10% Monthly Savings	$348.42	

Step 13

When you press enter, the spreadsheet will automatically update to show the new amount for total income and monthly savings.

	A	B	C
1	June Budget	Projected	Actual
2	Carlos' Income	$1,684.94	
3	Susan's Income	$2,104.16	
4	Total Income	$3,789.10	
5			
6	10% Monthly Savings	$378.91	

Step 14

Once you know the income and monthly savings, look at expenses. To stay organized, skip a row. In A8, type the name of the first expense. In this example, it's rent.

	A	B	C
1	June Budget	Projected	Actual
2	Carlos' Income	$1,684.94	
3	Susan's Income	$2,104.16	
4	Total Income	$3,789.10	
5			
6	10% Monthly Savings	$378.91	
7			
8	Rent		

Step 15

In B8, type in the projected amount for rent. The Garcias pay $800 per month for their apartment.

	A	B	C
1	June Budget	Projected	Actual
2	Carlos' Income	$1,684.94	
3	Susan's Income	$2,104.16	
4	Total Income	$3,789.10	
5			
6	10% Monthly Savings	$378.91	
7			
8	Rent	$800.00	

Using a Spreadsheet to Make a Budget

Step 16

Fill in the rest of the expenses and their projected amounts as they appear to the right. At the bottom of the list, type Total Expenses.

	A	B	C
8	Rent	$800.00	
9	Phone	$75.00	
10	Groceries & Household	$500.00	
11	Daycare	$515.00	
12	Gas	$75.00	
13	Magazine Subscription	$16.00	
14	Credit Card Payment	$40.00	
15	Student Loans	$225.00	
16	Car Insurance (2 cars)	$105.00	
17	Renter's Insurance	$14.00	
18	Health Insurance	$125.00	
19	Entertainment & Dining	$50.00	
20	Car Payment	$120.00	
21	Car Maintenance	$65.00	
22	Dental Appointments	$20.00	
23	Clothes	$40.00	
24	Internet	$40.00	
25	Total Expenses		

Step 17

To find total expenses, add all expenses. Start by selecting B25. Press `=`, type `=sum(` and select all expenses by clicking on the first one in B8, holding and dragging it to B24. Then close the parentheses `)` and press `enter`.

	A	B	C
8	Rent	$800.00	
9	Phone	$75.00	
10	Groceries & Household	$500.00	
11	Daycare	$515.00	
12	Gas	$75.00	
13	Magazine Subscription	$16.00	
14	Credit Card Payment	$40.00	
15	Student Loans	$225.00	
16	Car Insurance (2 cars)	$105.00	
17	Renters Insurance	$14.00	
18	Health Insurance	$125.00	
19	Entertainment & Dining	$50.00	
20	Car Payment	$120.00	
21	Car Maintenance	$65.00	
22	Dental Appointments	$20.00	
23	Clothes	$40.00	
24	Internet	$40.00	
25	Total Expenses	=SUM(B8:B24)	

Using a Spreadsheet to Make a Budget

Step 18

After creating their budget, the Garcias realize they forgot to include utilities. To add an expense, click on the row number where you want the new expense to go. It will highlight the entire row. In this case, click on row 20.

	A	B	C
8	Rent	$800.00	
9	Phone	$75.00	
10	Groceries & Household	$500.00	
11	Daycare	$515.00	
12	Gas	$75.00	
13	Magazine Subscription	$16.00	
14	Credit Card	$40.00	
15	Student Loans	$225.00	
16	Car Insurance (2 cars)	$105.00	
17	Renters Insurance	$14.00	
18	Health Insurance	$125.00	
19	Entertainment & Dining	$50.00	
20	Car Payment	$120.00	
21	Car Maintenance	$65.00	
22	Dental Appointments	$20.00	
23	Clothes	$40.00	
24	Internet	$40.00	
25	Total Expenses	$2,825.00	

Step 19

Right-click on that row number. A menu will appear. Click on Insert.

Note: If you have a Mac, hold control and click on the row number.

	A	B	C
8	Rent	$800.00	
9	Phone	$75.00	
10	Groceries & Household	$500.00	
11	Daycare	$515.00	
12	Gas	$75.00	
13	Magazine Subscription	$16.00	
14	Credit Card	$40.00	
15	Student Loans	$225.00	
16	Car Insurance (2 cars)	$105.00	
17	Renters Insurance	$14.00	
18	Health Insurance	$125.00	
19	Entertainment & Dining	$50.00	
20	Cut	$120.00	
21	Copy	$65.00	
22	Paste	$20.00	
23	Insert	$40.00	
24	Delete	$40.00	
25	Total Expenses	$2,825.00	

Using a Spreadsheet to Make a Budget

Step 20

A new row will be inserted. Type in the new expense. In this case, utilities average $45 per month. Press enter and the total expenses will automatically update to include your new expense.

	A	B	C
8	Rent	$800.00	
9	Phone	$75.00	
10	Groceries & Household	$500.00	
11	Daycare	$515.00	
12	Gas	$75.00	
13	Magazine Subscription	$16.00	
14	Credit Card	$40.00	
15	Student Loans	$225.00	
16	Car Insurance (2 cars)	$105.00	
17	Renters Insurance	$14.00	
18	Health Insurance	$125.00	
19	Entertainment & Dining	$50.00	
20	Utilities	$45.00	
21	Car Payment	$120.00	
22	Car Maintenance	$65.00	
23	Dental Appointments	$20.00	
24	Clothes	$40.00	
25	Internet	$40.00	
26	Total Expenses	$2,870.00	

Step 21

The Garcias decide they don't need the magazine subscription. To delete an expense, click on the row number for that expense. The entire row will be highlighted.

	A	B	C
8	Rent	$800.00	
9	Phone	$75.00	
10	Groceries & Household	$500.00	
11	Daycare	$515.00	
12	Gas	$75.00	
13	Magazine Subscription	$16.00	
14	Credit Card	$40.00	
15	Student Loans	$225.00	
16	Car Insurance (2 cars)	$105.00	
17	Renters Insurance	$14.00	
18	Health Insurance	$125.00	
19	Entertainment & Dining	$50.00	
20	Utilities	$45.00	
21	Utilities	$120.00	
22	Car Maintenance	$65.00	
23	Dental Appointments	$20.00	
24	Clothes	$40.00	
25	Internet	$40.00	
26	Total Expenses	$2,870.00	

Using a Spreadsheet to Make a Budget

Step 22

Right-click on the row number. A menu will appear. Since they decided to cancel the magazine subscription, click delete to remove it from their expenses.

Note: If you have a Mac, hold control and click on the row number.

	A	B	C
8	Rent	$800.00	
9	Phone	$75.00	
10	Groceries & Household	$500.00	
11	Daycare	$515.00	
12	Gas	$75.00	
13	Cut	$16.00	
14	Copy	$40.00	
15	Paste	$225.00	
16	Insert	$105.00	
17	Delete	$14.00	
18	Health Insurance	$125.00	
19	Entertainment & Dining	$50.00	
20	Utilities	$45.00	
21	Car Payment	$120.00	
22	Car Maintenance	$65.00	
23	Dental Appointments	$20.00	
24	Clothes	$40.00	
25	Internet	$40.00	
26	Total Expenses	$2,870.00	

Step 23

The spreadsheet will update the total of expenses to reflect the deletion of the magazine subscription expense that was in row 13.

	A	B	C
8	Rent	$800.00	
9	Phone	$75.00	
10	Groceries & Household	$500.00	
11	Daycare	$515.00	
12	Gas	$75.00	
13	Credit Card	$40.00	
14	Student Loans	$225.00	
15	Car Insurance (2 cars)	$105.00	
16	Renters Insurance	$14.00	
17	Health Insurance	$125.00	
18	Entertainment & Dining	$50.00	
19	Utilities	$45.00	
20	Car Payment	$120.00	
21	Car Maintenance	$65.00	
22	Dental Appointments	$20.00	
23	Clothes	$40.00	
24	Internet	$40.00	
25	Total Expenses	$2,854.00	

Using a Spreadsheet to Make a Budget

Step 24

After expenses, determine disposable income. To stay organized, skip a row. In A27, type Disposable Income.

	A	B	C
1	June Budget	Projected	Actual
25	Total Expenses	$2,854.00	
26			
27	Disposable Income		

Step 25

To find disposable income, subtract monthly savings and total expenses from total income. Start by selecting B27; press = ; click on Total Income in B4, subtract − the Monthly Savings in B6 and subtract − the Total Expenses in B25. Press enter.

	A	B	C
1	June Budget	Projected	Actual
2	Carlos' Income	$1,684.94	
3	Susan's Income	$2,104.16	
4	Total Income	$3,789.10	
5			
6	10% Monthly Savings	$378.91	
7			
8	Rent	$800.00	
9	Phone	$75.00	
10	Groceries & Household	$500.00	
11	Daycare	$515.00	
12	Gas	$75.00	
13	Credit Card	$40.00	
14	Student Loans	$225.00	
15	Car Insurance (2 cars)	$105.00	
16	Renters Insurance	$14.00	
17	Health Insurance	$125.00	
18	Entertainment & Dining	$50.00	
19	Utilities	$45.00	
20	Car Payment	$120.00	
21	Car Maintenance	$65.00	
22	Dental Appointments	$20.00	
23	Clothes	$40.00	
24	Internet	$40.00	
25	Total Expenses	$2,854.00	
26			
27	Disposable Income	=B4-B6-B25	

Step 26

Press enter and your disposable income shows as $556.19.

	A	B	C
27	Disposable Income	$556.19	

Using a Spreadsheet to Make a Budget

Step 27

The last section of your budget will be your financial goals. Under Disposable Income type the names of your goals. The Garcias' top three financial goals are to save for a vacation, a car, and a house.

	A	B	C
27	Disposable Income	$556.19	
28	Go on a Vacation (15%)		
29	Buy a Car (25%)		
30	Buy a House (60%)		

Step 28

Each goal is based on a percent of the disposable income. The Garcias decided to use 15% of their disposable income to go on a vacation. Select B28; press equals (=), click on Disposable Income in B27 and then multiply (*) it by 15%. Press (enter).

	A	B	C
27	Disposable Income	$556.19	
28	Go on a Vacation (15%)	=B27*15%	
29	Buy a Car (25%)		
30	Buy a House (60%)		

Step 29

The Garcias decided to use 25% of their disposable income to buy a car. Select B29, press equals (=), and click on the Disposable Income in B27. Then multiply (*) it by 25%. Press (enter).

	A	B	C
27	Disposable Income	$556.19	
28	Go on a Vacation (15%)	$83.43	
29	Buy a Car (25%)	=B27*25%	
30	Buy a House (60%)		

Step 30

The Garcias decided to use 60% of their disposable income to buy a house. Select B30; press equals (=) and click on the Disposable Income in B27. Then multiply (*) it by 60%. Press (enter).

	A	B	C
27	Disposable Income	$556.19	
28	Go on a Vacation (15%)	$83.43	
29	Buy a Car (25%)	$139.05	
30	Buy a House (60%)	=B27*60%	

Step 31

Press (enter) and you can see the amount of money that will go to each of the Garcias' goals each month.

	A	B	C
27	Disposable Income	$556.19	
28	Go on a Vacation (15%)	$83.43	
29	Buy a Car (25%)	$139.05	
30	Buy a House (60%)	$333.71	

Conclusion

Budgets help you stay organized, give you a realistic picture of your spending, and let you know how much money can go toward your goals.

1. Now Do the Math in a Spreadsheet ...

Create a budget in a spreadsheet for a family with a monthly income of $3,650. They save 10% of their income and have the following monthly expenses:

- Mortgage payment = $1,250
- Groceries & household = $575
- Health insurance = $140
- Car payment = $289
- Car insurance = $82
- Gas = $120
- Phone bill = $113.50
- Online movie subscription = $11.95

They also have the following financial goals:

- Retirement = 50% of their Disposable Income
- Craft Supplies = 40% of their Disposable Income
- Music & Concerts = 10% of their Disposable Income

Record your answers below.

	A	C	D
1	Monthly Budget	Projected	Actual
2	Income		
3			
4	10% Monthly Savings		
5			
6	Mortgage Payment		
7	Groceries and Household		
8	Health Insurance		
9	Car Payment		
10	Car Insurance		
11	Gas		
12	Phone Bill		
13	Online Movie Subscription		
14	Total Expenses		
15			
16	Disposable Income		
17	Retirement (50%)		
18	Craft Supplies (40%)		
19	Music and Concerts (10%)		

How Much Did You Actually Spend?

After using a spreadsheet to create a budget with your projected income and expenses, it is important to track your actual income and expenses to see if you are staying within budget. One way to do this is to look at your bank statements each month.

The Garcias' Bank Statement - June 2015

Date	Description	Deposits	Withdraws
6/1/2015	Rent		$800.00
6/1/2015	Daycare		$515.00
6/2/2015	Renters Insurance		$14.00
6/3/2015	Coffee Shop		$5.23
6/3/2015	Gas		$22.75
6/4/2015	Eating Out		$42.89
6/5/2015	Susan's Car Insurance		$105.00
6/7/2015	Groceries		$133.18
6/10/2015	Carlos' Paycheck	$842.47	
6/10/2015	Transfer to Savings Account		$378.91
6/12/2015	Susan's Paycheck	$1,052.08	
6/12/2015	Movies		$34.08
6/14/2015	Groceries & Household		$129.65
6/14/2015	Clothes		$12.99
6/14/2015	Health Insurance		$125.00
6/15/2015	Carlos' Student Loan Payment		$138.10
6/15/2015	Car Payment		$120.00
6/15/2015	Music Download		$12.99
6/15/2015	Internet		$40.00
6/17/2015	Gas		$36.08
6/18/2015	Coffee Shop		$6.14
6/19/2015	Oil Change		$65.00
6/20/2015	Utilities		$45.00
6/21/2015	Groceries		$122.77
6/24/2015	Carlos' Paycheck	$842.47	
6/25/2015	Credit Card Payment		$40.00
6/25/2015	Eating Out		$18.95
6/25/2015	Susan's Student Loan		$86.31
6/25/2015	Phone Bill		$75.00
6/25/2015	Gas		$31.79
6/26/2015	Susan's Paycheck	$1,052.08	
6/28/2015	Groceries		$146.08
6/29/2015	Transfer to Savings for Semiannual Dental Appointments		$20.00
6/30/2015	Gas		$39.02

2. Now Do the Math ...

Look at the bank statement on the previous page. Use it to determine the amount of money spent or earned in the following categories from the Garcias' budget.

Carlos' Income =

Susan's Income =

Savings =

Rent =

Phone =

Groceries & Household =

Daycare =

Gas =

Credit Card =

Student Loans =

Car Insurance =

Renter's Insurance =

Health Insurance =

Entertainment & Dining =

Utilities =

Car Payment =

Car Maintenance =

Dental Appointments =

Clothes =

Internet =

Including Your Actually Income and Expenses in Your Budget

Once you create your projected budget you can compare it to your actual spending. One way to do this is to look at your bank statements each month if you make most of your purchases with a debit or credit card. If you use cash for most of your spending, then you will need to keep track of that with receipts or in a journal. Let's fill in the actual spending for the budget you created based on a bank statement.

Step 1

Open the budget you made in the previous exercise.

	A	B	C
1	June Budget	Projected	Actual
2	Carlos' Income	$1,684.94	
3	Susan's Income	$2,104.16	

Including Your Actual Income and Expenses in Your Budget

Step 2

Use the information from the Garcias' bank statement to fill in the actual income and expenses.

	A	B	C
1	June Budget	Projected	Actual
2	Carlos' Income	$1,684.94	$1,684.94
3	Susan's Income	$2,104.16	$2,104.16
4	Total Income	$3,789.10	
5			
6	Monthly Savings	$378.91	$378.91
7			
8	Rent	$800.00	$800.00
9	Phone	$75.00	$75.00
10	Groceries & Household	$500.00	$531.68
11	Daycare	$515.00	$515.00
12	Gas	$75.00	$129.64
13	Credit Card Payment	$40.00	$40.00
14	Student Loans	$225.00	$224.41
15	Car Insurance	$105.00	$105.00
16	Renter's Insurance	$14.00	$14.00
17	Health Insurance	$125.00	$125.00
18	Entertainment & Dining	$50.00	$120.28
19	Utilities	$45.00	$45.00
20	Car Payment	$120.00	$120.00
21	Car Maintenance	$65.00	$65.00
22	Dental Appointments	$20.00	$20.00
23	Clothes	$40.00	$12.99
24	Internet	$40.00	$40.00
25	Total Expenses	$2,854.00	
26			
27	Disposable Income	$556.19	
28	Go on a Vacation (15%)	$83.43	
29	Buy a Car (25%)	$139.05	
30	Buy a House (60%)	$333.71	

Conclusion

Once the actual amounts are next to the projected amounts, you can see if you are on track with your goals. You can also see if there are areas that need to be adjusted. In this example, the Garcias spent more on groceries than they had planned. To fix this in the next month's budget, they can either increase the projected amount for groceries or figure out how to spend less in that category.

3. Now Do the Math in a Spreadsheet ...

Look at the following bank statement and fill in the actual amounts in the budget provided below.

Bank Statement - September 2015

Date	Description	Deposits	Withdraws
9/1/2015	Mortgage Payment		$1,120.00
9/2/2015	Transfer to Retirement Account		$130.00
9/3/2015	Eating Out		$5.59
9/4/2015	Paycheck	$1,325.00	
9/4/2015	Transfer to Savings Account		$132.50
9/6/2015	Groceries		$110.00
9/8/2015	Eating Out		$11.85
9/10/2015	Clothing		$55.00
9/13/2015	Groceries & Household		$88.00
9/16/2015	Eating Out		$14.33
9/18/2015	Paycheck	$1,450.00	
9/18/2015	Transfer to Savings Account		$145.00
9/20/2015	Groceries		$92.50
9/25/2015	Eating Out		$46.41
9/27/2015	Groceries		$107.00
9/30/2015	Savings for a Vacation		$55.00

	A	C	D
1	Monthly Budget	Projected	Actual
2	Income	$2,775.00	
3	Savings	$277.50	
4	Mortgage	$1,120.00	
5	Clothing	$30.00	
6	Groceries	$500.00	
7	Total Expenses	$2,110.00	
8	Disposable	$275.00	
9	Eating Out (30%)	$82.50	
10	Retirement (50%)	$137.50	
11	Vacation (20%)	$55.00	

4. What Do You Think?

In the exercise above, look at the projected amounts compared to their actual amounts. Which categories are over budget? Which categories are under budget?

Uncle Rob's Budget

Uncle Rob is a bachelor and lives in an apartment near Susan and Carlos. He loves to travel and dedicates 60% of his disposable income to taking trips. He is also generous and enjoys giving gifts to his friends and family. He dedicates 30% of his disposable income to this category. The remaining 10% goes toward buying a house one day, but he's in no hurry.

Section 1D: Budget Project

Part 1

Create a budget for Uncle Rob using the following information:

Income	Payroll	$4,825.00
Savings	Monthly Savings	10% of income
Expenses	Car Insurance	$98.22
	Credit Card	$25.00
	Gas	$110.00
	Groceries	$335.00

	Medical Insurance	$130.00
	Phone	$145.00
	Rent	$1,025.00
	Renter's Insurance	$18.00
	Utilities	$65.00
	Car Payment	$344.18
	Eating Out & Entertainment	$185.00
Financial Goals	Travel	60%
	Buy a House	10%
	Gifts	30%

Part 2

Using your own finances, create a budget for yourself. Use your own expenses, income and financial goals.

Note: Since finances are personal, this part of the project will be kept confidential. Your instructor will not share your project with anyone, and will hand it back to you once it has been graded.

Part 3

Use your personal budget from Part 2 and keep track of your expenses for the next month. Record your results in your budget under the column marked "Actual." Then answer the following questions.

a. How close were your projected amounts to your actual amounts? Which expense was the most different from what you had projected?

b. Were there any areas you over-spent or any expenses you forgot to include? If so, list them.

c. Are there any changes you want to make to your budget for the future? If so, list them.

CHAPTER 2: MANAGING DEBT

2A COMPOUND INTEREST

2B UNDERSTANDING TIME

2C PAYING OFF LOANS

2D USING CREDIT CARDS

Section 2A: Compound Interest

In Chapter 1, you learned how to create a personal budget, manage your expenses and save for long-term goals. Saving and borrowing both often involve interest. In Section 2A, you will learn how interest works.

Understand Interest Rates

Calculate Simple Interest

Calculate Compound Interest

Calculate Interest in a Spreadsheet

A Network of Lending

When you deposit money in the bank, it doesn't just sit there. Instead, the bank uses the money it has to make loans to people. In exchange for getting a loan people agree to pay interest as a fee for getting the money up front in one lump sum. In other words, the bank makes money by lending out money. In exchange for lending out your money, the bank pays you some of the interest.

Interest Vocabulary

Whether earning interest on your savings or on money you borrowed, the math of interest works the same way. The following vocabulary applies to situations involving interest.

Principal
The amount of money invested or borrowed.

Rate
The percentage used to calculate interest.

Interest
The money that accrues (adds up), as a percentage of the principal. In savings and investments, this is money you earn for saving or investing your money and not spending it.

1. What Do You Think?

A. How is interest different from the rate at which it accrues?

B. Why do you think calculating interest works the same way, regardless of whether you are saving or borrowing money?

Compound Interest

Compound interest means that interest you earn is added to your principal. When your principal gets larger, you earn more interest. Over time, compound interest can really add up.

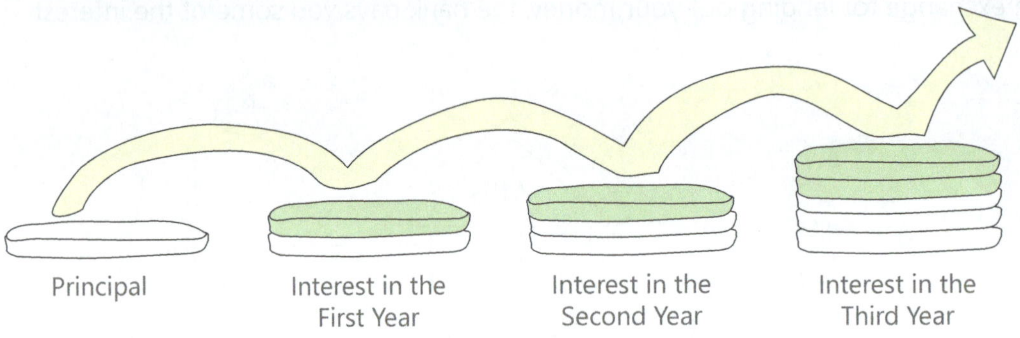

Calculating Interest for the First Year

The amount of interest earned in a year is based on the interest rate. Calculate the interest earned on a principal of $12,000 with a rate of 4%.

2. Now Do the Math ...

A. How much interest would you earn with a principal of $20,000 at a rate of 3.5% for one year?

B. What if you change the interest rate to 5%? How much interest would you earn in one year?

Using a Spreadsheet to Calculate Compound Interest

With compound interest, the principal continues to grow, and this causes the interest earned to increase as well. Spreadsheets make these complicated calculations simpler. In this example, you will find the compound interest for an account with a principal of $20,000.00 and a rate of 5% for 15 years.

Step 1

Open a new spreadsheet and double-click on Sheet 1 to highlight it.

	A	B	C	D
1				
2				
3				
	Sheet 1	+		

Step 2

Rename it Compound Interest and press enter.

	A	B	C	D
1				
2				
3				
	Compound Interest	+		

Step 3

Before making calculations, create the headings. Start in A1 and create the following headings (see right).

	A	B	C	D
1	Year	Principal	Rate	Interest
2				

Step 4

Fill in the information you know. In A2, type 1 for the first year. Type the principal ($20,000.00) in B2 and the rate (5%) in C2.

	A	B	C	D
1	Year	Principal	Rate	Interest
2	1	$20,000.00	5%	

Step 5

To calculate interest multiply the principal by the rate. Start by selecting D2, press =, click on the principal in B2, and multiply * it by the rate in C2.

	A	B	C	D
1	Year	Principal	Rate	Interest
2	1	$20,000.00	5%	=B2*C2

Using a Spreadsheet to Calculate Compound Interest

Step 6

Press (enter) and the spreadsheet will do the math showing $1,000 in interest the first year.

	A	B	C	D
1	Year	Principal	Rate	Interest
2	1	$20,000.00	5%	$1,000.00
3				

Step 7

To calculate the second year, start by clicking on A3 and type in the number 2 for the second year. Then, press (tab).

	A	B	C	D
1	Year	Principal	Rate	Interest
2	1	$20,000.00	5%	$1,000.00
3	2			

Step 8

When using compound interest, add the interest to the principal. In B3, press (=), click on the Principal in B2, and add (+) it to the Interest in D2. Then, press (tab).

	A	B	C	D
1	Year	Principal	Rate	Interest
2	1	$20,000.00	5%	$1,000.00
3	2	=B2+D2		

Step 9

With compound interest the principal will increase each year, but the rate will always stay the same. In C3, press (=), and click on the Rate in C2. Then, press the (tab) key.

	A	B	C	D
1	Year	Principal	Rate	Interest
2	1	$20,000.00	5%	$1,000.00
3	2	$21,000.00	=C2	
4				

Step 10

To find the interest for the second year you will multiply your new principal by the rate. In D3, press (=), click on the Principal in B3, and multiply (*) it by the rate in B3.

	A	B	C	D
1	Year	Principal	Rate	Interest
2	1	$20,000.00	5%	$1,000.00
3	2	$21,000.00	5%	=B3*C3

Using a Spreadsheet to Calculate Compound Interest

Step 11

Press enter and the spreadsheet does the math, showing $1,050 of interest in the second year. Notice how this is a little higher than interest earned in the first year. This is the effect of compounding.

	A	B	C	D
1	Year	Principal	Rate	Interest
2	1	$20,000.00	5%	$1,000.00
3	2	$21,000.00	5%	$1,050.00
4				

Step 12

To complete the rest of the years, select the bottom row. Click on A3, and hold and drag to D3. Then let go of the mouse.

	A	B	C	D
1	Year	Principal	Rate	Interest
2	1	$20,000.00	5%	$1,000.00
3	2	$21,000.00	5%	$1,050.00
4				

Step 13

Click on the fill handle and drag down until the number on the bottom right-hand corner shows the number of years you want. In this case it's 15 years.

	A	B	C	D	
1	Year	Principal	Rate	Interest	
2	1	$20,000.00	5%	$1,000.00	
3	2	$21,000.00	5%	$1,050.00	
16					15

Number of Years

Step 14

Let go of the mouse and the rest of the years will fill in automatically. Notice how the interest earned increases over time.

	A	B	C	D
1	Year	Principal	Rate	Interest
2	1	$20,000.00	5%	$1,000.00
3	2	$21,000.00	5%	$1,050.00
16	15	$39,598.63	5%	$1,979.93

Using a Spreadsheet to Calculate Compound Interest

Step 15

Once all the years have been completed, find the total interest earned over the 15 years. Select the cell underneath the interest column. In this case, it's D17. Type =sum(and then select your interest column by clicking on D2, holding, and dragging down to D16.

	A	B	C	D
1	Year	Principal	Rate	Interest
2	1	$20,000.00	5%	$1,000.00
3	2	$21,000.00	5%	$1,050.00
16	15	$39,598.63	5%	$1,979.93
17				=SUM(D2:D16)

Step 16

Press enter and the spreadsheet will do the math, showing that the total interest earned during the 15 years is $21,578.56 Make sure to save your work as 2A classwork.

	A	B	C	D
1	Year	Principal	Rate	Interest
2	1	$20,000.00	5%	$1,000.00
3	2	$21,000.00	5%	$1,050.00
16	15	$39,598.63	5%	$1,979.93
17				$21,578.56

Conclusion

When working with compound interest, the interest keeps adding to the principal, increasing the principal and the interest earned each year. The longer money is left in the account, the more interest it will earn. In this example, the investment doubled after 15 years because of compound interest.

3. Now Do the Math in a Spreadsheet ...

Use a spreadsheet to find the total compound interest with a principal of $15,500.00 and a rate of 3% for 8 years. Write your results below.

	A	B	C	D
1	Year	Principal	Rate	Interest
2	1	$15,500.00	3%	
3	2			
4	3			
5	4			
6	5			
7	6			
8	7			
9	8			
10				

4. What Do You Think?

A. What is the total interest in the exercise above when you

Double the principal?

Double the rate?

Double the time?

B. Earning compound interest requires a principal, an interest rate, and time. Which of the options from the question above has the greatest effects on your investment? Why do you think time is so important in compound interest?

Penny Learns How to Save

While Uncle Rob was babysitting Penny one day, he decided to show her the power of savings. They went to the bank together and explored the options.

Section 2A: Homework

1. Uncle Rob gave Penny $500 to put into a savings account that pays 3% interest compounded annually. He told her that she has to keep it in there until she turns 18. She is 5 years old at the moment.
    a. How many years will the money be in her account?
    b. Create a spreadsheet to track her savings. Record your results for the first year and the last year.

	A	B	C	D
1	Year	Principal	Rate	Interest
2				

    c. What is Penny's principal when she turns 18?
    d. How much interest did she earn?

2. Susan and Carlos found out about Uncle Rob's trip to the bank. They decided to add to Penny's account and gave her an additional $400.
    a. What is Penny's new principal?

b. Create a spreadsheet to track her savings with the new principal. Record your results for the first year and the last year.

	A	B	C	D
1	Year	Principal	Rate	Interest
2				

c. What is Penny's principal when she turns 18?
d. How much interest did she earn?

3. What is the difference between Penny's earnings from the first account and the second account?

4. Penny is curious and asks what would happen if she kept the money in there until she is as old as Uncle Rob, who is 38 years old.
   a. How many years will the money be in her account?
   b. Create a spreadsheet to track her savings. Record your results for the first year and the last year.

	A	B	C	D
1	Year	Principal	Rate	Interest
2				

   c. How much will she have in her account when she turns 38?
   d. How much interest did she earn?

5. What is the difference between Penny's earnings from saving until she was 18 years old compared to 38 years old?

6. Look at your personal budget from section 1D.
   a. What is your monthly savings?
   b. What is your yearly savings?
   c. If you put that in an account that pays compound interest at 3.5%, how much interest could you earn in 5 years?
   d. What would you do with the extra money?

Section 2B: Understanding Time

In Section 2A, you learned how to calculate interest when it is compounded once a year. Often, financial institutions compound your money more frequently. In this section you will learn the relationship between time and compound interest, and how much you can earn.

Time Value of Money

Compounding Time Periods

Compound Interest with Time Periods

Create Formulas in a Spreadsheet

Interest: A Tale of Marshmallows

In the 1960s, a research team at Stanford University conducted a study that has come to be known as the "Stanford marshmallow experiment." This experiment continues to be used to study children's willpower.

The experiment:

A child is presented with a marshmallow and told that she can eat the single marshmallow if she wants, or she can wait until the adult researcher returns and have two marshmallows.

The results:

Some children waited to earn the extra marshmallow (delayed gratification) and some children ate the single marshmallow (instant gratification). It was not easy for the children, and many of them gave in to temptation.

The consequences:

Years later, when researchers followed up with the children after they had grown up, they found that children willing to wait for the second marshmallow were generally more financially successful as adults. What do you think could explain that connection?

1. What Do You Think?

A. How does the marshmallow story relate to investing money?

B. If waiting meant that you could double your money, how long would you be willing to wait?

Time = Money

You might have heard the expression, "Time is money." Nowhere is that more true than when it comes to interest. When you invest money, it earns interest. The longer you wait to withdraw money, the more interest you will earn. And the sooner you invest money, the more time your money will have to earn interest. In the last section, you looked at interest that is compounded annually, but there are many other periods used for compounding. All other things being equal, the more frequently interest is compounded, the faster your investment grows.

Vocabulary of Interest

Calculating interest is straightforward when interest is compounded once per year, but interest is often compounded more frequently. In order to know how different frequencies of compounding affect investments, take a look at the vocabulary below.

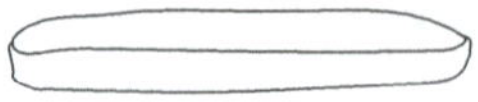

Principal
The amount of money invested or borrowed.

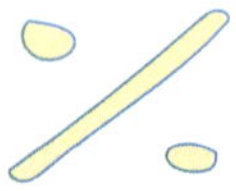

Rate
The percentage used to calculate interest.

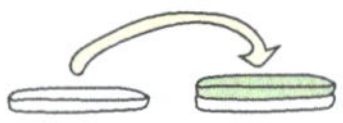

Interest
The money that accrues based on the principal.

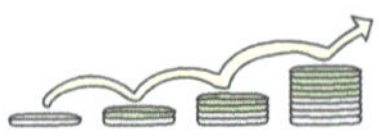

Compound Interest
Interest that is calculated periodically and then added to the principal.

Compound Periods
The frequency with which interest is added to the principal in a year.

Compounding Periods

Compounding interest means the interest earned is added to the principal invested. In Section 2A, compounding happens once each year, but it can happen more often. Every time interest is added to the principal, the principal grows.

Here is a list of common compounding periods.

Annually
1 time a year

Semiannually
2 times a year

Quarterly
4 times a year

Monthly
12 times a year

Weekly
52 times a year

Daily
365 times a year

Who Earns More Interest?

2. What Do You Think?

Of all the compounding periods listed in the image above, which one do you think will earn the most interest? Explain why the frequency of compounding is related to growth of the principal.

Calculating Interest with Time Periods

In Section 2A, you learned how to calculate interest compounded once a period. Often, financial institutions compound interest more frequently. In this example, you will learn how to calculate the interest for the first month of an account with a principal of $12,000 and a rate of 4% compounded monthly.

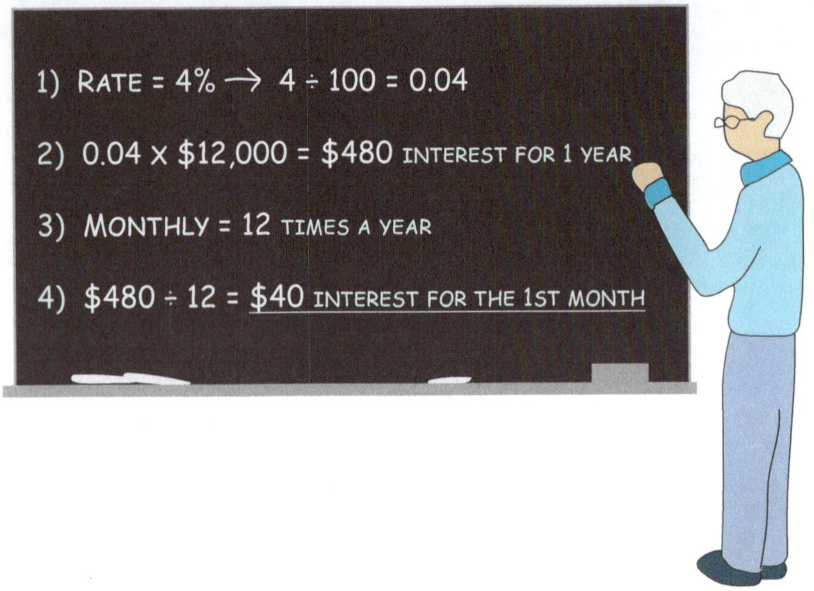

Step 1
Convert the rate into a decimal.

Step 2
Find the interest for one year by multiplying the decimal version of the rate by the principal.

Step 3
Determine the compounding frequency from the period. In this case, monthly means 12 times per year.

Step 4
Divide the interest for one year by the number of times it is compounded in a year. *Note: This interest is added to the principal and the interest for the next month is based on the new principal of $12,040.*

3. Now Do the Math ...

A. Find the interest for the first week for an account with a principal of $9,500 and a rate of 2.75% compounded weekly. Round your answer to the nearest hundredth. *For a review of rounding, refer to Appendix B.*

B. Find the interest for the first day of an account with a principal of $1,050 with a rate of 3% compounded daily. Round your answer to the nearest hundredth. *For a review of rounding, refer to Appendix B.*

Using a Spreadsheet to Find Compound Interest with Periods

With compound interest, the amount of interest you earn for each period will increase over time. Making the calculations by hand is tedious. Spreadsheets can calculate the amount of interest you earn each period. In this example, you will find the compound interest for 3 years for an account with a principal of $2,000.00 and a rate of 4% compounded monthly.

Step 1

Start by opening a blank spreadsheet. At the bottom of the page, double-click on Sheet 1 to highlight it.

	A	B	C	D	E
1					
2					
3					
	Sheet 1	+			

Step 2

Rename it to Compound Periods and then press enter.

	A	B	C	D	E
1					
2					
3					
	Compound Periods		+		

Step 3

Before making calculations create the headings. Start in A1 and type in the following headings.

	A	B	C	D	E
1	Period	Principal	Rate	Periods Per Year	Interest
2					
3					

Step 4

After creating headings, type in the information you know. In A2, type 1 for the first period. Type the Principal in B2 and the Rate in C2.

	A	B	C	D	E
1	Period	Principal	Rate	Periods Per Year	Interest
2	1	$2,000.00	4%		
3					

Step 5

In this example, compounding happens monthly (12 periods per year). In D2, type 12 and press tab.

Refer to the compounding periods chart on page 93 for more compounding periods.

	A	B	C	D	E
1	Period	Principal	Rate	Periods Per Year	Interest
2	1	$2,000.00	4%	12	
3					

Using a Spreadsheet to Find Compound Interest with Periods

Step 6

To find the interest, you will multiply the principal by the Rate and divide by the number of periods per year. Start by selecting E2, press (=), click on the Principal in B2, multiply (*) it by the Rate in C2, and divide (/) it by the Periods Per Year in D2. Then press (enter).

	A	B	C	D	E
1	Period	Principal	Rate	Periods Per Year	Interest
2	1	$2,000.00	4%	12	=B2*C2/D2
3					

Step 7

In the first month, you earned $6.67 in interest. To find the interest for the second month, start by selecting A3 and typing in a 2 for the second period. Then press (tab).

	A	B	C	D	E
1	Period	Principal	Rate	Periods Per Year	Interest
2	1	$2,000.00	4%	12	$6.67
3	2				
4					

Step 8

When using compound interest, you add the interest to the principal. In B3 press (=), click on the Principal in B2 and add (+) it to the Interest in E2. Then press (tab).

	A	B	C	D	E
1	Period	Principal	Rate	Periods Per Year	Interest
2	1	$2,000.00	4%	12	$6.67
3	2	=B2+E2			

Step 9

With compound interest, the principal will increase over time, but the Rate will stay the same. In C3 press (=) and click on the Rate in C2. Then press (tab).

	A	B	C	D	E
1	Period	Principal	Rate	Periods Per Year	Interest
2	1	$2,000.00	4%	12	$6.67
3	2	$2,006.67	=C2		

Step 10

The periods per year will also stay the same. In D3 press (=) and click on the Periods Per Year in D2 and then press (tab).

	A	B	C	D	E
1	Period	Principal	Rate	Periods Per Year	Interest
2	1	$2,000.00	4%	12	$6.67
3	2	$2,006.67	4%	=D2	

Using a Spreadsheet to Find Compound Interest with Periods

Step 11

To find the interest, select E3, press =, click on the Principal in B3, multiply * it by the Rate in C3, and divide / by the Periods Per Year in D3.

	A	B	C	D	E
1	Period	Principal	Rate	Periods Per Year	Interest
2	1	$2,000.00	4%	12	$6.67
3	2	$2,006.67	4%	12	=B3*C3/D3

Step 12

Press enter and your spreadsheet will do the math showing that the interest is $6.69 for the second month.

	A	B	C	D	E
1	Period	Principal	Rate	Periods Per Year	Interest
2	1	$2,000.00	4%	12	$6.67
3	2	$2,006.67	4%	12	$6.69
4					

Step 13

Once you set up the first two periods, your spreadsheet can do the rest. Select the bottom row by clicking on cell A3, holding down the mouse, and dragging it to cell E3. Then let go of the mouse.

	A	B	C	D	E
1	Period	Principal	Rate	Periods Per Year	Interest
2	1	$2,000.00	4%	12	$6.67
3	2	$2,006.67	4%	12	$6.69

Step 14

Click on the fill handle and drag it down until the number on the bottom right-hand corner tells you the total number of periods. To find the number of periods, multiply * the years times the periods per year.

	A	B	C	D	E
1	Period	Principal	Rate	Periods Per Year	Interest
2	1	$2,000.00	4%	12	$6.67
3	2	$2,006.67	4%	12	$6.69
4	3				
37	36				
38					

36 — Total Number of Periods

Step 15

Let go of the mouse and the spreadsheet will automatically do the math for the remaining months.

	A	B	C	D	E
1	Period	Principal	Rate	Periods Per Year	Interest
2	1	$2,000.00	4%	12	$6.67
3	2	$2,006.67	4%	12	$6.69
4	3	$2,013.36	4%	12	$6.71
37	36	$2,247.05	4%	12	$7.49

Using a Spreadsheet to Find Compound Interest with Periods

Step 16

To find the total amount of interest, you will total your interest column. Start by selecting the cell at the bottom of the interest column. In this case, it's E38. Then type =sum(. Select everything in the interest column by clicking on the first interest amount in E2, holding down the mouse, and dragging it to the last interest amount in E37.

	A	B	C	D	E
1	Period	Principal	Rate	Periods Per Year	Interest
2	1	$2,000.00	4%	12	$6.67
3	2	$2,006.67	4%	12	$6.69
37	36	$2,247.05	4%	12	$7.49
38					=SUM(E2:E37)

Step 17

Press enter and your spreadsheet will add all of the interest showing that you earned a total of $254.54 for the 3 years. Save your work as 2B Classwork.

	A	B	C	D	E
1	Period	Principal	Rate	Periods Per Year	Interest
2	1	$2,000.00	4%	12	$6.67
3	2	$2,006.67	4%	12	$6.69
37	36	$2,247.05	4%	12	$7.49
38					$254.54

Conclusion

Compound interest continues adding interest to the principal, thereby increasing how much interest you can earn. The more periods there are, the more frequently interest will be compounded.

The Power of Compound Interest

The power of compound interest is often underestimated. It is easy to put off investing if you don't have a lot of money to invest. You might think that you can wait a few more years to invest, but in this example you have seen the power of compound interest.

Albert Einstein is credited with this quote: "Compound interest is the eighth wonder of the world. He who understands it, earns it... he who doesn't... pays it." The sooner you start, even with a small sum of money, the sooner you can reap the rewards of compound interest.

4. Now Do the Math ...

For the following exercises, use your spreadsheet to find the total interest for the first year for different compounding periods on an account with a principal of $6,000 at a rate of 5%.

A. What would be the total interest earned if the account were compounded annually?

B. What if it were compounded semi-annually?

C. What if it were compounded quarterly?

D. What if it were compounded monthly?

E. What if it were compounded weekly?

F. What if it were compounded daily?

5. What Do You Think?

In the exercise above, which compounding period produced the greatest amount of interest? Explain why.

Send Penny to College

When Susan and Carlos were in college, they took out student loans and are still paying them back. They want to make sure Penny can go to college without loans. Uncle Rob will match Susan and Carlos' savings for Penny's college. Help the Garcias find a savings plan for Penny's college education.

Section 2B: Homework

1. One of the Garcia's financial goals is to save for a house and they put 60% of their disposable income towards this goal. Susan and Carlos decided to put this goal on hold for 6 months and use the money to save for Penny's education. If they have a disposable income of $556.19, how much would they save in 6 months?

2. Uncle Rob agreed to match their savings. With this contribution, how much money will the Garcias be able to put in Penny's account?

3. They place the money in an account for 15 years with a 4% interest rate that is compounded monthly.
   a. How many periods per year does this account have?
   b. How many total periods will there be?
   c. Create a spreadsheet for Penny's college fund. Record the first period and last period.

	A	B	C	D	E
1	Period	Principal	Rate	Periods Per Year	Interest
2					

   d. What is Penny's balance after the 15 years?
   e. Do you think this is enough for Penny to go to college without needing loans? Explain why or why not.

4. The Garcias decide that they want Penny to have more money. Instead of using their savings from the house for 6 months, they decided to use it for 1 year. They save 60% of their monthly disposable income of $556.19 for 1 year.
   a. How much would they be able to save?
   b. With Uncle Rob's contribution, how much would go into Penny's account?

5. They place the money in a similar account for 15 years with a 4% interest rate. This account is compounded weekly.
   a. How many periods per year does this account have?
   b. How many total periods will there be?
   c. Create a spreadsheet for Penny's college fund. Record the first period and last period.

	A	B	C	D	E
1	Period	Principal	Rate	Periods Per Year	Interest
2					

   d. What is Penny's balance after 15 years?
   e. Do you think this is enough for Penny to go to college without needing to take out loans? Explain why or why not.

6. Now think about your own life.
   a. What is one of your long-term goals?
   b. How many years do you need to be able to accomplish that goal?
   c. How much money will you need to reach your goal?

7. If you put $1,000 in an account that pays 4% interest compounded daily, see if you can reach your goal.
   a. How many periods per year does this account have?
   b. How many total periods will there be?
   c. Create a spreadsheet for your account and record the first period and the last period.

	A	B	C	D	E
1	Period	Principal	Rate	Periods Per Year	Interest
2					

   d. What is your ending balance?
   e. Were you able to reach your goal?

Section 2C: Paying Off Loans

In Sections 2A and 2B you learned how interest works. When you save money, interest is a good thing, but when you borrow money, you have to pay interest. In this section you will learn how interest on a loan works and how monthly payments are calculated.

Pros and Cons of Borrowing Money

Calculate the Monthly Payment

Create a Loan Repayment Schedule

Student Loans

Debt Happens ...

... and sometimes it can be hard to avoid. For most people, going to college, buying a car, or using a credit card means getting into debt. How much debt you get into, and how you plan to get out of debt are very important factors that affect your financial situation for years. When you go into debt to finance the things you want, you end up paying interest. Depending on the terms of the loan, you can end up paying a lot of interest. Understanding the true cost of financing can help you prioritize and decide how to use your budget to accomplish your financial goals.

The Pros and Cons of Borrowing Money

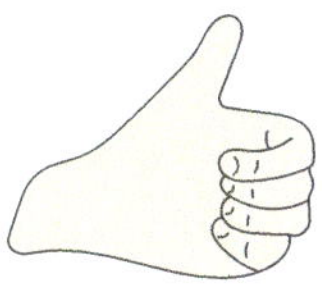

Pros

- Instant gratification
- Pay for emergencies
- Make large purchases (e.g. house or car)
- Opportunity to improve credit rating (more on this later)

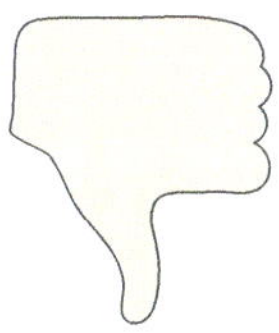

Cons

- Interest results in increased costs and makes saving more difficult
- Can lead to a debt cycle (opposite of the Saving Cycle on page 3)
- Lender owns the house or car until the loan is completely paid off
- Decreased credit rating for late payments or high credit card balance

1. What Do You Think?

A. What is an example of a time when going into debt could be a good idea?

B. What is an example of a time when going into debt could be a bad idea?

Types of Loans

There are many different kinds of loans, and the kind of loan you take out depends on what you plan to do with the money. Below are some of the most common loans.

Mortgages

A mortgage is a loan to buy a house. A mortgage is often the largest loan someone will ever take. Paying off a mortgage over 30 years is common.

Car Loans

A car loan is a loan to buy a car. It can be for a new or used car. Typically, interest rates for new cars are lower than for used cars, since new cars depreciate in value quickly and dealers have an incentive to sell off new car inventory.

Student Loans

Student loans are available to degree-seeking students enrolled in college. There are limits on how much a student can borrow in any one semester, and there are lifetime maximums for borrowing. There are two main kinds of student loans: subsidized and unsubsidized.

Personal Loans

Personal loans are loans issued for personal reasons. Qualifying for a personal loan requires a good credit rating and history and enough assets (savings and property) to be considered collateral for the loan.

Business Loans

Business loans are loans for starting, expanding, or improving a business. The amount you can borrow and the repayment terms are based on how old your business is, your personal credit history, your assets, and your business revenue. Most major financial institutions require businesses to be in business for at least 2 years, and the few that do lend to startups generally charge much higher interest rates.

Title Loans & Payday Loans

Title loans are loans where the title of a vehicle is signed over to a lending agency and a loan is made based on the value of the vehicle. If these are not repaid, the lender generally repossess the vehicle and sells it to cover the cost of the loan. Payday loans are loans based on pay-stubs and the employment history of the borrower. Title loans and payday loans are quite different, but they are both short-term loans that have the highest interest rates of any loans, often ranging from 30% to more than 300%.

Understanding Financial Aid and Student Loans

Financial aid is complicated, and understanding the different sources of funding to pay for college can be a challenge. This section will help you understand your financial aid award, so you can get back to your studies. If you have questions about your financial aid situation, see a financial aid professional.

FAFSA

The Free Application for Federal Student Aid (FAFSA) is the application you fill out in order to know what kinds of federal financial aid are available to you. You must complete the FAFSA annually in order to update your information. Based on this information, a Student Aid Report (SAR) is generated that details the kind of aid available to you.

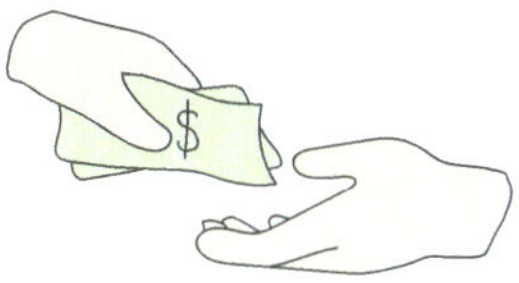

Scholarships

Scholarships are usually merit-based (based on academic performance) and do not have to be repaid. Often, specific scholarships target certain kinds of people: women, underrepresented ethnicities, and students in STEM majors are among the most commonly targeted groups. Academic advisors, counselors, and financial aid professionals can help you identify and apply for scholarships.

Grants

Grants are usually need-based (based on income) and most do not have to be repaid. One of the most common grants available is the Pell Grant. Amounts change every year, and the amount you are eligible for depends on your financial need, the cost of attendance, and whether you are a full-time or part-time student. You can only receive the Pell Grant for 12 full-time semesters.

Subsidized Student Loans

Subsidized student loans are the preferred kind of student loan, since the federal government pays the interest on the loan while you're in school. After graduation, you must repay the amount you borrowed. Perkins loans and some undergraduate Stafford loans fall into this category. There are limits on how much you can borrow in a year, and there is a lifetime maximum.

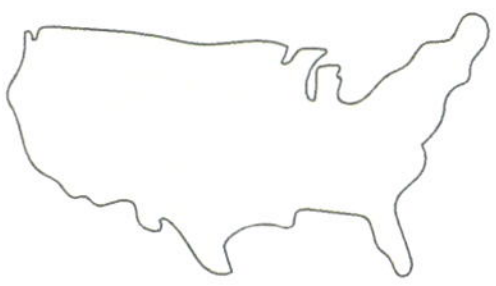

Unsubsidized Student Loans

Unsubsidized loans accrue interest immediately and that interest is added to your loan. When you graduate, you repay the amount you borrowed, plus interest. Furthermore, new interest is calculated based on the recapitalized amount (principal plus interest accrued). One way to avoid having interest recapitalized is to pay the interest while you are in school to avoid a bigger debt in the future. Some undergraduate, graduate, and all PLUS loans (for parents) fall into this category.

Private Student Loans

Private student loans are made directly by financial institutions and are not regulated directly by the federal government. As a result, they are unsubsidized loans and are generally at a higher interest rate. Financial aid professionals recommend that you avoid private loans, if possible.

The Costs of Borrowing Money

Down Payment
The amount of money you pay up front for a major purchase. The purchase price minus the down payment is the amount you have to finance.

Monthly Payment
The amount you pay each month, including interest.

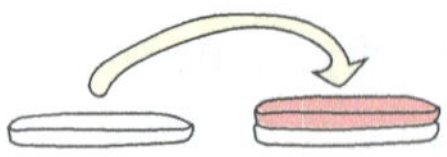

Interest
The money that accrues based on the principal of the loan. This is the fee for borrowing.

Total Amount Paid
The total sum of all payments made to repay the debt. This includes the original amount financed (the principal), all interest paid, and any fees.

Collateral
The assets (money or property) that "secures" certain loans. If the loan is not repaid, the assets used as collateral can be seized by the lender and sold to cover all or part of the loan.

Understanding Monthly Payments
When you make a monthly payment on a financed item, such as a car, part of the payment goes to pay for the car, and part goes to pay the lender (often a bank) as a fee for lending the money. How much of your monthly payment goes to pay off the car depends on the interest rate of the loan. If all the monthly payments made are added up, they will be more than amount borrowed since you have to pay back the money you borrowed plus interest.

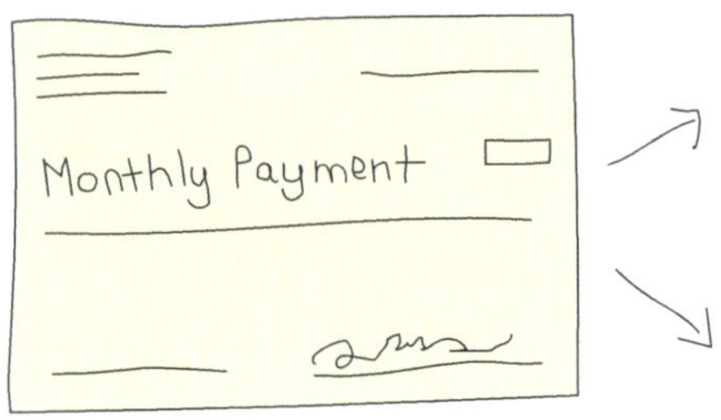

Interest
A portion of every monthly payment goes to pay interest.

Amount Paid on Principal
After paying interest, the rest of the monthly payment goes to pay off the principal of the loan.

Spreadsheet Abbreviations

Spreadsheets use abbreviations to represent common terms or functions. Here are some abbreviations or terms you will encounter in this section.

PMT

PMT stands for payment and is a spreadsheet function used to calculate the monthly payment on a loan.

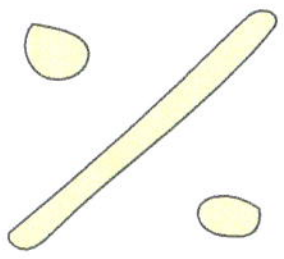

Rate

The percentage used to calculate interest on the principal.

NPER

NPER stands for the total numbers of periods in of your loan. Most loans are repaid monthly, so multiply the number of years by 12 months to find the total number of periods.

PV

PV stands for Present Value, which is the principal (the amount of money you are borrowing).

Using a Spreadsheet to Find the Monthly Payment

When you borrow money, you will be given a monthly payment. This payment will stay the same for the entire length of the loan. Spreadsheets have a function that can calculate the monthly payment for you. In this example, you will find the monthly payment for a loan of $20,000.00 with an Rate of 5% for 10 years.

Step 1

Start by opening a blank spreadsheet.

	A	B	C	D
1				
2				
3				
	Sheet 1	+		

Step 2

Rename Sheet 1 to Monthly Payment and press enter.

	A	B	C	D
1				
2				
3				
	Monthly Payment	+		

Using a Spreadsheet to Find the Monthly Payment

Step 3
Spreadsheets have a function called PMT that calculates your monthly payment. In A1, start by typing =pmt(.

	A	B	C	D
1	=PMT(			
2				

Step 4
The first piece of information needed is the rate per period. Type in your rate divided / by 12, since you are working with months. Then type a comma ,.

	A	B	C	D
1	=PMT(5%/12,			
2				

Step 5
The next piece of information needed is the total number of periods (NPER). Type in the number of years and multiply * it by 12 since you are working with months. Then type a comma ,.

	A	B	C	D
1	=PMT(5%/12,10*12,			
2				

Step 6
The last piece of information is your principal. Since you are dealing with debt it will be negative. Type a minus sign - before typing in the principal. Finish your function by closing the parentheses).

	A	B	C	D
1	=PMT(5%/12,10*12,-20000)			
2				

Step 7
Press enter and your spreadsheet will calculate your monthly payment. Save your work as 2C Classwork.

	A	B	C	D
1	$212.13			
2				

Conclusion
When applying for a loan, it is important to know what the monthly payment will be to make sure you can afford it. The PMT function can make this calculation.

2. Now Do the Math in a Spreadsheet ...

Use a spreadsheet to complete the chart below with the monthly payment for the following student loans. Record your answers in the chart below.

Name	Principal	Rate	Number of Years	Monthly Payment
Maria	$60,000.00	6.8%	20	
John	$40,000.00	6.8%	20	
Nancy	$20,000.00	6.8%	20	

3. What Do You Think?

A. Since all of the loans in the chart above have the same rate and number of years, how does the principal affects the monthly payment?

B. What is the difference between the highest and lowest monthly payments?

C. If you had a job that paid $15 per hour, how many hours per month would you have to work to cover the monthly payments for each loan scenario? *Round your answers to the nearest whole number.*

Maria = ____________________

John = ____________________

Nancy = ____________________

D. How many hours per week would that be? Assume there are 4 weeks per month. *Round your answers to the nearest whole number.*

Maria = ____________________

John = ____________________

Nancy = ____________________

Using a Spreadsheet to Create a Loan Repayment Schedule

A loan repayment schedule shows how much of your monthly payments go to pay interest. In this example, you will create a loan repayment schedule with a principal of $8,000.00 with an rate of 6% for 5 years.

Step 1

At the bottom of your spreadsheet, double-click the plus (+) sign next to the Monthly Payment sheet.

	A	B	C	D
1				
2				
3				

Monthly Payment | +

Step 2

Rename it to Loan Repayment and then press (enter).

	A	B	C	D
1				
2				
3				

Monthly Payment | Loan Repayment

Step 3

Before making calculations, create headings. Start in A1 and create the following headings.

	A	B	C	D	E	F
1	Month	Principal	Rate	Monthly Payment	Amount Paid on Interest	Amount Paid on Principal
2						

Step 4

After headings, type in the information you know. In A1, type the number 1 for the first month. In B2, type in your principal. In C2, type in your rate.

	A	B	C	D	E	F
1	Month	Principal	Rate	Monthly Payment	Amount Paid on Interest	Amount Paid on Principal
2	1	$8,000.00	6%			

Step 5

To find the monthly payment, you will use the PMT function. In D2, type (=pmt().

	A	B	C	D	E	F
1	Month	Principal	Rate	Monthly Payment	Amount Paid on Interest	Amount Paid on Principal
2	1	$8,000.00	6%	=PMT(		

Step 6

The first piece of information needed is the rate per period. Click on the rate in C2 and divide (/) it by 12 since you are working with months. Then type a comma (,).

	A	B	C	D	E	F
1	Month	Principal	Rate	Monthly Payment	Amount Paid on Interest	Amount Paid on Principal
2	1	$8,000.00	6%	=PMT(C2/12,		

Using a Spreadsheet to Create a Loan Repayment Schedule

Step 7

The next piece of information needed is the total number of periods (NPER). Type in the number of years and multiply * it by 12 since you are working with months. Then type a comma , .

	A	B	C	D	E	F
1	Month	Principal	Rate	Monthly Payment	Amount Paid on Interest	Amount Paid on Principal
2	1	$8,000.00	6%	=PMT(C2/12,5*12,		

Step 8

The last piece of information needed is the principal. Since you are dealing with debt, it will be negative. Type a minus sign - and click on your principal in B2. Then close the parentheses) to finish the function.

	A	B	C	D	E	F
1	Month	Principal	Rate	Monthly Payment	Amount Paid on Interest	Amount Paid on Principal
2	1	$8,000.00	6%	=PMT(C2/12,5*12,-B2)		

Step 9

Press enter and the spreadsheet will do the math showing that $154.66 is the monthly payment for this loan.

	A	B	C	D	E	F
1	Month	Principal	Rate	Monthly Payment	Amount Paid on Interest	Amount Paid on Principal
2	1	$8,000.00	6%	$154.66		

Step 10

The amount of interest you pay is based on your principal and rate. To find the interest, click on E2, type = , click on the Principal in B2, multiply * it by the Rate in C2, and divide / it by 12. Then press tab .

	A	B	C	D	E	F
1	Month	Principal	Rate	Monthly Payment	Amount Paid on Interest	Amount Paid on Principal
2	1	$8,000.00	6%	$154.66	=B2*C2/12	

Using a Spreadsheet to Create a Loan Repayment Schedule

Step 11

It shows that $40 of your monthly payment will go to interest. The rest will go towards paying off the loan. In F2, type (=), click on the Monthly Payment in D2, and subtract (-) the Amount Paid on Interest in E2.

	A	B	C	D	E	F
1	Month	Principal	Rate	Monthly Payment	Amount Paid on Interest	Amount Paid on Principal
2	1	$8,000.00	6%	$154.66	$40.00	=D2-E2

Step 12

Press (enter) and your spreadsheet will do the math showing that $114.66 of your monthly payment goes to pay off the loan.

	A	B	C	D	E	F
1	Month	Principal	Rate	Monthly Payment	Amount Paid on Interest	Amount Paid on Principal
2	1	$8,000.00	6%	$154.66	$40.00	$114.66
3						

Step 13

To calculate the second month, select A3 and type the number 2 for the second month.

	A	B	C	D	E	F
1	Month	Principal	Rate	Monthly Payment	Amount Paid on Interest	Amount Paid on Principal
2	1	$8,000.00	6%	$154.66	$40.00	$114.66
3	2					

Step 14

Since you paid $114.66 on your loan, your principal will be a little less in the second month. In B3, type (=), click on the Principal in B2, and subtract (-) the Amount Paid on Principal in F2. Then press (tab).

	A	B	C	D	E	F
1	Month	Principal	Rate	Monthly Payment	Amount Paid on Interest	Amount Paid on Principal
2	1	$8,000.00	6%	$154.66	$40.00	$114.66
3	2	=B2-F2				

Step 15

The principal will get a little smaller each month., but the Rate will stay the same. In C3, type (=) and click on the Rate in C2. Then press (tab).

	A	B	C	D	E	F
1	Month	Principal	Rate	Monthly Payment	Amount Paid on Interest	Amount Paid on Principal
2	1	$8,000.00	6%	$154.66	$40.00	$114.66
3	2	$7,885.34	=C2			

Using a Spreadsheet to Create a Loan Repayment Schedule

Step 16

The monthly payment will also stay the same. In D3, type = and click on the Monthly Payment in D2. Then press tab.

	A	B	C	D	E	F
1	Month	Principal	Rate	Monthly Payment	Amount Paid on Interest	Amount Paid on Principal
2	1	$8,000.00	6%	$154.66	$40.00	$114.66
3	2	$7,885.34	6%	=D2		

Step 17

Since your principal is a little smaller, you will pay a little less interest in your second month. In E3, type =, click on the Principal in B3, multiply * it by the Rate in C3, and divide / it by 12 months. Then press tab.

	A	B	C	D	E	F
1	Month	Principal	Rate	Monthly Payment	Amount Paid on Interest	Amount Paid on Principal
2	1	$8,000.00	6%	$154.66	$40.00	$114.66
3	2	$7,885.34	6%	$154.66	=B3*C3/12	

Step 18

It shows that $39.43 of your monthly payment will go toward interest in month 2. To find how much of your payment will go toward the loan, select F3, type =, click on the Monthly Payment in D3, and subtract − the Amount Paid on Interest in E3.

	A	B	C	D	E	F
1	Month	Principal	Rate	Monthly Payment	Amount Paid on Interest	Amount Paid on Principal
2	1	$8,000.00	6%	$154.66	$40.00	$114.66
3	2	$7,885.34	6%	$154.66	$39.43	=D3-E3

Step 19

Press enter and your spreadsheet will do the math showing that you will pay $115.24 on the principal of your loan in the second month.

	A	B	C	D	E	F
1	Month	Principal	Rate	Monthly Payment	Amount Paid on Interest	Amount Paid on Principal
2	1	$8,000.00	6%	$154.66	$40.00	$114.66
3	2	$7,885.34	6%	$154.66	$39.43	$115.24
4						

Using a Spreadsheet to Create a Loan Repayment Schedule

Step 20

Once the first 2 months are complete, your spreadsheet can do the rest. Select the bottom row by clicking on A3, holding down the mouse, and dragging it to cell F3. Then let go of the mouse.

	A	B	C	D	E	F
1	Month	Principal	Rate	Monthly Payment	Amount Paid on Interest	Amount Paid on Principal
2	1	$8,000.00	6%	$154.66	$40.00	$114.66
3	2	$7,885.34	6%	$154.66	$39.43	$115.24

Step 21

Click on the fill handle and drag it down so that the number on the bottom right-hand corner shows the total number of months of the loan (to find the total months multiply * the number of years by 12). In this case there are 60 total months.

	A	B	C	D	E	F	
1	Month	Principal	Rate	Monthly Payment	Amount Paid on Interest	Amount Paid on Principal	
2	1	$8,000.00	6%	$154.66	$40.00	$114.66	
3	2	$7,885.34	6%	$154.66	$39.43	$115.24	
60							
61							60

Total Number of Months

Step 22

Let go of the mouse and the rest of the spreadsheet will fill in.

	A	B	C	D	E	F
1	Month	Principal	Rate	Monthly Payment	Amount Paid on Interest	Amount Paid on Principal
2	1	$8,000.00	6%	$154.66	$40.00	$114.66
3	2	$7,885.34	6%	$154.66	$39.43	$115.24
60	59	$307.02	6%	$154.66	$1.54	$153.13
61	60	$153.89	6%	$154.66	$0.77	$153.89

Step 23

To find the total amount of interest you will pay on this loan, select the cell underneath the interest column. In this case, it's cell E62. Type =sum(. Then, select everything in that column.

	A	B	C	D	E	F
1	Month	Principal	Rate	Monthly Payment	Amount Paid on Interest	Amount Paid on Principal
2	1	$8,000.00	6%	$154.66	$40.00	$114.66
3	2	$7,885.34	6%	$154.66	$39.43	$115.24
60	59	$307.02	6%	$154.66	$1.54	$153.13
61	60	$153.89	6%	$154.66	$0.77	$153.89
62					=SUM(E2:E61)	

Using a Spreadsheet to Create a Loan Repayment Schedule

Step 24

Press enter and your spreadsheet will do the math showing that you will pay a total of $1,279.77 in interest over the life of the loan. Make sure to save your work.

	A	B	C	D	E	F
1	Month	Principal	Rate	Monthly Payment	Amount Paid on Interest	Amount Paid on Principal
2	1	$8,000.00	6%	$154.66	$40.00	$114.66
3	2	$7,885.34	6%	$154.66	$39.43	$115.24
60	59	$307.02	6%	$154.66	$1.54	$153.13
61	60	$153.89	6%	$154.66	$0.77	$153.89
62					$1,279.74	

Conclusion

When you take out a loan, you pay a monthly payment each month until the loan is paid off. Part of each payment will go towards interest, and that interest can really add up over the life of the loan.

4. Now Do the Math ...

Use a spreadsheet to create a repayment schedule for the following loan that is to be paid within 10 years. Record the answers to the first 2 months and the last 2 months below.

	A	B	C	D	E	F
1	Month	Principal	Rate	Monthly Payment	Amount Paid on Interest	Amount Paid on Principal
2	1	$35,000.00	4.5%			
3	2					
120	119					
121	120					
122						

5. What Do You Think?

A. When you look at the spreadsheet above, what do you notice about the amount paid on the principal? Does it increase or decrease over time?

B. Does the amount paid on interest increase or decrease over time?

Paying Off Student Loans

When Susan and Carlos were still in school, they both took out student loans and 5 years later, they are still paying them off.

Section 2C: Homework

1. Carlos took out $4,000 each year in subsidized federal student loans. His loans have a 6.8% interest rate and he was in school for 3 years.
   a. What was his principal when he graduated?
   b. If Carlos decides to pay the loan off in 10 years, what will his monthly payment be?
   c. How many payments will he make over 10 years?
   d. What is the total of all of these payments?
   e. Use a spreadsheet to create a loan repayment schedule for Carlos. Record your results for the first month and last month.

	A	B	C	D	E	F
1	Month	Principal	Rate	Monthly Payment	Amount Paid on Interest	Amount Paid on Principal
2						

   f. Use your spreadsheet to find the total amount of interest Carlos will pay over the course of 10 years.

2. Carlos has the option of paying his loans off in 25 years instead of 10 years.
   a. What would his new monthly payment be?
   b. How many payments will he make in the course of 25 years?
   c. What will the total of all of his payments be?
   d. Use a spreadsheet to create a new repayment schedule for Carlos. Record your results for the first month and the last month.

	A	B	C	D	E	F
1	Month	Principal	Rate	Monthly Payment	Amount Paid on Interest	Amount Paid on Principal
2						

   e. Use your spreadsheet to find the total amount of interest.

3. Carlos could also pay the loan off faster. He could pay it in 5 years instead of 10 years.
   a. What would his new monthly payment be?
   b. How many payments will he make in the course of 25 years?
   c. What will the total of all of his payments be?
   d. Use a spreadsheet to create a new repayment schedule for Carlos. Record your results for the first month and the last month.

	A	B	C	D	E	F
1	Month	Principal	Rate	Monthly Payment	Amount Paid on Interest	Amount Paid on Principal
2						

   e. Use your spreadsheet to find the total amount of interest.

4. Based on your results to problems 1-3, compare the repayment options for Carlos.
   a. What is the difference between the monthly payment of the 10 year loan and the 25 year loan?
   b. What is the difference between the monthly payment of the 5 year loan and the 10 year loan?
   c. How much more interest did Carlos pay for the 25 year plan than the 10 year plan?
   d. How much less interest did Carlos pay for the 5 year plan than the 10 year plan?

5. If you were Carlos, which repayment plan would you choose? Explain why.

6. Susan also took out student loans, but she decided to work and take out less. Instead of taking out $4,000 a year like Carlos, she took out $2,500 a year.
   a. What is the difference between Carlos' loans each year and hers?
   b. If she worked a job that paid $12 an hour, how many hours a year did she have to work to make up that difference? Round your answer to the nearest whole number.
   c. How many hours a week would that be? Round your answer to the nearest whole number. *Assume there are 52 weeks in a year.*

7. Assuming Susan took out $2,500 a year for the 3 years she was in school, calculate her loan details.
   a. What was her principal when she graduated?
   b. If Susan decides to pay the loan off in 10 years, what will her monthly payment be?
   c. How many payments will she make over 10 years?
   d. What is the total of all of these payments?
   e. Use a spreadsheet to create a loan repayment schedule for Susan. Record your results for the first month and last month.

	A	B	C	D	E	F
1	Month	Principal	Rate	Monthly Payment	Amount Paid on Interest	Amount Paid on Principal
2						

   f. Use your spreadsheet to find the total amount of interest Susan will pay over the course of 10 years.

8. What is the difference between Carlos' interest and Susan's interest if they both pay the loan off in 10 years?

9. In your opinion, what do you think are the pros and cons of taking out student loans? List at least 3 pros and 3 cons.

10. When you think about your own life, what has your experience been with loans? If you have taken out loans, do you think they were worth the extra cost of interest? Explain why or why not. If you haven't taken out any loans, do you think you will? Explain why or why not.

Section 2D: Using Credit Cards

In Section 2C, you learned about paying off loans and how interest is calculated. Credit cards are another form of debt. Unlike on a loan, the amount you owe when you use a credit card can change over time, which causes the amount you have to pay each month to change. In this section, you will learn the pros and cons of credit cards, how payments are calculated, and ways to reduce credit card interest.

Calculate Minimum Payments

Understand Credit Ratings

Explore the Pros and Cons of Credit Cards

Calculate the Long Term Costs of Credit Cards

Are you Leaving Money on the Table?

When you use credit cards they often come with a reward system, such as cash back on certain purchases or points that can be redeemed for plane tickets and other rewards. This makes credit cards different from other kinds of debt, such as loans. These "perks" for credit card use can be enticing, but are only worth it if the credit card balance is paid off every month. Often, you have to make $15,000 in purchases before you have enough points to redeem for rewards. Paying off the entire credit card balance every month means you don't pay interest, you improve your credit rating, and you can take advantage of the rewards of credit card use.

The Pros and Cons of Credit Cards

As with every kind of debt, there are pros and cons to using credit cards. Credit cards can be a convenient way to pay for purchases and earn rewards, but they can also be a fast track to a debt cycle.

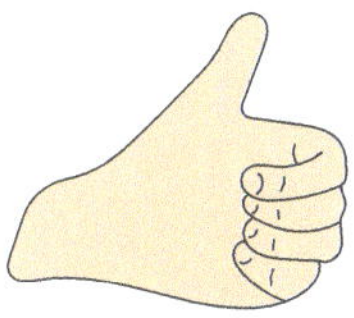

Pros

- Rewards, such as cash back or redeemable points
- Build a credit history
- Instant gratification
- Helpful in emergencies

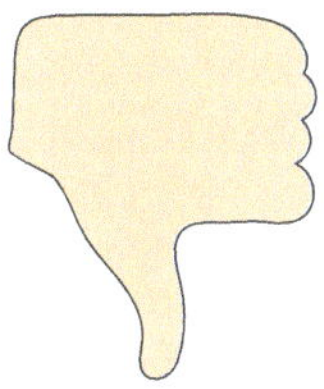

Cons

- High interest rates
- Easy to spend more than you make
- Difficult to pay off
- Penalties and fees

1. What Do You Think?

A. What is your experience with credit cards?

B. What is an example of when a credit card would be useful?

C. What is an example of when a credit card can be dangerous?

Credit Scores

Factors that Influence Credit Scores

Many factors influence how credit scores are calculated. Higher credit scores mean lower interest rates and less interest paid when you do borrow. More and more, credit scores are being used to make all kinds of decisions, including whom to hire.

Payment History

A record of whether payments have been on time or late.

Debt to Balance Ratio

How much debt you have compared to your credit limit.

Debt to Income Ratio

How much debt you have compared to your income.

Credit History

Whether previous lines of credit have been paid off or are in good standing.

Types of Credit

The different lines of credit you have (credit card, auto loan, mortgage, personal loan, etc.).

New Credit

How many of your lines of credit are recently opened.

2. What Do You Think?

Describe situations when having a good credit score is useful.

Credit Card Vocabulary

The vocabulary of credit cards is similar to other kinds of debt, but it includes the concept of minimum payment. With loans, the loan amount (principal) and the monthly payment are set and do not change. With credit cards, the balance and minimum payment are based on how you use it.

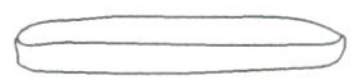

Balance

The amount of money you owe to the credit card company. It is similar to the principal for a loan.

Minimum Payment

The minimum amount you must pay each month, usually 2% of the balance. Generally, most of this money goes to pay interest and not to pay the balance.

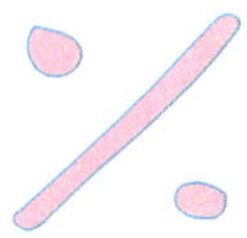

Rate

The percentage that determines how much interest you have to pay.

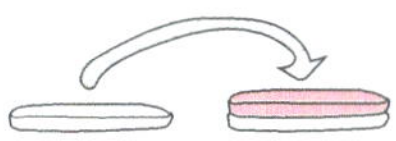

Interest

The money you pay as a fee for borrowing money.

Calculating the Minimum Payment

For most credit cards, the minimum payment is 2% of the average balance on your card. Calculate the minimum payment for a credit card that has a balance of $500.

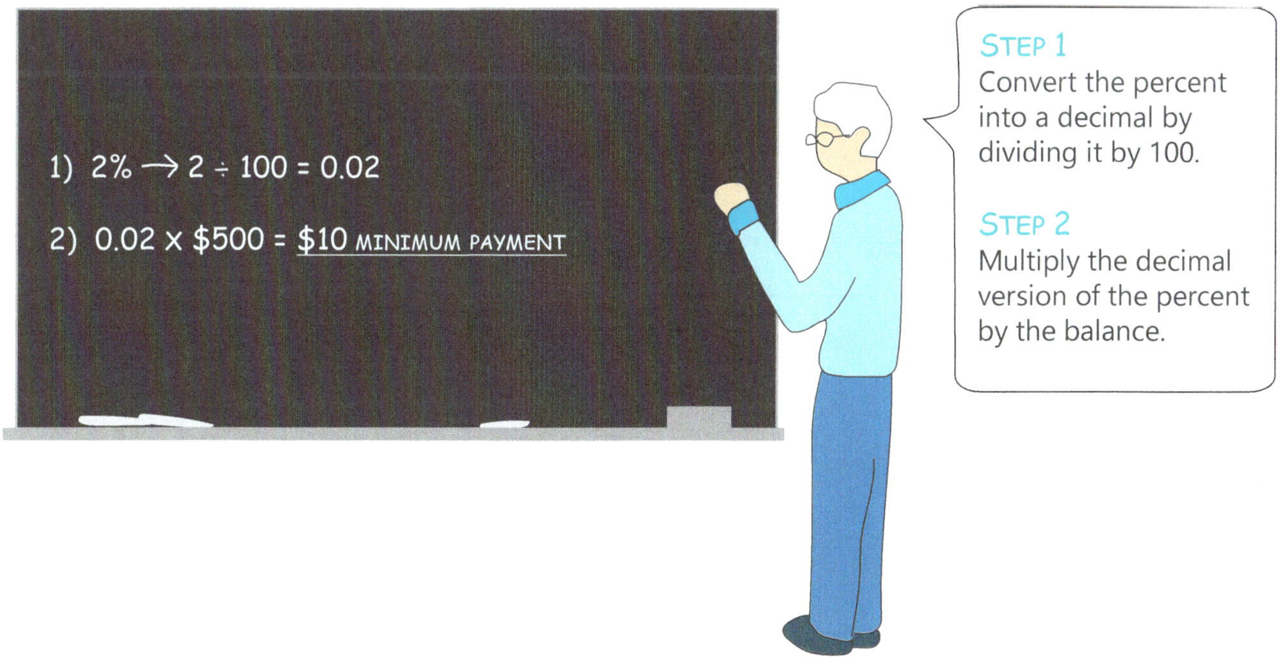

3. Now Do the Math ...

A. What would the minimum payment be for a credit card that has a $2,000 balance if the minimum payment is 2% of the balance?

B. If the credit card doesn't charge any interest, how many months would it take to pay it off if you paid that much each month?

C. If the credit card has an interest rate of 14%, take a guess as to how long it would take to pay off the card if you only made the minimum payments.

Using a Spreadsheet to Pay Off a Credit Card

In the previous exercise, you guessed how long it would take to pay off a credit card with a balance of $2,000.00 that had an interest rate of 14% if you only made minimum payments. Now use a spreadsheet to find out.

Step 1

Open a new spreadsheet.

	A	B	C	D
1				
2				
3				
	Sheet 1	+		

Step 2

Rename Sheet 1 to Credit Card and press enter.

	A	B	C	D
1				
2				
3				
	Credit Card	+		

Step 3

Start in A1 and create the following headings.

	A	B	C	D	E	F
1	Month	Balance	Rate	2% Minimum Payment	Amount Paid on Interest	Amount Paid on Balance
2						

Using a Spreadsheet to Pay Off a Credit Card

Step 4

After headings, type in what you know. In A2, type the number 1 for the first month. In B2, type the balance. In C2, type the rate.

	A	B	C	D	E	F
1	Month	Balance	Rate	2% Minimum Payment	Amount Paid on Interest	Amount Paid on Balance
2	1	$2,000.00	14%			

Step 5

Most minimum payments are 2% of the balance. In D2, type =, click on the Balance in B2, and multiply * it by 2%. Then press tab.

	A	B	C	D	E	F
1	Month	Balance	Rate	2% Minimum Payment	Amount Paid on Interest	Amount Paid on Balance
2	1	$2,000.00	14%	=B2*2%		

Step 6

The interest is the balance times the Rate, divided by 12 months. In E2, type =, click on the Balance in B2, multiply * it by the Rate in C2, and divide / it by 12. Then press tab.

	A	B	C	D	E	F
1	Month	Balance	Rate	2% Minimum Payment	Amount Paid on Interest	Amount Paid on Balance
2	1	$2,000.00	14%	$40.00	=B2*C2/12	

Step 7

According to the spreadsheet, you will pay $40.00, and $23.33 of it will go toward interest. The rest will go toward paying off the balance. In F2, type =, click on the Minimum Payment in D2, and subtract - the Interest in E2. Then press enter.

	A	B	C	D	E	F
1	Month	Balance	Rate	2% Minimum Payment	Amount Paid on Interest	Amount Paid on Balance
2	1	$2,000.00	14%	$40.00	$23.33	=D2-E2

Step 8

You paid $16.67 , the Balance in the second month will decrease. In B3, type =, click on the Balance in B2, and subtract - the Amount Paid on the Balance in F2. Then press tab.

	A	B	C	D	E	F
1	Month	Balance	Rate	2% Minimum Payment	Amount Paid on Interest	Amount Paid on Balance
2	1	$2,000.00	14%	$40.00	$23.33	$16.67
3	2	=B2-F2				

Using a Spreadsheet to Pay Off a Credit Card

Step 9

The Balance decreased a little, but the Rate will stay the same. In C3, type (=) and click on the Rate in C2. Then press (tab).

	A	B	C	D	E	F
1	Month	Balance	Rate	2% Minimum Payment	Amount Paid on Interest	Amount Paid on Balance
2	1	$2,000.00	14%	$40.00	$23.33	$16.67
3	2	$1,983.33	=C2			

Step 10

The minimum payment is 2% of the balance. In D3, type (=), click on the balance in B3, and multiply (*) it by 2%. Then press (tab).

	A	B	C	D	E	F
1	Month	Balance	Rate	2% Minimum Payment	Amount Paid on Interest	Amount Paid on Balance
2	1	$2,000.00	14%	$40.00	$23.33	$16.67
3	2	$1,983.33	14%	=B3*2%		

Step 11

To find the interest, select E3, type (=), click on the Balance in B3, multiply (*) it by the Rate in C3, and divide (/) by 12 months. Then press (tab).

	A	B	C	D	E	F
1	Month	Balance	Rate	2% Minimum Payment	Amount Paid on Interest	Amount Paid on Balance
2	1	$2,000.00	14%	$40.00	$23.33	$16.67
3	2	$1,983.33	14%	$39.67	=B3*C3/12	

Step 12

To find the amount paid on balance, select F3, type (=), click on the Minimum Payment in D3, and subtract (-) the Interest in E3. Then press (tab).

	A	B	C	D	E	F
1	Month	Balance	Rate	2% Minimum Payment	Amount Paid on Interest	Amount Paid on Balance
2	1	$2,000.00	14%	$40.00	$23.33	$16.67
3	2	$1,983.33	14%	$39.67	$23.14	=D3-E3

Step 13

Once the first 2 months are set up, the spreadsheet can do the rest. Select the bottom row by clicking on A3, holding the mouse down, and dragging it to F3. Then let go of the mouse.

	A	B	C	D	E	F
1	Month	Balance	Rate	2% Minimum Payment	Amount Paid on Interest	Amount Paid on Balance
2	1	$2,000.00	14%	$40.00	$23.33	$16.67
3	2	$1,983.33	14%	$39.67	$23.14	$16.53

Using a Spreadsheet to Pay Off a Credit Card

Step 14

Click on the fill handle and drag it down until the balance is close to but not under $100. Note: this will take a while.

	A	B	C	D	E	F
1	Month	Balance	Rate	2% Minimum Payment	Amount Paid on Interest	Amount Paid on Balance
2	1	$2,000.00	14%	$40.00	$23.33	$16.67
3	2	$1,983.33	14%	$39.67	$23.14	$16.53
?						

Step 15

It will take 358 months to get the balance close to $100. To find the number of years, divide / 358 by 12.

358 ÷ 12 = 29.8 years

	A	B	C	D	E	F
1	Month	Balance	Rate	2% Minimum Payment	Amount Paid on Interest	Amount Paid on Balance
359	358	$100.83	14%	$2.02	$1.18	$0.84

Step 16

To find the amount of interest over that time, select the cell underneath the amount of interest. In this case, it's cell E360. Type =sum(. Then select everything in the interest column.

	A	B	C	D	E	F
1	Month	Balance	Rate	2% Minimum Payment	Amount Paid on Interest	Amount Paid on Balance
359	358	$100.83	14%	$2.02	$1.18	$0.84
360						

Step 17

Press enter and the spreadsheet will show that you will pay $2,660.01 in interest in addition to the $2,000 balance charged on the credit card. It will also take 30 years. Save your work as 2D Classwork.

	A	B	C	D	E	F
1	Month	Balance	Rate	2% Minimum Payment	Amount Paid on Interest	Amount Paid on Balance
359	358	$100.83	14%	$2.02	$1.18	$0.84
360					$2,660.01	

Conclusion

Paying the minimum payment on a credit card may seem like the most affordable option in the short term, but it takes a long time to pay off the card and causes you to pay more interest.

4. Now Do the Math in a Spreadsheet ...

A. Use a spreadsheet to find the number of months it would take to pay off $1,500 with an interest rate of 18% if you only make the minimum payment of 2% of the balance. Stop when your balance gets close to but not under $100. Record your answers below for the first two months and the last month. Record your answers in the chart below.

	A	B	C	D	E	F
1	Month	Balance	Rate	2% Minimum Payment	Amount Paid on Interest	Amount Paid on Balance
2	1	$1,500.00	18%			
3	2					

B. What if you doubled your payments? Redo the problem above and change the minimum payment from 2% to 4% of the balance. How many months would it take to pay it off? Record your answers in the chart below.

	A	B	C	D	E	F
1	Month	Balance	Rate	4% Minimum Payment	Amount Paid on Interest	Amount Paid on Balance
2	1	$1,500.00	18%			
3	2					

5. What Do You Think?

A. Considering the exercise above, why do you think it takes so long to pay off a credit card balance if only the minimum payment is made?

B. How much time was saved by doubling the monthly payment?

What About Rewards?

Credit cards usually have high interest rates, but credit card companies often advertise rewards or incentives to attract customers. Some offer cash back on purchases, others give frequent flier miles, and others promote introductory interest rates that are lower for the first few months. The way to take advantage of these rewards is to completely pay your balance each month. That way, you won't pay any interest and you'll benefit from the rewards.

Types of Rewards

Each credit card company is different. Here are some common rewards offered to credit card holders.

Cash Back

Many credit cards give you a percentage of your purchase back. For example, if you spend $100 on an item, you might get 1% or 2% ($1 or $2) back as "cash back." You only get cash back for purchases once.

Points

Credit cards also offer points. For each dollar you charge on your card, you'll receive points which you can redeem for gift cards, plane tickets, and other rewards.

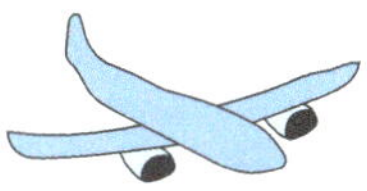

Frequent Flier Miles

Another incentive credit card companies offer is frequent flier miles. For each dollar you charge, you earn miles, which can be redeemed for plane tickets. This is a popular reward for people who love to travel.

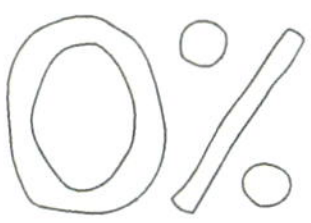

Introductory Rate

Many credit card companies offer low or no interest for the first few months. Make sure to pay off your balance during this time period, as your interest rates will increase quickly.

Calculating Cash Back Rewards

Calculate the reward for a charge of $138.75 on a credit card that offers 1% cash back.

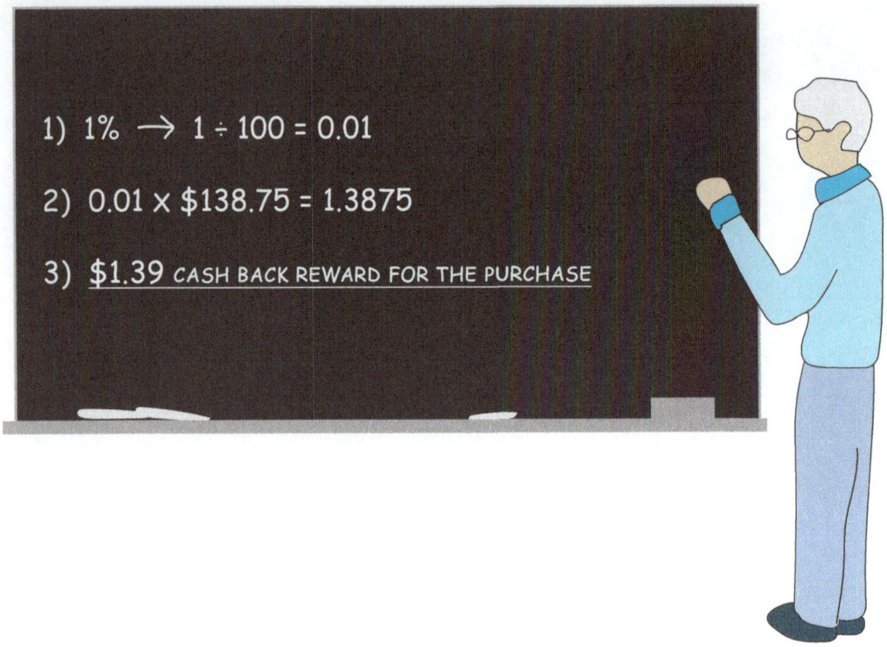

Step 1
Turn the percentage into a decimal.

Step 2
Multiply the decimal version of the percentage by the dollar amount.

Step 3
Round your answer to the nearest hundredth.

Comparing Cash Back to Interest

Calculate the amount of interest for the first month for the same credit card charge of $138.75 if the interest rate is 22%.

Step 1
Since the rate is based on a year, divide it by 12 months.

Step 2
Turn the percentage into a decimal.

Step 3
Multiply the decimal version of the percentage by the dollar amount.

Step 4
Round your answer to the nearest hundredth.

6. Now Do the Math ...

A. Compare the cash back rewards of 1.5% on purchases of $2,000 with the interest that accrues for 1 month for a credit card balance of $2,000 and interest rate of 16.9%.

Cash Back = ______________________

Interest = ________________________

B. Compare the cash back rewards of 2% on purchases of $1,200 with the interest that accrues for 1 month for a credit card balance of $1,200 and interest rate of 10.9%.

Cash Back = ______________________

Interest = ________________________

C. Compare the cash back rewards of 3% on purchases of $5,000 with the interest that accrues for 1 month for a credit card balance of $5,000 and interest rate of 18.9%.

Cash Back = ______________________

Interest = ________________________

7. What Do You Think?

Look at the two examples on the chalkboards on the previous page. Which was the higher amount: the cash back or the interest?

Paying Off the Credit Card

If the Garcias pay off their entire credit card balance each month, they won't have to pay interest and they will earn rewards for using a credit card. If they can't pay the entire balance, they will pay interest on their debt. Since they want to pay off all their debt so they can save more money toward their financial goals, they need to know how different credit card terms will affect how much of their money is going to interest, rather than toward their goals. Help the Garcias make informed decisions about using a credit card and how paying interest will affect their ability to save!

Section 2D: Homework

1. The Garcias currently owe $4,800 on their credit card.
   a. Calculate their (2%) minimum payment.
   b. If the card charged no interest, how many months would it take to pay off the card if they paid that much each month?
   c. How many years is that? *Round to the nearest year.*

2. Now assume their credit card has an interest rate of 11.75%.
   a. Use a spreadsheet to determine how many months it would take to get their balance close to but not under $100. Record your answers for the first month and last month.

	A	B	C	D	E	F
1	Month	Balance	Rate	2% Minimum Payment	Amount Paid on Interest	Amount Paid on Balance
2						

   b. How many months did it take to pay it off?

c. How many years is that? *Round to the nearest year.*
d. How much interest did they pay?

3. Compare your answers from problems 1 and 2.
   a. How many more years did it take to pay the credit card when there is interest than when there was no interest?
   b. How much more did the Garcias have to pay when there was interest?

4. Carlos accidentally made a late payment, which increased the interest rate to 18%.
   a. Create another spreadsheet with the new interest rate. Record your answers for the first month and last month.

	A	B	C	D	E	F
1	Month	Balance	Rate	2% Minimum Payment	Amount Paid on Interest	Amount Paid on Balance
2						

   b. How many months does it take to pay it off with the new interest rate?
   c. How many years is that? *Round to the nearest year.*
   d. How much interest do they have to pay?

5. Susan and Carlos decide they want to pay off their credit card faster. Instead of paying the minimum payment which is 2% of the balance, they decided to pay 10% of the balance. Assume they still have the interest rate of 18%.
   a. Create a spreadsheet with the new payment method. Record your answers for the first month and last month.

	A	B	C	D	E	F
1	Month	Balance	Rate	10% Payment	Amount Paid on Interest	Amount Paid on Balance
2						

   b. How many months does it take to pay it off with the new interest rate?
   c. How many years is that? *Round to the nearest year.*
   d. How much interest do they have to pay?

6. Compare your answer to problems 4 and 5.
   a. How many years did the Garcias save by paying 10% of the balance instead of 2%?
   b. How much interest did they save?

7. What do you think are some of the pros and cons (advantages and disadvantages) to using credit? List at least 3 of each.

Chapter 3: Financial Stability

3A Calculating Risk

3B Retirement

3C Property & Auto Insurance

3D Health Insurance

Section 3A: Calculating Risk

In Chapter 2, you learned about interest. Whenever interest is involved, there are risks. When you invest money, you have the opportunity to earn interest, but you can also lose the interest you earned, depending on the state of the economy. In risky investing, you can even lose your principal. When borrowing money, there is always a risk that your financial situation may change making it difficult to make your monthly payments. In this section, you will learn how to look at risk from a mathematical perspective to make informed decisions.

Calculate Probability

Make Pie Charts to Show Probability

Understand Risk and Reward

Calculate the Expected Value

Manage Risk

People calculate probability all the time. Mostly, you calculate how probable (likely) an event is from real life experiences. When you reach into a drawer for socks in the morning, what is the probability that the two socks you grab are matching? Well, the answer to that question depends on several factors, such as how many socks you have and how many different patterns there are. But you don't usually think about that—you just keep grabbing socks until you have a pair. In this section, you will look at the math behind how you calculate probability. Whether you're talking about card games, the lottery, or what kind of insurance to purchase, knowing the odds can help you make informed decisions.

1. What Do You Think?

A. Do you prefer to take a lot of risks with the hopes of getting a bigger reward or do you prefer to play it safe with smaller rewards?

B. If you could invest in an account that would double your money, but it could also cause you to lose all of your money, would you do it? Why or why not?

Probability

Probability is the likelihood of something happening. It is the relationship between the desired outcome compared to the total possible outcomes.

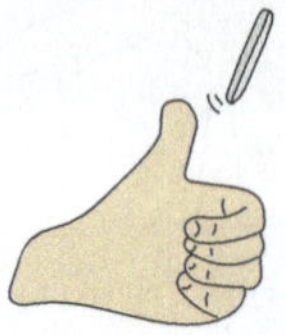

Flipping a Coin

The probability of getting heads from a coin toss is 1 out of 2, since there is 1 desired outcome out of 2 possible sides of a coin.

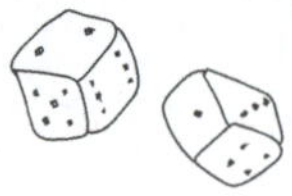

Rolling a Die

The probability of rolling a "2" on a die is 1 out of 6, since there is 1 desired outcome out of 6 possible sides of a die.

Drawing a Card

The probability of drawing the ace of diamonds is 1 out of 52 because there is 1 desired outcome out of 52 possible cards in a standard deck.

Calculating Probability

Probability can be expressed as a fraction, decimal, or percent. In this section you will work with it as a decimal. Find the probably of getting heads on a coin toss.

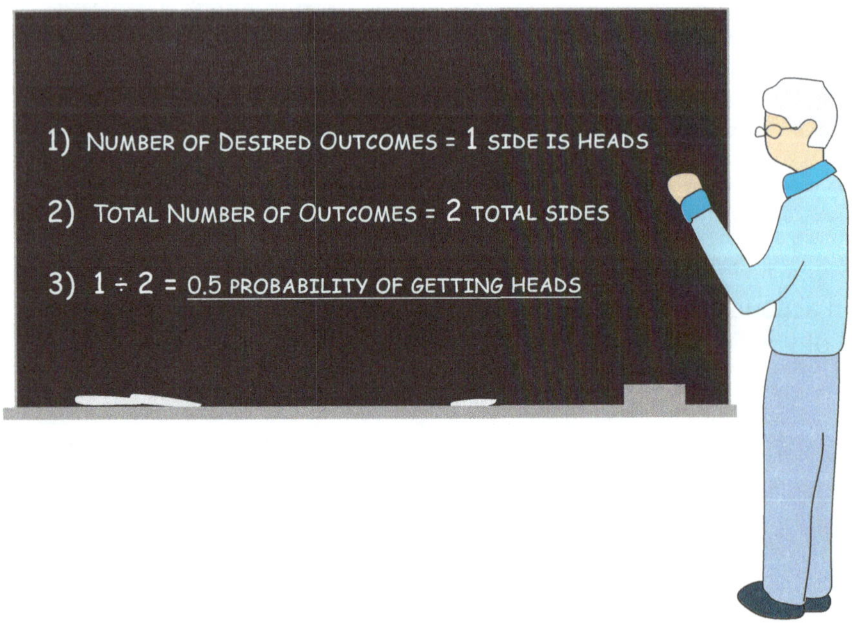

Step 1

Determine the number of desired outcomes. In this case, 1 side of the coin is heads.

Step 2

Determine the number of total possible outcomes. In this case, there are 2 sides on the coin.

Step 3

Divide the number of desired outcomes by the number of total possible outcomes.

2. Now Do the Math …

A. What is the probability of rolling a "2" on a six-sided die? *Round your answer to the nearest hundredth.*

B. What is the probability of drawing an ace in a 52-card deck? *Round your answer to the nearest hundredth.*

C. What is the probability of rolling an even number on a six-sided die?

D. What is the probability that a randomly selected month of the year will end with the letter "y"?

Risk and Financial Decisions

Understanding risk is an important part of making financial decisions. The following are some areas where the concept of risk comes in handy.

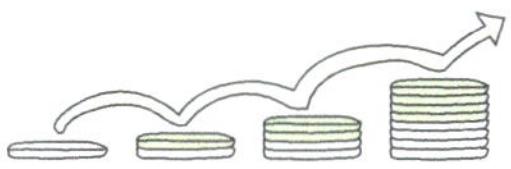

Investing

Anytime you invest money, you have the opportunity to earn interest, but there is always risk. You could lose all or part of the money you put into the investment, depending on the terms of the investment. Generally, higher interest rates for investments correspond to more risk.

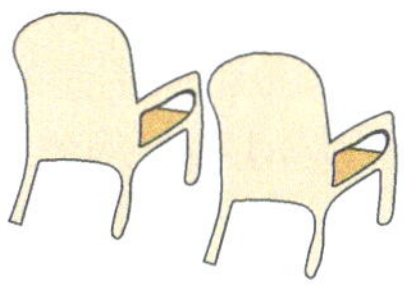

Retirement

Saving in a retirement fund is a form of investing. It has the chance of earning interest, but there is also the chance of losing some or all of the money in the account. Retirement savings accounts vary, so talk with your employer or a financial professional for the specifics of your plan.

Debt

Taking out a loan is a risk because life events happen and can make it difficult to continue making payments.

Insurance

Whether insuring your personal property or your health, there is always a risk of unexpected events happening that will cost money. Buying insurance is a way to manage the risk of unexpected costs. The level of your insurance should correspond to the level of risk in your life.

Expected Value

It is impossible to truly know what will happen in the future. There is always the element of risk in life, but probability can show you what is likely to happen in a given circumstance. This information can help you make informed decisions about your finances. In the case of money, Expected Value is the average amount of money you can expect to gain or lose when you take a risk.

Calculating Expected Value

Find the expected value of a roulette game. The probability of winning is 1 out of 38. If you win, you win $100 on top of your bet. If you lose, you lose $10. Since the Expected Value was -$7.11, you would expect to average a loss of $7.11 every time you played roulette. You might win occasionally, but you will lose much more often.

Step 1
Calculate the probability of winning.

Step 2
Multiply the probability of winning by the amount of money you would receive.

Step 3
Calculate the probability of losing.

Step 4
Multiply the probability of losing by the amount of money you would lose.

Step 5
Subtract the amount you would win from the amount you would lose.

3. Now Do the Math ...

A. John plays the lottery. The odds of winning the lottery are 1 in 175,000,000. If he wins, he wins $35,000,000 and if he loses, he loses $1. What is his expected value? *Round your answer to the nearest hundredth.*

B. John also puts money in a retirement fund that pays interest. The probability of being able to retire with $300,000 is 48 out of 50. However, there is a 2 out of 50 chance of losing the $175,000 he invested. What is his expected value?

4. What Do You Think?

A. If you could set aside $1 a day for 30 years, how much money would you be able to save? Assume there are 365 days in a year.

B. Would you rather use that money to buy lottery tickets or put it in a retirement fund? Why?

What are the Odds?

Penny Garcia enjoys magic tricks and she wants to know the probabilities involved with randomly getting some of her tricks right. Since probability affects many aspects of life, Penny will be prepared to apply what she learns about magic to real life. Help Penny figure out some of the probabilities involved in her favorite tricks!

Section 3A: Homework

1. What is the probability of getting tails when you flip a coin?

2. A deck of cards has 52 cards.
    a. What is the probability of drawing a "2" from a deck of cards?
    b. What is the probability of drawing a "3"?
    c. What is the probability of drawing a "2" or a "3"?

3. Which probability is greater: drawing a face card or rolling an odd number on a six-sided die?

4. A test has a multiple choice question with 5 possible answers.
    a. What is the probability of guessing the correct answer?
    b. If you eliminate two of the answers that you know are wrong, does this increase or decrease your probability of guessing correctly?

5. Find the expected value for a $1 bet on a slot machine. If you win, you win $50, but the odds of winning are 1 out of 100.

6. Find the expected value for the Garcias' lottery ticket if a lottery ticket costs $1 and the odds of winning $1,000,000 are 1 out of 2,000,000.

7. The Garcias have the chance to invest $5,000 of their savings in a risky mutual fund that could double their money. The odds of doubling their money are 3 out of 4, but there is a 1 out of 4 chance that they'll lose their entire $5,000 investment. Find their expected value for this investment.

8. The Garcias have another investment opportunity to invest $5,000 of their savings in a safer mutual fund that would increase their $5,000 to $6,500. The odds of earning the extra $1,500 are 9 out of 10, but there is a 1 out of 10 chance that they'll lose their entire $5,000 investment. Find their expected value for this investment.

9. Of the two mutual fund investment opportunities above, which one had the higher expected value? Which one would you recommend the Garcias invest in?

10. Why are probabilities never less than 0.00 or greater than 1.00? Why are probabilities always values between 0 and 1? What is an example of probability of 0? What is an example of probability of 1?

Section 3B: Retirement

In Section 3A, you learned about risk and how to calculate probability. One of the areas that involves risk is planning for retirement. Many retirement saving options earn interest, but the interest you earn on your savings often depends on the strength of the economy. Since riskier investment options attract investors with higher interest rates, you need to know when to play it safe.

Retirement Options

Risk and Reward

Create an Annuity

Social Security

Save for the Future

There are many ways to save for the future, depending on your goals. For many, saving for the future means saving for retirement. Unless you inherit a lot of money or win the lottery, you will need a retirement plan. In this section, you will look at one way to save for the future – an annuity. Though there are many kinds of annuities, you will look at an annuity in which you invest money monthly. After so many years of investing in your annuity, the annuity will pay you regular monthly payments for the rest of your retirement.

Retirement Options

There are several ways to save for retirement; the most common options are provided through the government, employers, and financial institutions.

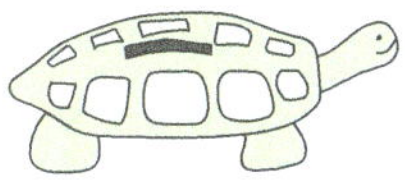

Regular Savings

You can save for retirement by saving money in a regular savings account at a bank or credit union. This offers little, if any, interest, but is the most secure. Deposits at banks and credit unions are insured by the Federal Deposit Insurance Corporation (FDIC) and the National Credit Union Share Insurance Fund (NCUSIF), respectively.

Social Security

For every paycheck you receive, a percentage is deducted for social security. When you reach retirement age, you receive monthly benefits (payments) from social security. You can claim benefits starting at age 62, but the longer you wait to claim them, the greater your financial benefit. Visit ssa.gov for more information and details about social security benefits and the retirement age.

401(k)

A 401(k) is a retirement savings plan offered through some employers. A portion of every paycheck goes into an account and is often matched proportionately by the employer. Similar employer-sponsored defined-benefit plans exist, such as 403(b) and 457(b).

IRA

An IRA (Individual Retirement Account) is a retirement savings plan through many financial institutions, such as banks, credit unions, and investment firms. It allows you to set aside money each month and earn interest. Once you reach retirement age, you can take money out of your retirement account. There are many different kinds of IRAs, so contact your bank, credit union, or financial advisor for information.

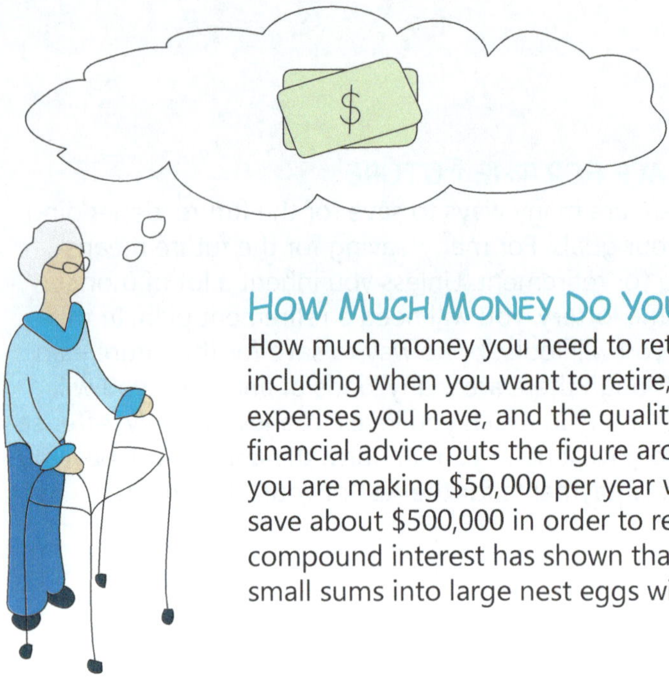

How Much Money Do You Need to Retire?

How much money you need to retire depends on many different factors, including when you want to retire, how long you think you will live, what expenses you have, and the quality of life you want to enjoy. Commonly, financial advice puts the figure around 10 times your final annual income. If you are making $50,000 per year when you retire, you would be advised to save about $500,000 in order to retire securely. This might seem like a lot, but compound interest has shown that starting early and saving regularly can turn small sums into large nest eggs with the power of time.

Is Social Security Enough?

Social Security benefits are designed to be a social safety net and provide basic income for retirees, widow(er)s, and individuals with disabilities. Social Security benefits will help you retire, but they are rarely enough on their own. According to the Social Security Administration, average retiree benefits are almost $1,300 per month. Your actual benefit amount depends on how much you contribute during your working years and at what age you claim benefits. In any event, you will want to plan on saving more than just your Social Security benefit.

1. Now Do the Math ...

A. How many more years to do you plan to work before you retire?

B. How much money do you want to have when you retire?

C. How much money will you have to save each year to be able to save that much?

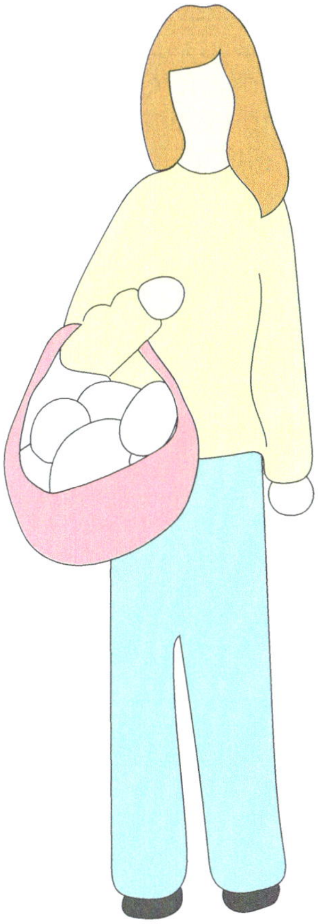

All Your Eggs in One Basket?

Saving for the future in a 401(k) or IRA comes with risk. Investment options range from secure options, such as certificates of deposit (CD) and savings bonds, to riskier options, such as stocks and mutual funds. The opportunity for greater interest earnings with financial instruments, such as stocks, is often proportional to the risk of losing money. Many financial advisors encourage investors to have diverse portfolios to protect their savings from market volatility. While markets might go up and down in the short-term, low-risk options that are designed for long-term investment are ideal for investors who start early and save consistently.

2. What Do You Think?

A. Do you think social security is enough to cover your retirement?

B. Do you already have a retirement savings plan? If so, what kind? If not, what kind of retirement plan will you start?

C. Would you rather have a higher risk retirement plan that pays more interest or a lower risk plan that pays less interest?

Using a Spreadsheet to Create an IRA

An IRA (Individual Retirement Plan) allows you to save money each month and earn interest on those savings. Once you reach retirement age, you can withdraw your money. In this example, you will use a spreadsheet to calculate your total savings for an IRA lasting 40 years, with an interest rate of 4.5% if you save $75.00 per month.

Step 1

Start by opening a blank spreadsheet.

	A	B	C	D
1				
2				
3				
	Sheet 1	+		

Step 2

Rename it to *IRA* and press enter.

	A	B	C	D
1				
2				
3				
	IRA	+		

Step 3

Start in A1 and create the following headings.

	A	B	C	D	E
1	Month	Balance	Rate	Interest	Payment
2					
3					

Step 4

In A2, type the number 1 for the first month. In the first month, the Balance in B2 will be 0. In C2, type in the Rate.

	A	B	C	D	E
1	Month	Balance	Rate	Interest	Payment
2	1	$0.00	4.5%		
3					

Step 5

To find the interest, multiply the Balance by the Rate divided by 12 months. In D2, type =, click on the Balance in B2, multiply * it by the Rate in C2, and divide / it by 12. Then press tab.

	A	B	C	D	E
1	Month	Balance	Rate	Interest	Payment
2	1	$0.00	4.5%	=B2*C2/12	
3					

Step 6

In E2, type the amount of money invested in the IRA each month.

	A	B	C	D	E
1	Month	Balance	Rate	Interest	Payment
2	1	$0.00	4.5%	$0.00	$75.00
3					

Using a Spreadsheet to Create an IRA

Step 7

In A3, type the number 2 for the second month.

	A	B	C	D	E
1	Month	Balance	Rate	Interest	Payment
2	1	$0.00	4.5%	$0.00	$75.00
3	2				

Step 8

To find the new balance, add the original balance, interest, and payment together. In B3, type = , click on the Balance in B2, add + the Interest in D2, and add + it to the Payment in E2. Then press tab.

	A	B	C	D	E
1	Month	Balance	Rate	Interest	Payment
2	1	$0.00	4.5%	$0.00	$75.00
3	2	=B2+D2+E2			

Step 9

The Rate will stay the same. In C3, type = and click on the Rate in C2. Then press tab.

	A	B	C	D	E
1	Month	Balance	Rate	Interest	Payment
2	1	$0.00	4.5%	$0.00	$75.00
3	2	$75.00	=C2		

Step 10

In D3, type =, click on the Balance in B3, multiply it by the Rate in C3, and divide / it by 12 months. Then press tab.

	A	B	C	D	E
1	Month	Balance	Rate	Interest	Payment
2	1	$0.00	4.5%	$0.00	$75.00
3	2	$75.00	4.5%	=B3*C3/12	

Step 11

The Payment will stay the same. In E3, type = and click on the Payment in E2.

	A	B	C	D	E
1	Month	Balance	Rate	Interest	Payment
2	1	$0.00	4.5%	$0.00	$75.00
3	2	$75.00	4.5%	$0.28	=E2

Step 12

Once you have the first 2 months, the spreadsheet can calculate the rest. Start by selecting the bottom row.

	A	B	C	D	E
1	Month	Balance	Rate	Interest	Payment
2	1	$0.00	4.5%	$0.00	$75.00
3	2	$75.00	4.5%	$0.28	$75.00

Using a Spreadsheet to Create an IRA

Step 13

Click on the fill handle and drag it down to the total number of months. In this example, 40 years time 12 months per year equals 480 months.

	A	B	C	D	E
1	Month	Balance	Rate	Interest	Payment
2	1	$0.00	4.5%	$0.00	$75.00
3	2	$75.00	4.5%	$0.28	$75.00
481						480

Step 14

Let go of the mouse and the rest of the spreadsheet will fill in. The balance shows that you will have $100,135.79 when you retire if you save $75 per month for 40 years.

	A	B	C	D	E
1	Month	Balance	Rate	Interest	Payment
2	1	$0.00	4.5%	$0.00	$75.00
3	2	$75.00	4.5%	$0.28	$75.00
481	480	$100,135.79	4.5%	$375.51	$75.00

Step 15

To find the total amount of interest earned, select the cell beneath the last row of the interest column. In this case, it's D482. Type =sum(. Then select everything in that column.

	A	B	C	D	E
1	Month	Balance	Rate	Interest	Payment
2	1	$0.00	4.5%	$0.00	$75.00
3	2	$75.00	4.5%	$0.28	$75.00
481	480	$100,135.79	4.5%	$375.51	$75.00
				=SUM(D2:D481)	

Step 16

Press enter and the spreadsheet shows that you will earn $64,586.30 in interest over the course of 40 years.

	A	B	C	D	E
1	Month	Balance	Rate	Interest	Payment
2	1	$0.00	4.5%	$0.00	$75.00
3	2	$75.00	4.5%	$0.28	$75.00
481	480	$100,135.79	4.5%	$375.51	$75.00
				$64,586.30	

Conclusion

Even saving a small amount of money each month into a retirement account can add up over time. In this case, saving $75.00 a month turned into $100,135.79 after 40 years.

3. Now Do the Math in a Spreadsheet ...

A. If every month you put $200 dollars in a shoebox and didn't earn any interest, how much money you would you have after 30 years?

B. Instead of putting it in a shoebox, how much would you have if you put the $200 a month into an IRA that earns 5% interest for 30 years? Fill in the first 2 months and the last 2 months.

	A	B	C	D	E
1	Month	Balance	Rate	Interest	Payment
2	1				
3	2				
360	359				
361	360				

4. What Do You Think?

In the exercise above, what is the difference between the earnings in a shoebox savings and the savings with compound interest after 30 years?

Planning for Retirement

Susan and Carlos are working hard to provide the life they want for their family, but they don't want to work forever. If they want to retire with any kind of financial security, then they need to know how different ways to save will affect their investment. They don't want Penny to feel that she will have to take care of them when they get older, so the Garcias need to get to work on a plan! Help the Garcias make a plan for how to save for retirement!

Section 3B: Homework

1. Susan and Carlos plan to retire in 40 years. Currently, they save 10% of their income of $3,789.10 each month.
    a. How much money do they save each month?
    b. If they saved that much each month, how much would they have in 40 years?

2. Susan and Carlos plan to retire at age 65 and want enough money to last for 25 years of retirement.
    a. How much will Susan and Carlos have each year of their retirement if they live off of the savings you found in question number 1? *Round your answer to the nearest hundredth.*
    b. How much money a month would that be? *Round your answer to the nearest hundredth.*

3. Susan and Carlos decide to put their 10% monthly savings in an IRA account that pays 6% interest for 40 years.
    a. Use a spreadsheet to create their IRA plan. Record your answers for the first 2 months and the last 2 months.

	A	B	C	D	E
1	Month	Balance	Rate	Interest	Payment
2					
3					

    b. What is the total amount they will save with this plan when they retire?
    c. If they live off these savings, how much will they have each year of their retirement if they plan to be retired for 25 years?
    d. How much money a month would that be?

4. How much more money were they able to save for retirement when they used the IRA instead of the regular savings account?

5. Susan and Carlos have been saving 10% of their take home pay after taxes have been deducted from their paycheck. They decide to save 10% of their gross income (the amount they make before taxes).

a. If their gross income is $2,160 per month, what is their new monthly savings?
b. They decide to put that money in the IRA created in question number 3. Use a spreadsheet to create a new IRA plan. Record your answers for the first 2 months and the last 2 months.

	A	B	C	D	E
1	Month	Balance	Rate	Interest	Payment
2					
3					

c. What is the total amount they will save with this plan when they retire?
d. If they live off these savings, how much will they have each year of their retirement if they plan to be retired for 25 years?
e. How much money a month would that be?

6. How much more money did they save in the second IRA?

7. Carlos and Susan are still young and would enjoy using their money in other ways. They are curious what would happen if they decide to wait another 10 years before starting their IRA. This would mean they would save for retirement for 30 years instead of 40 years.
   a. Create a new IRA plan for the Garcias and record your answers for the first 2 months and the last 2 months. *Assume they will save 10% of their gross income of $2,160 a month for 30 years and their income stays the same for that period of time.*

	A	B	C	D	E
1	Month	Balance	Rate	Interest	Payment
2					
3					

   b. What is the total amount they will save with this plan when they retire?

8. How much money did Carlos and Susan lose by waiting 10 years to start their retirement?

9. What do you think are the pros and cons of saving for retirement? List at least 3 pros and 3 cons.

10. What is your retirement plan? Explain your reasoning behind it.

Section 3C: Property & Auto Insurance

In Section 3B, you learned about saving for retirement to protect you in the future. You can take measures to protect yourself in the present by insuring your possessions. In this section, you will learn about property insurance and types of coverage.

Types of Insurance

Deductibles

Comparing Costs

Premiums

Protect It

Insurance protects your investments and property and can save you from financially crippling situations. Liability car insurance is required by law and is an example of the protection insurance can provide. If you don't have liability car insurance, you will be responsible for paying for all repairs to another car if you have an accident. If you don't have thousands of dollars on-hand to pay for costly repairs, then liability insurance is a must. If you don't have enough cash on-hand to replace your car if it is totaled, then full coverage car insurance might be a worthwhile investment for you. The rule: if you can't afford to replace it or be without it, then you should insure it.

Auto Insurance

- Liability insurance is required by law. It pays for damage to other vehicles, people, and property. Every state has its own minimum coverage laws.
- Comprehensive and collusion coverage provides financial protection for damage done to your vehicle. If another driver does not have liability insurance or leaves the scene of the accident, full coverage may be the only way for you to afford repairs to your vehicle. Full coverage is usually only required for vehicles that aren't paid off. Every state has its own requirements.

Renters Insurance

- Renters insurance protects your belongings if you are renting a home or apartment. If your property is damaged or stolen, renters insurance can help pay to replace your property. Taking pictures of all your belongings now will make it easier to file a claim.

Homeowners Insurance

- Homeowners insurance protects your home. Often, mortgage lenders require a home buyer to have homeowners insurance until the mortgage is paid off. Consult with an insurance professional to determine the specific kind of insurance (flood, fire, etc.) and the level of protection you need.

1. What Do You Think?

A. Which kinds of insurance do you have?

B. Describe a time in your life when insurance was useful.

C. Do you think insurance is a need or a want? Explain why or why not.

Insurance Vocabulary

While there are many different kinds of property insurance, they all work basically the same way: pay a premium for the insurance policy, and pay a deductible if you file a claim with your insurance company.

Premium

The cost of having insurance protection. Annual or semiannual premiums are often paid monthly.

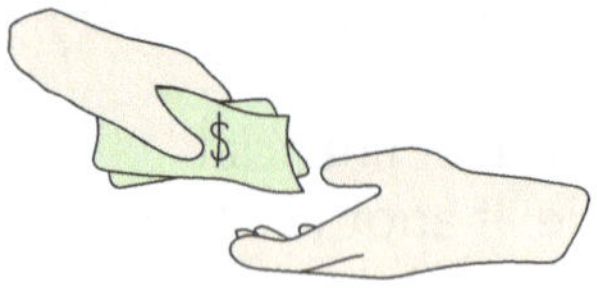

Deductible

The amount you have to pay before insurance starts paying.

Have You Met Your Deductible?

Just because you have insurance doesn't mean all your costs are covered. In fact, all kinds of insurance have deductibles. If your deductible is $500, for example, you will have to cover the first $500 of your repair bill before insurance will start paying. The lower your deductible, the less you have to pay out of your own pocket, but the higher your monthly premium will be. Be sure to choose a deductible you can afford and monthly premiums that work in your budget. If the repair bill is less than your deductible, then you will have to pay the entire bill on your own and insurance won't help. Deductibles are usually based on a year of coverage, so if you meet the deductible within the year, then insurance will help pay costs above the deductible.

Finding Total Costs When You Meet Your Deductible

In the event of a car accident and subsequent repairs, your insurance company will pay part of the cost. Use this spreadsheet to find your costs when you've met your deductible. In this example you pay an annual premium of $875.00 and have a deductible of $1,000.00 Car repairs cost $3,000.00.

Step 1

Start by opening a blank spreadsheet.

	A	B	C	D	
1					
2					
3					
	Sheet 1	+			

Step 2

Rename it to Met Deductible and press enter.

	A	B	C	D	
1					
2					
3					
	Met Deductible	+			

Step 3

Start in A2 and create the following headings.

	A	B	C	D	E
1	Cost of Repairs	Deductible	Annual Premium	What Insurance Pays	What You Pay
2					

Step 4

Fill in what you know. In this case, repairs from an accident cost $3,000 with an Annual Premium of $875.

	A	B	C	D	E
1	Cost of Repairs	Deductible	Annual Premium	What Insurance Pays	What You Pay
2	$3,000.00	$1,000.00	$875.00		

Step 5

If you meet your deductible, then insurance will pay the difference between the repair costs and the deductible. In D2, type =, click on the Cost of Repairs in A2, and subtract - the Deductible in B2. Then, press tab.

	A	B	C	D	E
1	Cost of Repairs	Deductible	Annual Premium	What Insurance Pays	What You Pay
2	$3,000.00	$1,000.00	$875.00	=A2-B2	

Finding Total Costs When You Meet Your Deductible

Step 6
You will still have to pay your premium and the deductible. In E2, type =, click on the Deductible in B2, and add + it to the Annual Premium in C2.

	A	B	C	D	E
1	Cost of Repairs	Deductible	Annual Premium	What Insurance Pays	What You Pay
2	$3,000.00	$1,000.00	$875.00	$2,000.00	=B2+C2

Step 7
Press enter and the spreadsheet shows that the insurance company will pay $2,000 and you will pay $1,875 for the year. Save your work as 3C Classwork.

	A	B	C	D	E
1	Cost of Repairs	Deductible	Annual Premium	What Insurance Pays	What You Pay
2	$3,000.00	$1,000.00	$875.00	$2,000.00	$1,875.00
3					

Conclusion
When you have insurance, and you need to make repairs, your insurance company will pay a portion of your costs as long as you meet your deductible.

2. Now Do the Math in a Spreadsheet ...

For the following problems, use the spreadsheet you created for the previous example.

A. Find the total annual costs you would pay on a $5,458 repair bill with a deductible of $500 and an annual premium of $1,275. Record your answers below.

	A	B	C	D	E
1	Cost of Repairs	Deductible	Annual Premium	What Insurance Pays	What You Pay
2					

B. Find the total annual costs you would pay on a $1,530 repair bill with a deductible of $1,000 and a semiannual premium of $549. First, find the annual premium. Then use the spreadsheet and record your answers below.

	A	B	C	D	E
1	Cost of Repairs	Deductible	Annual Premium	What Insurance Pays	What You Pay
2					

Finding Total Costs When You Do Not Meet Your Deductible

When you make an insurance claim that doesn't meet your deductible, you end up paying the repair bill out of pocket. Use this spreadsheet to find your costs when you pay an annual premium of $875.00 and have a deductible of $1,000.00. In this example you only need $150 worth of repairs on a fender bender.

Step 1

Start by creating a new sheet.

	A	B	C	D	E
1					
2					
3					
	Met Deductible	+			

Step 2

A new sheet will appear.

	A	B	C	D	E
1					
2					
3					
	Met Deductible	Sheet 2			

Step 3

Rename it to Did Not Meet Deductible.

	A	B	C	D	E
1					
2					
3					
	Met Deductible	Did Not Meet Deductible			

Step 4

Start in A2 and create the following headings.

	A	B	C	D	E
1	Cost of Repairs	Deductible	Annual Premium	What Insurance Pays	What You Pay
2					

Step 5

Fill in what you know. In this case, it is minor repairs for $150 and an annual premium of $875.

	A	B	C	D	E
1	Cost of Repairs	Deductible	Annual Premium	What Insurance Pays	What You Pay
2	$150.00	$1,000.00	$875.00		

Step 6

If you don't meet your deductible, than your insurance company will not pay for your repairs. In D2, type 0.

	A	B	C	D	E
1	Cost of Repairs	Deductible	Annual Premium	What Insurance Pays	What You Pay
2	$150.00	$1,000.00	$875.00	$0.00	

Finding Total Costs When You Do Not Meet Your Deductible

Step 7

When you do not meet your deductible, you will have to pay for your repairs and your premium. In E2, type =, click on the Cost of Repairs in A2, and add + it to the Annual Premium in C2.

	A	B	C	D	E
1	Cost of Repairs	Deductible	Annual Premium	What Insurance Pays	What You Pay
2	$150.00	$1,000.00	$875.00	$0.00	=A2+C2

Step 8

Press enter and the spreadsheet shows that the insurance company will pay nothing and you will pay $1,025.00 for the year. Make sure to save your work.

	A	B	C	D	E
1	Cost of Repairs	Deductible	Annual Premium	What Insurance Pays	What You Pay
2	$150.00	$1,000.00	$875.00	$0.00	$1,025.00
3					

Conclusion

Insurance only pays when you meet your deductible. Until then, you must continue to pay your annual premium and the cost of any repairs.

3. Now Do the Math in a Spreadsheet ...

A. Karla had an accident and her car needs $5,860 worth of repairs. Her deductible is $500 and her annual premium is $922. Use a spreadsheet to find out how much she has to pay. How much does insurance pay? Record your answers below.

	A	B	C	D	E
1	Cost of Repairs	Deductible	Annual Premium	What Insurance Pays	What You Pay
2					

B. John had a fender bender and his car needed $315 worth of repairs. His deductible is also $500, with an annual premium of $922. How much does he have to pay? How much does insurance pay? Record your answers below.

	A	B	C	D	E
1	Cost of Repairs	Deductible	Annual Premium	What Insurance Pays	What You Pay
2					

4. What Do You Think?

A. In the exercise on the previous page, who benefited the most from insurance?

B. When does insurance start paying off?

Preventive Maintenance

Insurance is similar to preventive maintenance in that smaller periodic payments stave off costly expenses. Just the way regular oil changes keep you from being saddled with a big car repair bill, the right level of property insurance means that theft or damage to your property doesn't result in repair and replacement costs that you can't afford. Don't buy the level of insurance you can afford; buy the level of insurance you can't afford to live without.

Rainy Day Fund

The Garcias worked hard to save enough to accomplish major financial goals, such as buying a car, so they want to protect their property with insurance. In the homework for this section, you will help them compare and analyze insurance coverage.

Section 3C: Homework

1. Susan Garcia's car is worth $8,000. Her monthly car insurance premium is $77.48 for full coverage.
    a. If Susan were to save the $77.48 instead of paying for insurance, how many months would it take to save up the $8,000 to replace it? *Round to the nearest month.*
    b. How many years would that be? *Round to the nearest year.*

2. Carlos and Susan have renter's insurance to protect their belongings from theft or damage. The coverage and peace of mind costs them $22.80 per month.
    a. If they saved that money instead of paying for insurance, how many months would it take to save to replace their belongings ($4,500)? *Round to the nearest month.*
    b. How many years would that be? *Round to the nearest year.*

3. The Garcia's have to file a car insurance claim this year and the repairs will cost $3,700.
    a. Plan A offers a monthly premium of $115 with a deductible of $500. Use a spreadsheet to find their costs and record your answers below.

	A	B	C	D	E
1	Cost of Repairs	Deductible	Annual Premium	What Insurance Pays	What You Pay
2					

b. Plan B offers a monthly premium of $75 with a deductible of $1,500. Use a spreadsheet to find their costs and record your answers below.

	A	B	C	D	E
1	Cost of Repairs	Deductible	Annual Premium	What Insurance Pays	What You Pay
2					

c. Which plan is better for the Garcias?

4. Heavy summer rains during New Mexico's monsoon season create a leak in the Garcia's roof damaging their bed ($400), a TV ($500) and a computer ($1,800).
   a. Plan A offers a monthly premium of $35 with a $500 deductible. Use a spreadsheet to find their costs and record your answers below.

	A	B	C	D	E
1	Cost of Repairs	Deductible	Annual Premium	What Insurance Pays	What You Pay
2					

   b. Plan B offers a monthly premium of $22.50 with a $1,000 deductible. Use a spreadsheet to find their costs and record your answers below.

	A	B	C	D	E
1	Cost of Repairs	Deductible	Annual Premium	What Insurance Pays	What You Pay
2					

   c. Which plan is a better deal for the Garicas?

5. If the Garcias are saving 5% of their monthly income ($3800) in a "rainy day fund," how many months will it take them to save to cover the $500 deductible?

6. If the Garcias have $40 more disposable income than they thought, should they save that money or use it to pay a higher premium and lower their deductible?

7. If you are just starting out, you might not have a lot of savings built up. Suppose you don't have any savings yet, would you prefer a higher premium with a lower deductible? Explain ...

8. Think of a time when insurance helped you. If you have never needed to file an insurance claim, is the peace of mind that insurance provides worth it?

Section 3D: Health Insurance

In Section 3C, you learned about property insurance and how to protect your physical belongings. Another important insurance consideration is your health. Unexpected illnesses or accidents can happen, and medical care can be expensive. In this section, you will learn about health insurance and different kinds of coverage.

Deductibles and Premiums

Types of Health Insurance

Levels of Coverage

Comparing Plans using a Spreadsheet

Healthcare and Risk

Like liability car insurance, health insurance is required law. Since anyone can get sick at anytime and healthcare costs can add up quickly, health insurance is protection to make sure you get the healthcare services you need and that you can afford them. Even a short hospital stay can cost thousands of dollars. If you don't have the money to pay healthcare costs out of pocket, then health insurance can end up saving you money if you get sick.

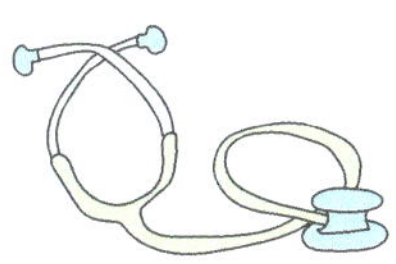

Health Insurance

Health insurance protects individuals and families from expensive healthcare costs. There are several levels of health insurance coverage available.

Life Insurance

Life insurance pays a designated family member or beneficiary if the insured individual dies.

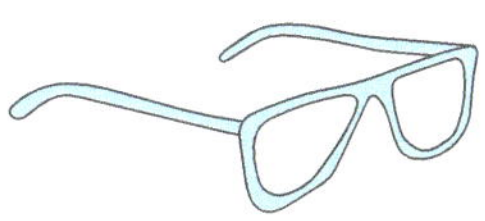

Vision Insurance

Vision insurance covers many kinds of vision care costs, including eye exams and other procedures, glasses, and contact lenses. Premiums, coverage, and deductibles vary widely.

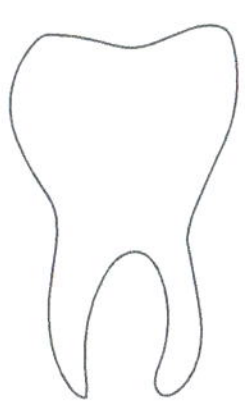

Dental Insurance

Dental insurance covers dental care costs, including cleanings, x-rays, and other procedures. Premiums, coverage, and deductibles vary widely.

1. What Do You Think?

Do you think health insurance is a want or need? Explain your answer.

Parts of a Healthcare Plan

Younger, healthier consumers often choose higher deductible plans. Individuals with more risk factors and those who have more healthcare needs often choose lower deductible plans since they know they will need the healthcare. How much risk you're willing to take on and how much you're willing to pay in monthly premiums depends on many factors. Not all healthcare costs are covered by all health insurance plans. Be sure to choose a plan that meets your coverage needs. Visit healthcare.gov for more information.

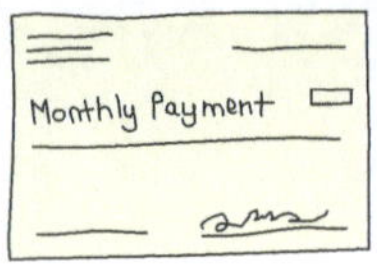

Premium

The cost of having insurance protection. Annual or semiannual premiums are often paid monthly.

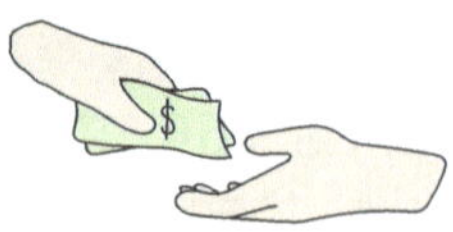

Deductible

The amount you have to pay before insurance starts paying.

Out Of Pocket Maximum

The most you pay during a policy period (usually one year) before your health insurance plan starts to pay 100% of eligible healthcare costs.

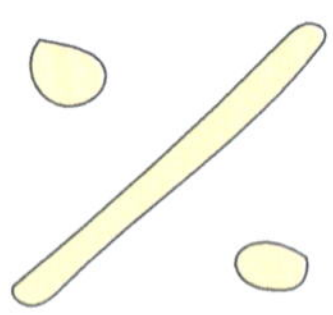

Co-Insurance

A kind of insurance in which you and your insurance company each pay a portion of healthcare costs after your deductible has been met. Co-insurance is similar to a co-pay, except that co-insurance is usually based on a percentage of your healthcare costs, while a co-pay is a fixed amount.

2. What Do You Think?

A. What is your current premium and deductible?

B. What would you change about your health insurance plan to make it a better fit for you and your healthcare needs?

Balancing Premiums and Deductibles

When you are healthy, you can sign up for a low-risk plan that gives you a low monthly premium with a high deductible. If you have health conditions or are at a higher risk of getting sick, it's better to have a plan with a higher premium and a lower deductible.

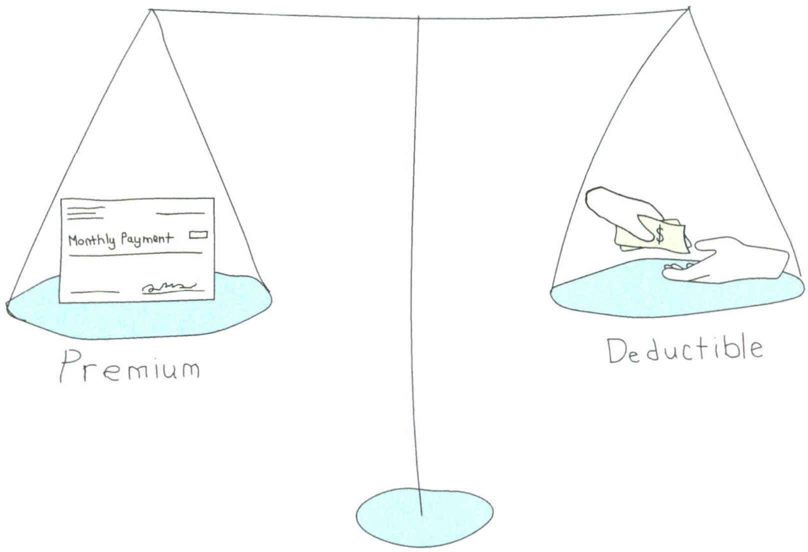

Healthcare Plans Based on Risk

How much risk you're willing to take on and how much you're willing to pay each month in premiums depends on many factors. Younger, healthier consumers often choose higher deductible plans. Individuals with more risk factors and those who have more healthcare needs often choose lower deductible plans since they are likely to use their coverage.

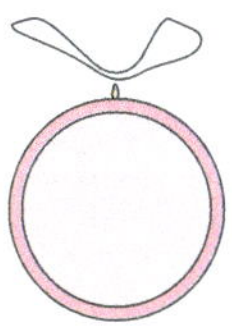

Bronze

Bronze plans are for individuals with the lowest health risks and healthcare costs. They offer the lowest premiums with the highest deductibles.

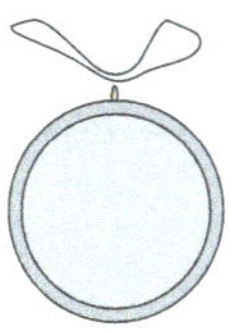

Silver

Silver plans are for individuals with moderate health risks and healthcare costs. They offer moderate premiums with moderate deductibles.

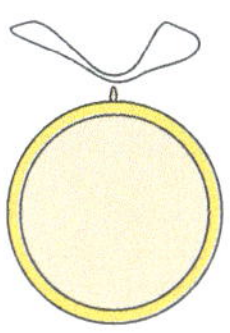

Gold

Gold plans are for individuals with higher health risks and healthcare costs. They offer higher premiums with lower deductibles.

Platinum

Platinum plans are for individuals with the highest health risks and healthcare costs. They offer the highest premiums with the lowest deductibles.

Healthcare Costs When You Meet Your Deductible

Once you have met your deductible, your insurance company starts to cover part of your healthcare costs. Use a spreadsheet to find the costs for someone who has $1,300.00 worth of healthcare costs if the plan has an annual premium of $2,496.00, a deductible of $750.00, and 20% co-insurance.

Step 1

Start by opening a blank spreadsheet.

	A	B	C	D	E
1					
2					
3					
	Sheet 1	+			

Step 2

Rename it to Met Deductible and press enter.

	A	B	C	D	E
1					
2					
3					
	Met Deductible	+			

Step 3

Start in A1 and create the following headings.

	A	B	C	D	E
1	Healthcare Costs	Deductible	Annual Premium	Co-Insurance	What You Pay
2					

Step 4

Fill in the information you know.

	A	B	C	D	E
1	Healthcare Costs	Deductible	Annual Premium	Co-Insurance	What You Pay
2	$1,300.00	$750.00	$2,496.00		

Step 5

Once you meet your deductible, you still have to pay co-insurance. In D2, press =, type the percentage of co-insurance, and multiply * it by the difference between the Healthcare Costs in A2 and the Deductible in B2. Then, press tab.

	A	B	C	D	E
1	Healthcare Costs	Deductible	Annual Premium	Co-Insurance	What You Pay
2	$1,300.00	$750.00	$2,496.00	=20%*(A2-B2)	

Healthcare Costs When You Meet Your Deductible

Step 6

To find What You Pay, add your deductible, premium, and co-insurance together. In E2, press =, click on the Deductible in B2, add + the Annual Premium in C2, and add + the Co-Insurance in D2.

	A	B	C	D	E
1	Healthcare Costs	Deductible	Annual Premium	Co-Insurance	What You Pay
2	$1,300.00	$750.00	$2,496.00	$110	=B2+C2+D2

Step 7

Press enter and your spreadsheet shows that you have to pay $3,356.00 for the year. Save your work as 3D Classwork.

	A	B	C	D	E
1	Healthcare Costs	Deductible	Annual Premium	Co-Insurance	What You Pay
2	$1,300.00	$750.00	$2,496.00	$110	$3,356.00
3					

Conclusion

In this example, you ended up paying more than your healthcare costs alone. Had your costs been higher, insurance would have been more useful. There are many different kinds of health insurance plans so you can find the one that fits your needs the best.

Healthcare Costs When You Do Not Meet Your Deductible

Once you meet your deductible, your insurance company starts to cover part of your healthcare costs. Use a spreadsheet to find the costs for someone who has $255.00 worth of healthcare costs if the plan has an annual premium of $2,496.00, a deductible of $750.00, and 20% co-insurance.

Step 1

Start by creating a new sheet. Click on the plus + symbol next to the sheet named Met Deductible.

	A	B	C	D	E
1					
2					
3					
	Met Deductible	+			

Healthcare Costs When You Do Not Meet Your Deductible

Step 2
Double-click on Sheet 2.

	A	B	C	D	E
1					
2					
3					

Tabs: Met Deductible | Sheet 2

Step 3
Rename it to Did Not Meet Deductible.

	A	B	C	D	E
1					
2					
3					

Tabs: Met Deductible | Did Not Meet Deductible

Step 4
Start in A1 and create the following headings.

	A	B	C	D	E
1	Healthcare Costs	Deductible	Annual Premium	Co-Insurance	What You Pay
2					

Step 5
Fill in the information you know.

	A	B	C	D	E
1	Healthcare Costs	Deductible	Annual Premium	Co-Insurance	What You Pay
2	$255.00	$750.00	$2,496.00		

Step 6
You do not pay co-insurance until you meet your deductible. In this case, your co-insurance will be $0.

	A	B	C	D	E
1	Healthcare Costs	Deductible	Annual Premium	Co-Insurance	What You Pay
2	$255.00	$750.00	$2,496.00	$0.00	

Step 7
When you don't meet your deductible, you pay your healthcare costs and your premium. In E2, press =, click on the Healthcare Costs in A2, and add + it to the Annual Premium in C2.

	A	B	C	D	E
1	Healthcare Costs	Deductible	Annual Premium	Co-Insurance	What You Pay
2	$255.00	$750.00	$2,496.00	$110	=A2+C2

Healthcare Costs When You Do Not Meet Your Deductible

Step 8

Press enter and your spreadsheet shows that you will have to pay $2,751.00 Make sure to save your work.

	A	B	C	D	E
1	Healthcare Costs	Deductible	Annual Premium	Co-Insurance	What You Pay
2	$255.00	$750.00	$2,496.00	$110	$2,751.00
3					

Conclusion

In this example, you ended up paying more than your healthcare costs alone. Health insurance is designed to protect you from financial ruin in the event of expensive or catastrophic care, but does not always save you money when healthcare costs are low and deductibles are high.

3. Now Do the Math in a Spreadsheet ...

A. Sarah needs surgery on her shoulder. She also takes medication for high blood pressure. Without health insurance her health care costs for the year would be $1,260. Before making any calculations, which kind of plan (platinum, gold, silver, or bronze) would you recommend for her?

B. Use a spreadsheet to compare the costs of each of the following healthcare plans if Sarah has healthcare costs of $1,260. Record your answers below.

Platinum Plan Annual Premium = $2,760.00 Deductible = $200.00 Co-Insurance = 10% Sarah Pays ____________	Gold Plan Annual Premium = $1,325.00 Deductible = $850.00 Co-Insurance = 20% Sarah Pays ____________
Silver Plan Annual Premium = $1,210.00 Deductible = $1,750.00 Co-Insurance = 30% Sarah Pays ____________	Bronze Plan Annual Premium = $944.00 Deductible = $5,000.00 Co-Insurance = 50% Sarah Pays ____________

4. What Do You Think?

In the exercise above, which plan is best for Sarah? Explain why.

Keep Penny and the Piggy Bank Healthy

Although she is usually a very healthy young girl, Penny has the flu that has been going around. This is making her parents question whether they have enough health insurance to protect their family. In the homework for this section, you will help the Garcias analyze some different scenarios that could happen and how to protect themselves.

Section 3D: Homework

For this assignment, use the following information:

Plan	Monthly Premium	Deductible	Co-Pay
Platinum	$335	$100	10%
Gold	$208	$750	20%
Silver	$180	$2,000	30%
Bronze	$137	$4,000	50%

1. Carlos needs to have a $2,500 surgery to repair a hernia.
    a. How much would they pay with each plan?
    b. Which plan would save the Garcias the most money for the year?

2. Susan gets sick and needs a prescription for medicine costing $130.
    a. How much would they pay with each plan?
    b. Which plan would save the Garcias the most money for the year?

3. Penny breaks her leg and it costs $700 to put her leg in a cast.
    a. How much would they pay with each plan?
    b. Which plan would save the Garcias the most money for the year?

4. What if all of the scenarios from problems 1, 2 and 3 all happen in the same year?
    a. How much would they pay with each plan?
    b. Which plan would save the Garcias the most money for the year?

5. Susan goes to acupuncture once a week and it costs $40 each time.
    a. What would it cost her without insurance for 1 year?
    b. If she got insurance, how much would she save with each plan?
    c. Which plan would save her the most money?

6. Carlos faints at work and the doctor wants him to go for a $2,200 MRI.
    a. How much would each plan cost Carlos?
    b. Which plan would save the Garcias the most money for the year?

7. Penny hasn't been feeling well. The doctors want to run test to see if she's diabetic. If she is, insulin will cost the family $175 a month.
    a. How much would her insulin cost a year?
    b. How much would she pay with each plan?
    c. Which plan would save the Garcias the most money for the year for Penny's insulin?

8. What if all of the scenarios from problems 5, 6 and 7 all happen in the same year?
    a. How much would they pay with each plan?
    b. Which plan would save the Garcias the most money for the year?

9. Which type of plan do you think is best for the Garcias? Explain your answer.

10. Describe a time when having insurance made a difference in your life.

CHAPTER 4: INFORMED DECISIONS

4A Creating Value

4B Buying a Car

4C Buying a House

4D Planning a Vacation

Section 4A: Creating Value

In Chapter 3, you learned about the effect of time on investments and how insurance can protect your financial well-being as well as your personal well-being. In Chapter 4, you will explore the math behind making informed decisions, starting with different ways to think about the effect purchases have on your ability to save.

Reducing Financial Waste

Selling Unused Goods

Useful Life of Products

Making Informed Purchases

Are You Sitting on Money?

Chances are that if you really work at it, you could find some way to reduce expenses. Even if the reduction in expenses is temporary, it might be enough to help you save for what you really want. If your expenses are as low as they can be, you can look at generating more income. If you have material goods you are sure you no longer want or need, consider selling them. Getting rid of excess cargo could bring in a little extra income, but it might also have added benefits for your state of mind.

Opportunities to Increase Value

There are many ways to increase value, including decreasing an expense's prorated cost or increasing income.

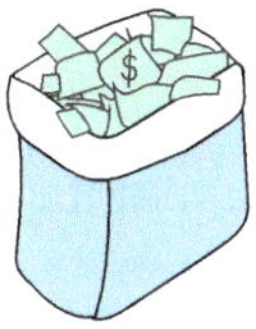

Reduce Financial Waste

Identifying and reducing financial waste can be challenging. Whenever you spend money you can ask yourself, "Is there a way I could save money on this purchase?"

Consider the Useful Life of Products

Products are designed to last for a certain period of time. Higher quality products are more expensive, but they often last longer then cheaper products. The useful life of a product changes its prorated cost to you.

Make Informed Purchases

Knowing the true cost of purchases allows you to make informed decisions about what you want.

Sell Unused Goods

Selling unused material goods can be a source of one-time income. If you are looking to boost your savings and declutter, this can be a good option.

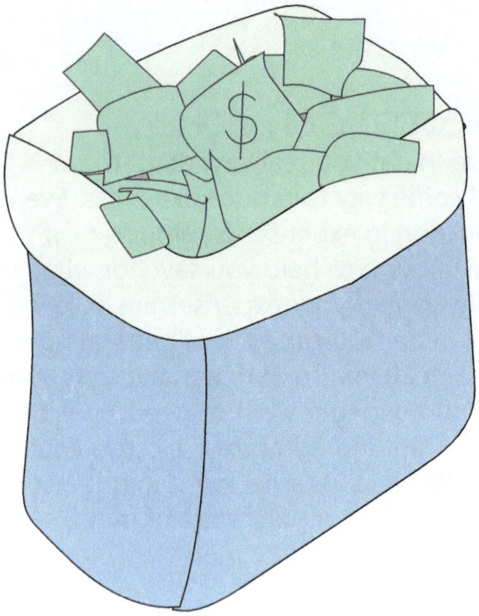

Financial Waste

It is easy to overlook financial waste if it's small, but even small amounts add up quickly. Saving just an extra dollar per day could turn into enough money for you to retire a whole year earlier. Financial waste is personal. Only you know if you are wasting money and have an opportunity to cut expenses and save more. Only you can decide what pleasures in life you're willing to live without in order to save for your financial goals.

Common Forms of Waste

You can't avoid all waste, but you can work to minimize it. Below are some common forms of waste.

Unused Data

If you regularly have unused smartphone data on your current plan, then you might save money by reducing your data plan.

Unused Groceries

If you end up throwing away food because it goes bad before you can eat it, then you have an opportunity to reduce waste and expenses.

Unused Memberships/Subscriptions

If you are paying a membership or subscription fee that you don't use, then you could consider canceling your membership or subscription to save money. You can always reactivate it in the future if you decide it's an expense worth keeping.

Overused Utilities

Setting your heat high in the winter and leaving the lights on when you are not at home are examples of how utility expenses can vary widely, depending on how they are used. Many appliances use electricity, even when they're off. Consider unplugging appliances you rarely use.

Late Fees and Penalties

Late fees are a classic example of financial waste. Avoid late fees by paying bills on time or early, and consider setting up auto pay to avoid unnecessary penalties.

Trading in Your Waste for Your Financial Goals

Having clearly defined financial goals is the best way to start thinking about reducing financial waste. If you know exactly what you'd do with the money, then it will be easier to identify and reduce waste. Every time you save instead of wasting, consider putting that money somewhere visible, such as in a jar in the kitchen. Before long, the jar will start to fill up and you will be even closer to your financial goals.

1. Now Do the Math ...

A. If Uncle Rob cancels the unused gym membership that costs him $38.50 per month and starts taking walks in his neighborhood, how much money could he save in a year?

B. Uncle Rob tends to buy more groceries than he can eat in a week. If he only buys what he needs, he could save $18 per week. How much money would he save in a year?

2. What Do You Think?

A. What is the total amount Uncle Rob saved in the exercises above?

B. If you were able to save that much money, what would you do with it?

How Little Things Add Up

An example of how little expenses can add up is daily coffee. One cup of coffee is not a huge expense, but keep buying coffee for a week and you can see how it adds up. One daily coffee for a year ends up costing a lot, even though one coffee did not seem very expensive.

Coffee for one day.

Coffee for one week.

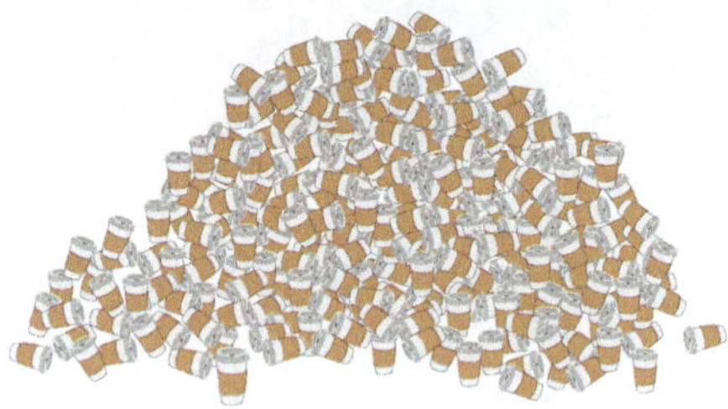

Coffee for one year.

The Cost of Daily Coffee

Just like the physical waste produced, the potential financial waste of one coffee per day really adds up over time. The price of coffee, coffee makers, and coffee beans varies, so below is an example of some typical prices you might expect to see.

The Price of a Cup of Coffee from a Coffee Shop

A cup of coffee at a coffee shop costs $2.85.

The Price of a Coffee Maker

A coffee maker costs $29.99.

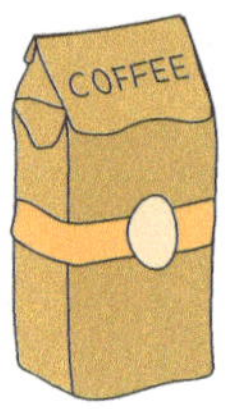

The Price of a Bag of Coffee Beans

A bag of coffee beans costs $9.95 and makes 15 cups of coffee.

3. Now Do the Math ...

A. Based on the prices listed on the previous page, how much would it cost to buy a cup of coffee at a coffee shop every day for one month? *Assume there are 30 days in a month.*

B. How much would it cost to buy a cup of coffee at a coffee shop every day for one year? *Assume there are 365 days in a year.*

C. If you made your own coffee, how many bags of coffee beans would you need to buy in order to drink a cup of coffee every morning for a year? *Round your answer to the nearest whole number.*

D. Including the price of a coffee maker and coffee beans, how much would it cost to make your own coffee everyday for one year?

4. What Do You Think?

A. In the exercises above, how much more money would you save from making your own coffee instead of buying it from a coffee shop over the course of a year?

B. Are there other benefits to going to the coffee shop that make the extra expense worth it? Explain.

Useful Life of Products

Another important consideration in reducing unnecessary spending is the useful life of a product. Products eventually wear out, tear up, or break after a certain amount of time. Often, products that are cheaper initially don't last as long and need to be replaced more frequently. The balance between initial cost and long-term value is the big trade off between quality and quantity. There are situations in which it is a better deal to pay more upfront for a product that will last longer and save you money in the long run.

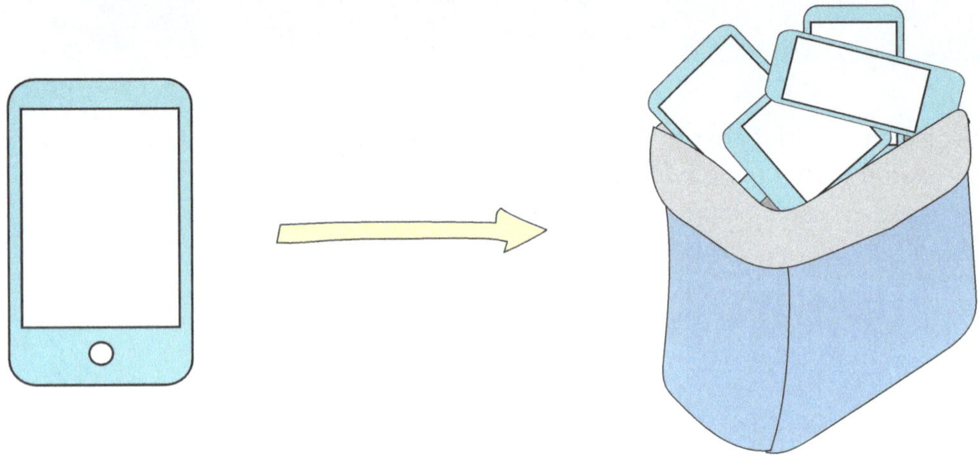

Comparing Products Over Time

Use a spreadsheet to compare the costs of the following types of shoes over a 2 year time period:

- Beige shoes that have a selling price of $29.00 and a useful life of 6 months.
- Brown shoes that have a selling price of $59.95 and a useful life of 2 years.

Step 1

Start by opening a blank spreadsheet.

	A	B	C	D	E
1					
2					
3					
	Sheet 1	+			

Step 2

Rename it to Comparing Products and press enter.

	A	B	C	D	E
1					
2					
3					
	Comparing Products	+			

Step 3

Start in A1 and create the following headings.

	A	B	C	D	E
1	Product Name	Selling Price	Useful Life (in months)	Number of Purchases	Total Cost
2					

Comparing Products Over Time

Step 4

In columns A and B, type in the product names and their selling prices.

	A	B	C	D	E
1	Product Name	Selling Price	Useful Life (in months)	Number of Purchases	Total Cost
2	Beige Shoes	$29.99			
3	Brown Shoes	$59.95			

Step 5

In column C, type in the Useful Life. Since the useful life of the beige shoes is given in months, simply type the number 6. Since the useful life of the brown shoes is given in years, multiply * the years times 12 months.

	A	B	C	D	E
1	Product Name	Selling Price	Useful Life (in months)	Number of Purchases	Total Cost
2	Beige Shoes	$29.99	6		
3	Brown Shoes	$59.95	=12*2		

Step 6

To find the number of purchases, divide the total number of months by the useful life. In D2, press =, type the total number of months in 2 years (24), and divide / by the Useful Life in C2. Then, press enter.

	A	B	C	D	E
1	Product Name	Selling Price	Useful Life (in months)	Number of Purchases	Total Cost
2	Beige Shoes	$29.99	6	=24/C2	
3	Brown Shoes	$59.95	24		

Step 7

The spreadsheet shows you will need to buy 4 pairs of beige shoes over the course of 2 years. Repeat the process for the brown shoes. In D3, press =, type the total number of months (24), and divide / by the Useful Life in C3. Then, press enter.

	A	B	C	D	E
1	Product Name	Selling Price	Useful Life (in months)	Number of Purchases	Total Cost
2	Beige Shoes	$29.99	6	4	
3	Brown Shoes	$59.95	24	=24/C3	

Comparing Products Over Time

Step 8

To find the total cost, multiply the Selling Price by the Number of Purchases. In E2, press =, click on the Selling Price in B2, and multiply * it by the Number of Purchases in D2. Then, press enter.

	A	B	C	D	E
1	Product Name	Selling Price	Useful Life (in months)	Number of Purchases	Total Cost
2	Beige Shoes	$29.99	6	4	=B2*D2
3	Brown Shoes	$59.95	24	1	

Step 9

Repeat the process for the brown shoes. In E2, press =, click on the Selling Price in B2, and multiply * it by the Number of Purchases in D2. Then, press enter.

	A	B	C	D	E
1	Product Name	Selling Price	Useful Life (in months)	Number of Purchases	Total Cost
2	Beige Shoes	$29.99	6	4	$119.96
3	Brown Shoes	$59.95	24	1	=B3*D3

Conclusion

The beige shoes cost less at the time of purchase, but they don't last as long as the brown shoes. Since you have to keep buying beige shoes every six months, they end up being more expensive than the brown shoes.

5. What Do You Think?

A. Which pair of shoes in the exercise above, was the most affordable over a 2 year period?

B. Do you think it is better to pay more upfront with a longer useful life, or to pay less upfront with a shorter useful life? Explain why.

Cleaning Out the Closet

If you have a lot of stuff you don't use or need, consider cleaning out the closet. Having stuff you don't want, but others might, is like a store having a bunch of merchandise it never sells. Selling a nice pair of shoes you never wear, or that guitar you never play can put you that much closer to achieving your financial goals, thereby increasing the value and quality of your life. And if there's stuff you can't sell, donate it and ask for a receipt. Charitable donations are tax deductions (more on this in Chapter 6).

6. What Do You Think?

A. List 3 things you bought but never used or regretted buying afterward.

B. List 3 things you bought that have improved your life or that you are glad you bought.

The Yard Sale

The Garcias want to make sure they are maximizing income and minimizing expenses so they can reach their financial goals. They know that they have stuff they don't need anymore and decide to have a yard sale to see if they can declutter and make a little money at the same time.

Section 4A: Homework

1. It's spring cleaning time and the Garcias want to sell their old stuff. Carlos has 22 used books he wants to sell.
    a. If he prices them for $2 a book, he can sell 14 of them. How much would he make?
    b. If he prices them for $5 a book, he can sell 8 books. How much would he make?
    c. If he prices them as 2 books for $3, he can sell 18 books. How much would he make?
    d. Which price makes the most money?

2. Susan has 2 pieces of fabric she wants to sell. The first piece is 5 yards long and the second piece is 3 yards long.
    a. How many total yards does she have?
    b. If she wants to receive $2.50 for each yard, how much does she need to charge for each piece?

3. The Garcias are also looking to cut their expenses in other areas. Carlos recently signed up for a gym membership that costs $48 per month. He exercises 1 day a week for 2.5 hours each day.

a. How many hours a month does he work out? *Assume there are 4 weeks in a month.*
b. How much money does he spend per hour working out?
c. The gym also offers a pay as you go plan for $10 a day with no monthly fee. If he used this plan, how much would it cost him per month?
d. Which is the better plan for Carlos?

4. Susan wants to join Carlos' gym. The gym offers a family share plan that costs $55 per month. Carlos still works out 1 day a week for 2.5 hours each day, but Susan manages to go 2 times a week for 1 hours each time.
   a. Now that Susan joined the gym, how many hours do they spend a month working out in total?
   b. How much money do they spend per hour working out on their new family share plan?
   c. If they decided to use the pay as you go plan instead ($10 a day), how much would they spend in a month?
   d. Which is the better plan Carlos and Susan?

5. Susan ran out of ink for her ink jet printer. She prints on average 30 pages per month.
   a. A basic ink cartridge costs $38.95 and prints 120 pages. What is its useful life in months?
   b. The deluxe ink cartridge costs $59.95 and prints 240 pages. What is its useful life in months?
   c. Use a spreadsheet to compare the costs over a 2 year time period. Record your answers below.

	A	B	C	D	E
1	Product Name	Selling Price	Useful Life (in months)	Number of Purchases	Total Cost
2	Basic				
3	Deluxe				

   d. Which type of ink is the better buy?

6. The Garcias like to make salads. Each week they buy lettuce ($1.99), spinach ($2.95), arugula ($2.89), and spring greens ($1.49).
   a. How much do they spend a week on their salad greens?
   b. If they tend to throw away 50% of their greens, how much money do they waste each week?
   c. If they saved that money each week instead, how much would they have at the end of 1 year?

7. Describe an area in your life where you could reduce spending.
   a. How much do you currently spend each month on this area?
   b. How would you reduce its cost?
   c. How much would you save in a month?
   d. How much would you save in a year?

Section 4B: Buying a Car

In Section 4A, you learned some ways to think about purchases and decisions using mathematics to show you value in the short-term and in the long-term. One common financial goal is buying a car, so this section will focus on the math behind making the decision to buy a car, including depreciation and operating costs.

Down Payments

Monthly Payments

Gas Mileage

Budgeting for Other Car Related Expenses

Getting Clear

Creating goals is important. Clearly defined financial goals inform your budget about what your priorities are. Choosing goals that meet your needs and are within your reach are important parts of achieving those goals. In combination, your budget and goals will be your road map to success.

1. Prioritizing ...

Consider the following wants when buying a car:

- Paying a low monthly payment
- Getting great gas mileage
- Having a low interest rate
- Driving a reliable car
- Purchasing a particular brand or model
- Getting features like navigation, entertainment, or heated seats
- Buying a new car
- Having a car with high safety ratings

Prioritize these wants by putting the most important first and the least important last. Note: there is no right or wrong answer to this exercise. Making informed decisions is about being clear about your priorities.

1. ____________________
2. ____________________
3. ____________________
4. ____________________
5. ____________________
6. ____________________
7. ____________________
8. ____________________

Options for Buying a Car

There are many options for buying a car, depending on your goals. The one that's right for you depends on many factors, including your financial situation and how you plan to use the car.

New

New cars are the most expensive option when buying a car. Advantages of new cars include warranties, state-of-the-art safety, reliability, and comfort.

Used

Used cars are generally a better value because car prices decline precipitously in the first few years. However, their age and previous driving history can make them less reliable than a new car.

Certified Pre-Owned

Certified Pre-Owned cars are certified through a rigorous inspection by the manufacturer to be high quality, reliable used cars that often come with a warranty.

Lease

Leasing a car means paying a monthly fee to drive a new vehicle for a certain period of time. Often, leases are for 2-3 years and require a large upfront payment at lease signing.

The Useful Life of a Car

A car will only last so long, no matter how well you take care of it. How long you anticipate your car to last before it requires major mechanical repairs is an important factor in determining the car's value to you. You could expect to drive a new car for 10 years before having expensive repairs, whereas you might expect to only get 5 years of problem-free use out of a used car. However, not all new cars are problem-free for 10 years, and many used cars last longer that expected, so these are just general trends to consider.

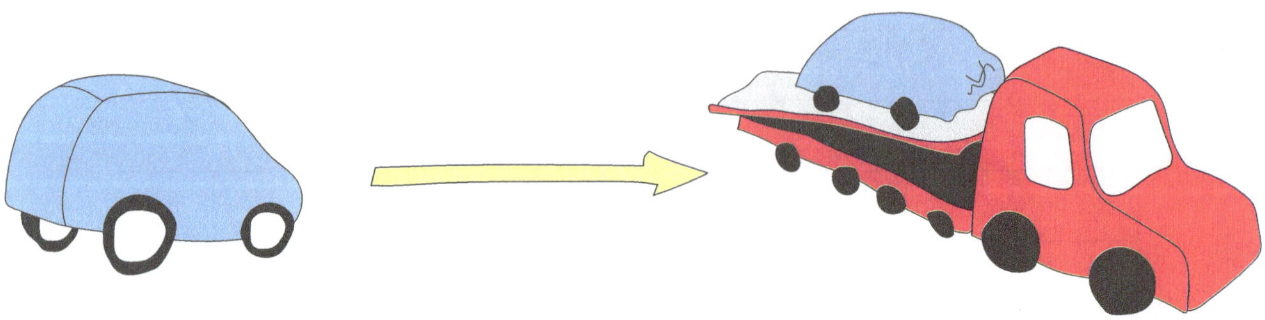

Depreciation

The value of a car decreases over time as it reaches the end of its useful life. This decrease in value over time is known as depreciation. Cars depreciate rapidly in the beginning and after 5 years are generally worth half what they were worth new. This is good news for used car buyers, but bad news for new car buyers. Depreciation means that buying a new car is the most expensive option because the car's resell value declines so quickly. Nowadays, cars are increasingly more reliable and are lasting longer. The useful life of a new car today could easily be close to 20 years, or even longer with proper preventive maintenance.

Graphing Depreciation

Use a line graph to show how the value of a car decreases over time for a $24,000 car that is expected to last 18 years. Vehicles don't actually depreciate in a linear (straight line) way, but using a line graph to show depreciation is very useful for making informed decisions about purchases.

Step 1

Start by drawing a blank graph.

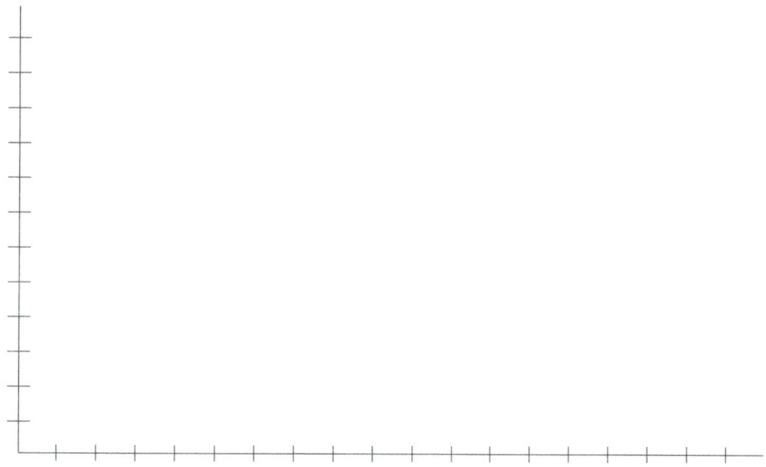

Step 2

The horizontal axis on graphs often represents time. In this example, let it represent the number of years you will own the car. Label each tick mark with the years 1 to 18.

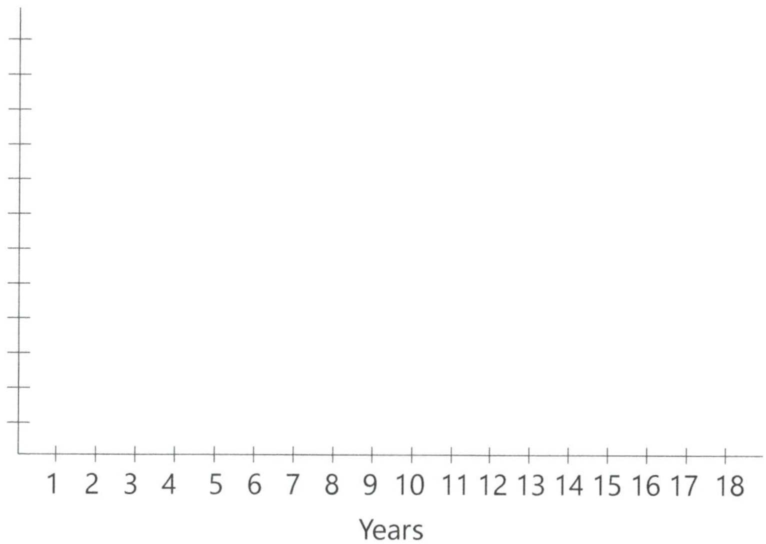

Graphing Depreciation

Step 3

The vertical axis will be the value of the car. To save space each tick mark will increase by $2,000.

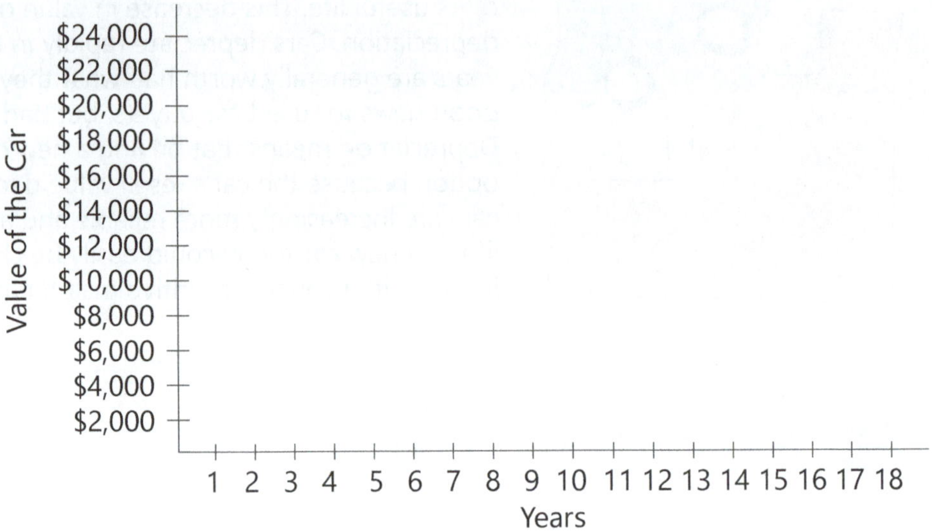

Step 4

When you buy the car, it is worth $24,000. Mark a dot on $24,000.

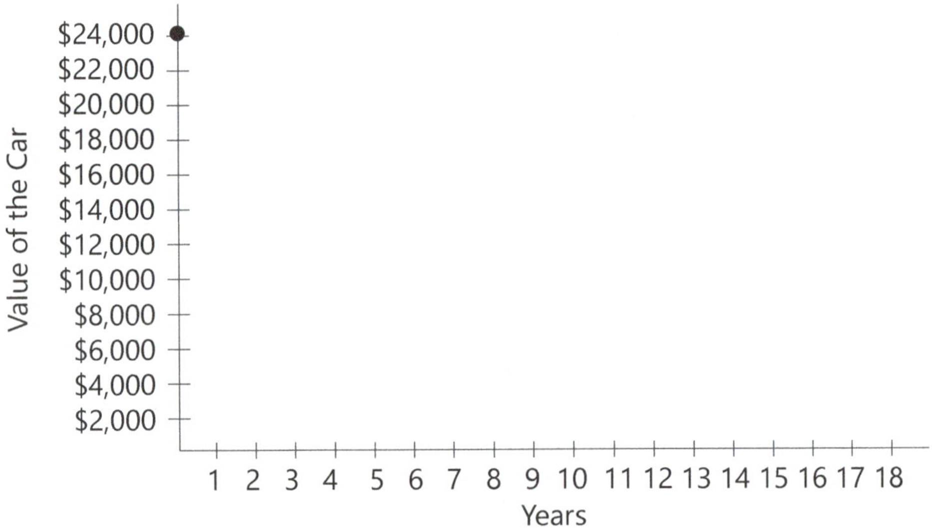

Step 5

The car has an expected useful life of 18 years. That means after 18 years, the car will no longer be worth any money. Mark a dot on 18 years.

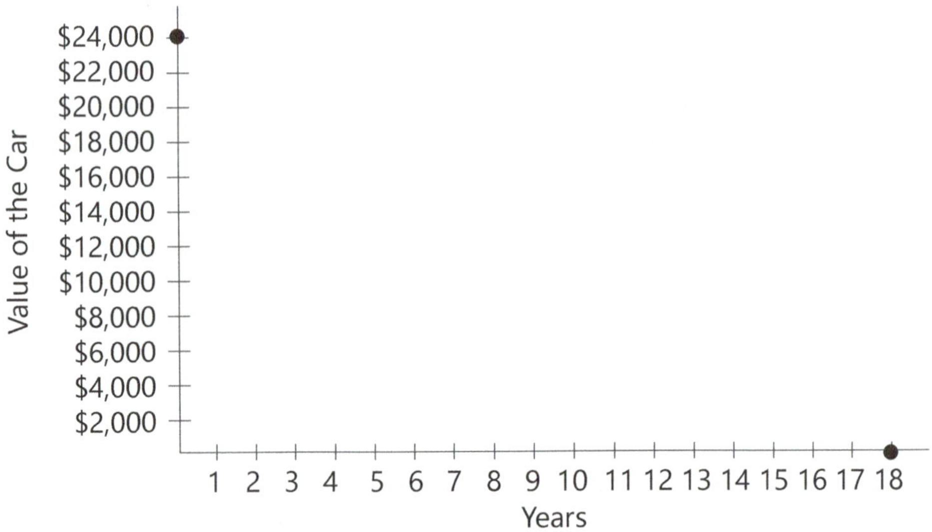

Graphing Depreciation

Step 6

Draw a line connecting the dots to show how the value of the car decreases over time.

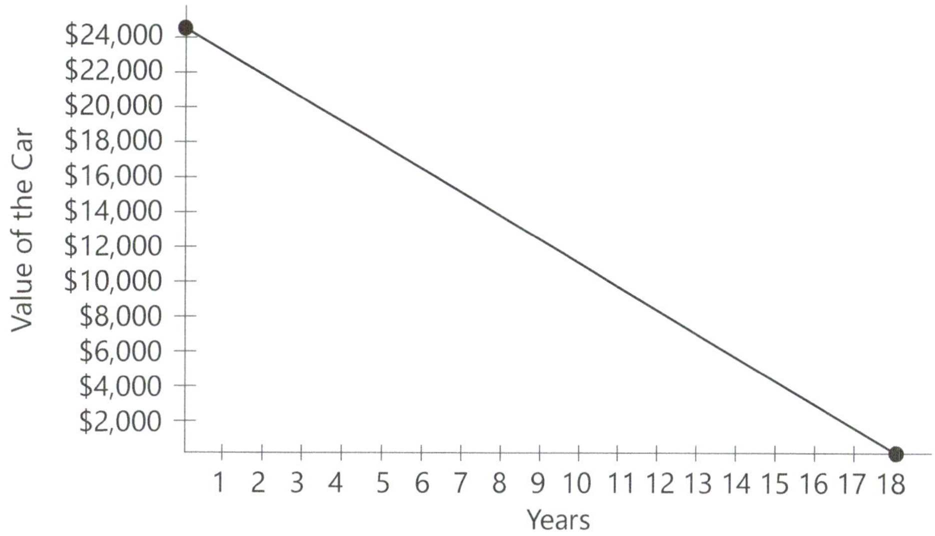

Step 7

Once you make your graph, you can use it to find information. To see what the car is worth after 6 years, find 6 years on your horizontal axis and look up to find the corresponding point on your line.

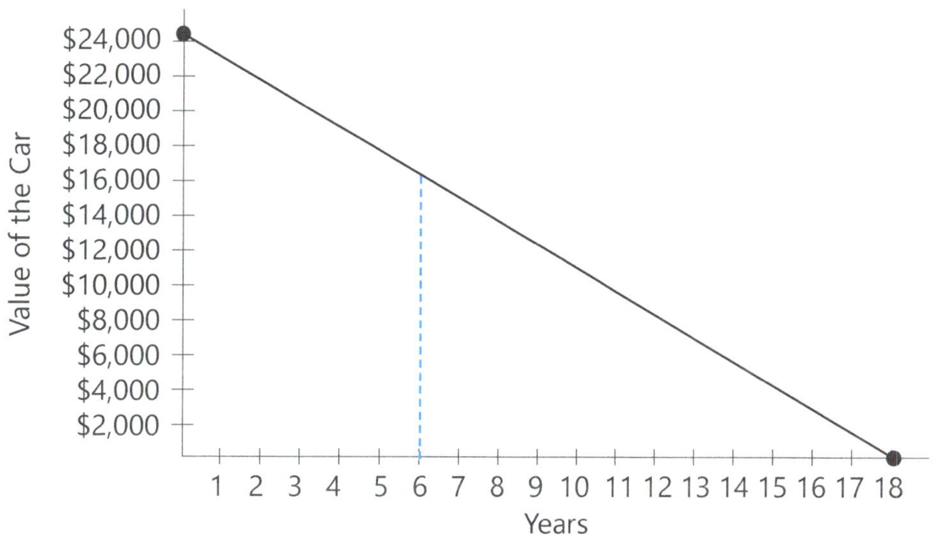

Step 8

Then look to the left to find the corresponding value.

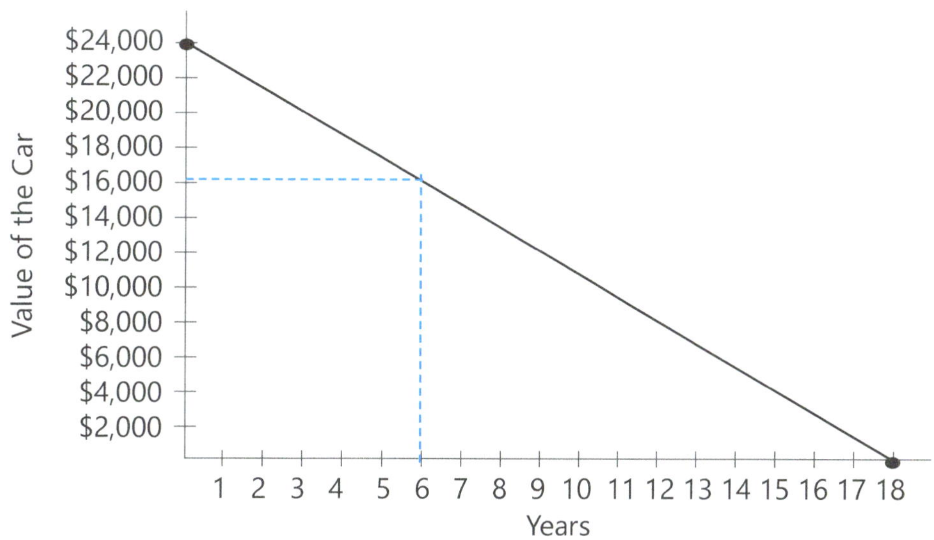

Conclusion

Graphs can show you how the value of a car decreases over time. In this case, the car is worth $16,000 after 6 years.

2. Now Do the Math ...

A. The Garcias are considering buying a new car for $32,000 that has a useful life of 20 years. Graph the depreciation and find the value of the car after 5 years. How much value does the car lose in 12 years?

B. The Garcias are also considering buying a used car for $14,000 that has a useful life of 12 years. Graph the depreciation and find the value of the car after 5 years. How much value does the car lose in 5 years? *Round your answers to the nearest thousand.*

3. What Do You Think?

A. In the exercise on the previous page, which do you think is the better option for the Garcias? Why?

B. What has been your experience with vehicle depreciation?

Other Factors to Consider

If you can't afford to buy a car outright, you will need to take out a loan. Consider some the other expenses that go into operating a vehicle before you make a decision.

Down Payment

A percentage of the list price you pay before getting a loan for the car. The percentage can vary depending on your credit history, the terms of the loan, and whether you buy new or used.

Monthly Payment

A set payment you make every month until the car is completely paid off.

Gas Mileage

The fuel economy of a vehicle. Fuel is a major operating cost.

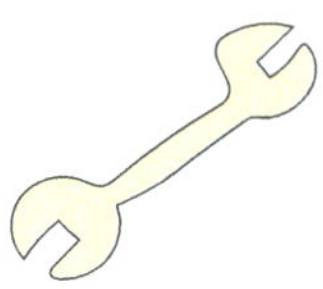

Maintenance Costs

As cars age, they require maintenance. Saving for this makes it more affordable than being surprised by a big repair bill that you knew would come eventually.

Calculating the Down Payment

When buying a car, you will be required to make a down payment before getting a loan. The standard down payment for a car is about 20% of the selling price. Find the down payment for a car that costs $18,000.

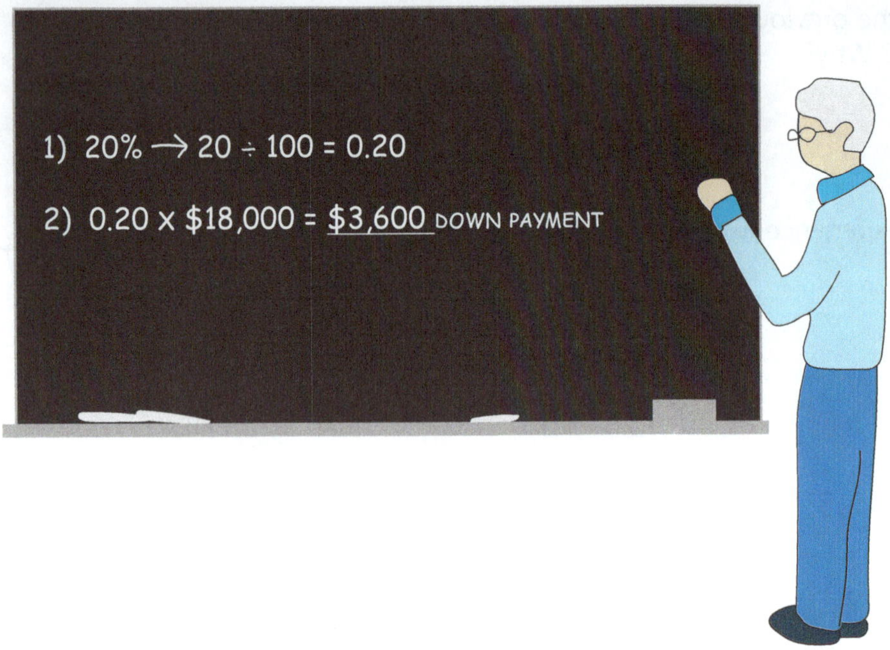

Step 1

Turn 20% into a decimal by dividing it by 100.

Step 2

To find the down payment, multiply the decimal form of the percentage by the selling price of the car.

4. Now Do the Math ...

A. Barb is getting a new car that costs $27,000. At 20% upfront, what would her down payment be?

B. If she saves $300 a month, how many months will it take Barb to save enough for her down payment?

Using a Spreadsheet to Find the Monthly Payment

When you buy a car, you will be given a monthly payment. This payment will stay the same for the entire length of your loan. Spreadsheets have a function that can calculate the monthly payment. In this example, you will find the monthly payment for a loan of $18,450 and an interest rate of 5% for 4 years.

Step 1

Start by opening a blank spreadsheet. At the bottom of the page, double-click on Sheet 1 to highlight it.

	A	B	C	D
1				
2				
3				
	Sheet 1	+		

Using a Spreadsheet to Find the Monthly Payment

Step 2

Rename it to Monthly Payment and then press enter.

	A	B	C	D
1				
2				
3				
	Monthly Payment	+		

Step 3

Spreadsheets have a function called PMT that calculates your monthly payment. In A1, start by typing =pmt(.

	A	B	C	D
1	=PMT(			
2				

Step 4

First is your rate per period. Type in your rate divided / by 12 since you are working with months. Then type a comma ,.

	A	B	C	D
1	=PMT(5%/12,			
2				

Step 5

Next is the total number of periods. Type in the number of years and multiply * it by 12 since you are working with months. Then type a comma ,.

	A	B	C	D
1	=PMT(5%/12,4*12,			
2				

Step 6

Last is your principal. Since you are dealing with debt, it will be negative - Finish your function by closing the parentheses).

	A	B	C	D
1	=PMT(5%/12,10*12,-18450)			
2				

Step 7

Press enter and the spreadsheet will calculate your monthly payment. Save your work as 4A Classwork.

	A	B	C	D
1	$424.89			
2				

Conclusion

When getting a loan, it is important to know what the monthly payment will be to make sure you can afford it. The PMT function can make this calculation.

Finding the Gas Mileage

Knowing your vehicle's gas mileage or miles per gallon (mpg) allows you to do all sorts of things, such as estimate how much money you will spend on fuel when you travel. It can also help you estimate how many more miles you can drive before you need to refuel. Another benefit of checking your gas mileage periodically is that a sudden change in gas mileage can be an early indication that your vehicle needs maintenance. Factors that negatively influence gas mileage include improper tire pressure, driving fast, and frequent acceleration or deceleration.

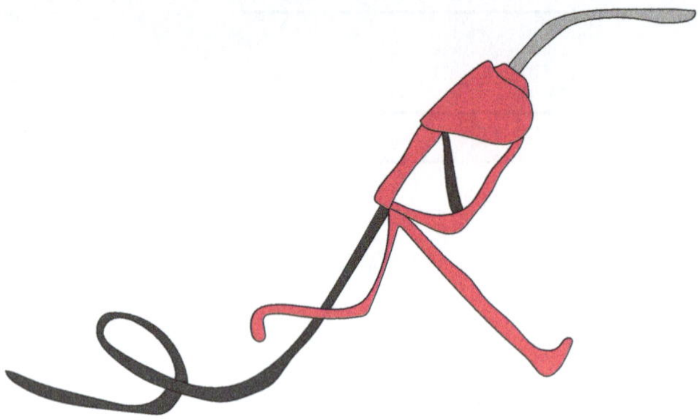

Step 1
Fill your tank.

Step 2
Reset your car's odometer to 0.

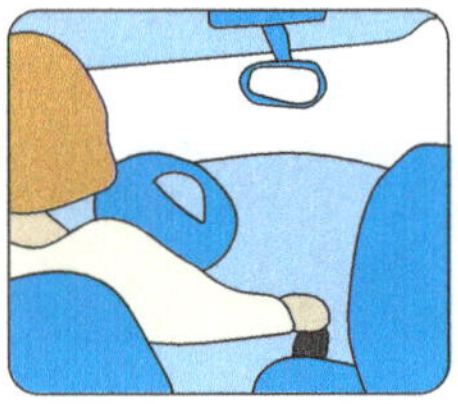

Step 3
Drive.

Step 4
Fill your tank again.

Step 5
Record the gallons dispensed.

Step 6
Divide the number of miles driven by the number of gallons dispensed.

5. Now Do the Math ...

Find the gas mileage for a car that travels 456 miles on 12 gallons of gas.

Finding the Monthly Cost of Gas

Once you know the gas mileage, you can estimate the monthly cost of gas. It will only be an estimate because the price of gas fluctuates and so do your driving habits. Calculate the monthly cost of gas for a car that gets 35 miles per gallon and drives an average of 700 miles each month.

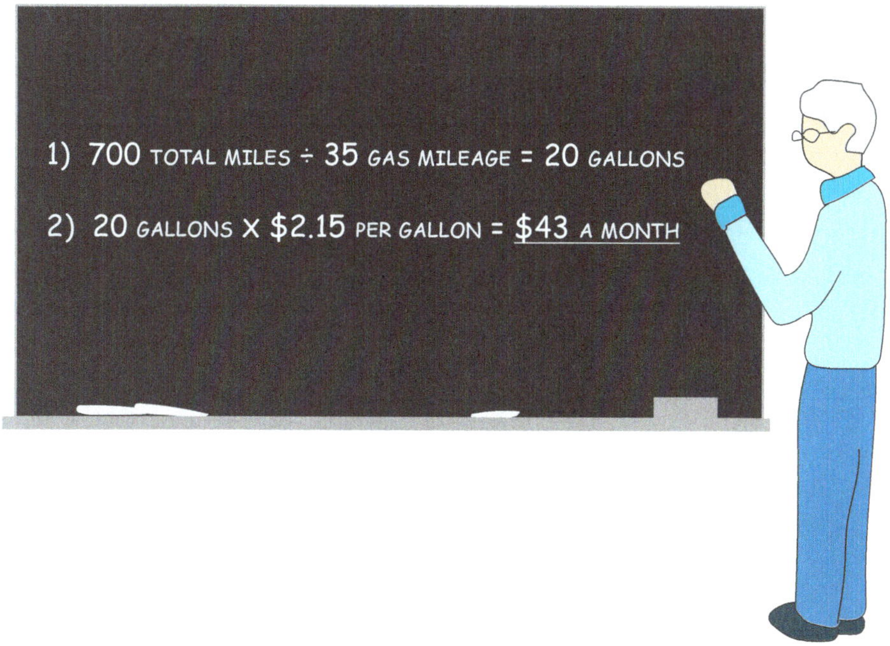

Step 1
Determine the number of gallons you will need to purchase by dividing the total miles by the gas mileage.

Step 2
Multiply the number of gallons by the price of gas. This will give you the cost of gas for the month.

6. Now Do the Math ...

A. Find the monthly cost of gas for a car that gets 44 miles per gallon and is driven 650 miles per month. Assume the price of gas is $2.89 per gallon. *Round your answer to the nearest hundredth.*

B. Find the monthly cost of gas for an SUV that gets 18 miles per gallon and is driven 650 miles per month. Assume the price of gas is $2.89 per gallon.

7. What Do You Think?

A. If you were planning on buying a car, how important would the price of gas be in your decision-making process?

B. What would be the minimum gas mileage on a car you would be willing to buy?

Buying a Car

In order to avoid taking on unnecessary new debt, the Garcias plan how to save as much as possible to purchase the things they need. While it would be very difficult to save the entire amount they need to make a major purchase outright, they know the more they save, the less they have to borrow and the less interest they'll pay. The money they save paying less interest will go toward a family vacation and extra savings to start their small business.

Section 4B: Homework

1. Carlos and Susan have been saving a portion of their disposable income for a down payment for a car.
   a. If their monthly income is $3,789.10 and they save 10% of it and their total expenses are $2,854.00, what is their disposable income?
   b. If they have been saving 25% of their disposable income each month for a car, how much money were they saving each month?
   c. They have been saving 25% for 2 years now. How much money do they still need for a down payment for a car?

2. Carlos wants to get a new truck. He found one that sells for $28,000. It requires a 20% down payment.
   a. How much is the down payment for this truck?
   b. Based on your answer to question number 1, can the Garcias afford this down payment?
   c. How much more money would they need?
   d. If they continue to save the same amount of money each month, how many months would they need to save in order to have enough to get the new truck? Round your answer to the nearest month.

3. Carlos decides that the new truck isn't worth the wait. Susan suggests a new compact car that costs $16,000. It also requires a 20% down payment.

a. How much is its down payment?
b. Can the Garcias afford the compact car?
c. If they decided to get this car, what will their principal be?
d. They can sign up for a 5 year auto loan with an interest rate of 3.5%. What will their monthly payment be?

4. The dealer said Carlos can probably drive about 424 miles on a full tank of gas.
   a. If the tank holds 10.6 gallons, what is the gas mileage of the compact car?
   b. How many gallons of gas will Carlos need each month if he tends to drive about 900 miles each month?
   c. Assuming that the price of gas will average $3.15, what will his monthly cost of gas be for the compact car?

5. New cars tend to be reliable and have few repair needs. The useful life of the compact car is expected to be about 20 years.
   a. Graph the depreciation of the compact car.
   b. Use your graph to estimate the amount of money the car will be worth after 5 years.

6. Carlos isn't thrilled about driving a compact car and still wants a truck. He found a certified pre-owned truck for $18,000. It requires a 10% down payment.
   a. How much is its down payment?
   b. If they decided to get this truck, what would their principal be?
   c. They can sign up for a 5 year auto loan with an interest rate of 3.5%. What will their monthly payment be?

7. The dealer said Carlos can probably drive the truck about 250 miles on a full tank of gas.
   a. If the tank holds 12.5 gallons, what is the gas mileage of the used truck?
   b. How many gallons of gas will Carlos need each month if he tends to drive about 900 miles each month?
   c. Assuming that the price of gas will average $3.15, what will his monthly cost of gas be for the used truck?

8. Susan likes the compact car and Carlos wants the truck. Compare the prices of each to help them decide.
   a. Since new cars tend to be more reliable, the Garcias plan to set aside $50 a month for any maintenance costs. Including the monthly payment, price of gas and their maintenance savings, how much will they pay each month for the compact car?
   b. Since used cars tend to need more maintenance, the Garcias plan to set aside $100 a month for any needed repairs. Including the monthly payment, price of gas, and the maintenance savings, how much will they pay each month for the used truck?
   c. If you were Carlos, which car would you choose? Explain why?

9. When you plan to buy a car, what factors do you plan to take into consideration?

Section 4C: Buying a House

In Section 4A, you learned about the costs that go into buying a car and how to compare your options. Another major purchase is buying a house. In this section, you will look at the pros and cons of renting versus owning your home. You will also explore the short-term and long-term costs of home ownership.

Pros and Cons of Home Ownership

Calculate Monthly Payments

Create an Amortization Table

Learn Ways to Save on Interest

Why Buy A House?

In the last few sections, you explored how interest works and how it can really add to the cost of a loan, which poses a question: why would anyone want to buy a house? Buying a house can be an exciting endeavor, but is also a major financial commitment. Being able to calculate the short-term and long-term costs of owning a home can help you plan ahead, avoid financial crisis, and make more informed decisions.

1. What Do You Think?

A. What are some pros to owning your own home?

B. What are some cons to owning a home?

C. What are some pros to renting an apartment or house?

D. What are some cons to renting an apartment or house?

Creating a Plan

In this section, you will learn how to calculate the monthly payment for different houses. You will also look at the factors that influence the cost of those monthly payments, the long term costs of owning a home, and how much interest you will pay over the life of a mortgage. Lastly, you will examine different ways to reduce the monthly payment and the amount of interest you will have to pay.

Vocabulary for Buying a House

There are many factors to consider when buying a house. Each will influence the total cost you will pay for your house.

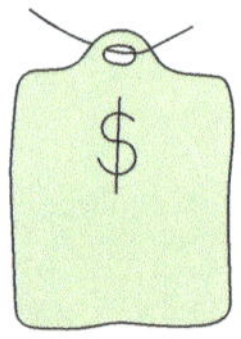

Selling Price

The price of the house.

Down Payment

A percentage of the selling price you pay before getting a loan for the house. Depending on the strength of the economy and your credit history, the down payment can be anywhere from 3% to 20%.

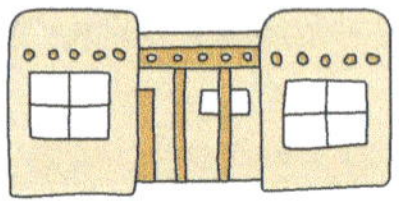

Mortgage

The name of a loan used to buy a house.

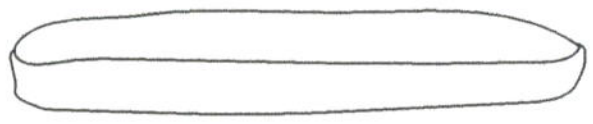

Principal

The amount you have to borrow after paying the down payment.

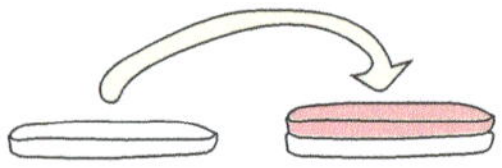

Interest

The additional amount of money you pay for borrowing money.

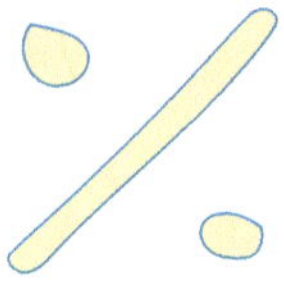

Rate

The percentage used to calculate interest.

Monthly Payment

A set payment you pay every month until the house is completely paid off.

Using a Spreadsheet to Find the Monthly Payment

When you buy a house, you will be given a monthly payment. Assuming a fixed rate loan, this payment will stay the same for the entire length of the mortgage. Spreadsheets have a function that can calculate the monthly payment. In this example, you will find the monthly payment for a $250,000 mortgage with an interest rate of 6% for 30 years.

Step 1

Start by opening a blank spreadsheet. At the bottom of the page, double-click on Sheet1 to highlight it.

	A	B	C	D
1				
2				
3				
	Sheet 1	+		

Step 2

Rename it to Monthly Payment and then press enter.

	A	B	C	D
1				
2				
3				
	Monthly Payment	+		

Step 3

Spreadsheets have a function called PMT that calculates your monthly payment. In A1, start by typing =pmt(.

	A	B	C	D
1	=PMT(			
2				

Step 4

The first piece of information needed is the rate per period. Type in the Interest Rate divided / by 12 since you are working with months. Then type a comma , .

	A	B	C	D
1	=PMT(6%/12,			
2				

Step 5

The next piece of information needed is the total number of periods. Type in the number of years and multiply * it by 12 since you are working with months. Then type a comma , .

	A	B	C	D
1	=PMT(6%/12,30*12,			
2				

Using a Spreadsheet to Find the Monthly Payment

Step 6

The last piece of information is your principal. Since you are dealing with debt, it will be negative. Finish your function by closing the parentheses).

	A	B	C	D
1	=PMT(6%/12,30*12,-250000)			
2				

Step 7

Press enter and the spreadsheet will calculate your monthly payment. Save your work as 4C Classwork.

	A	B	C	D
1	$1,498.88			
2				

Conclusion

When buying a house, it is important to know what the monthly payment will be to make sure you can afford it. The PMT function can make this calculation.

2. Now Do the Math ...

A. Calculate the monthly payment for a mortgage of $340,000 with an interest rate of 4% for 30 years.

B. Calculate the monthly payment for the same house for 15 years.

3. What Do You Think?

A. In the exercise above, which length of time produced the higher monthly payment?

B. Why do you think it was higher?

Finding the Total Cost of Interest on a Mortgage

Once you know the monthly payment, you can find the total amount you'll pay for the mortgage. This will tell you how much interest you'll end up paying over the life of your loan. In this example, find the total interest for a mortgage of $250,000 with an interest rate of 6% for 30 years if the monthly payment is $1,498.88

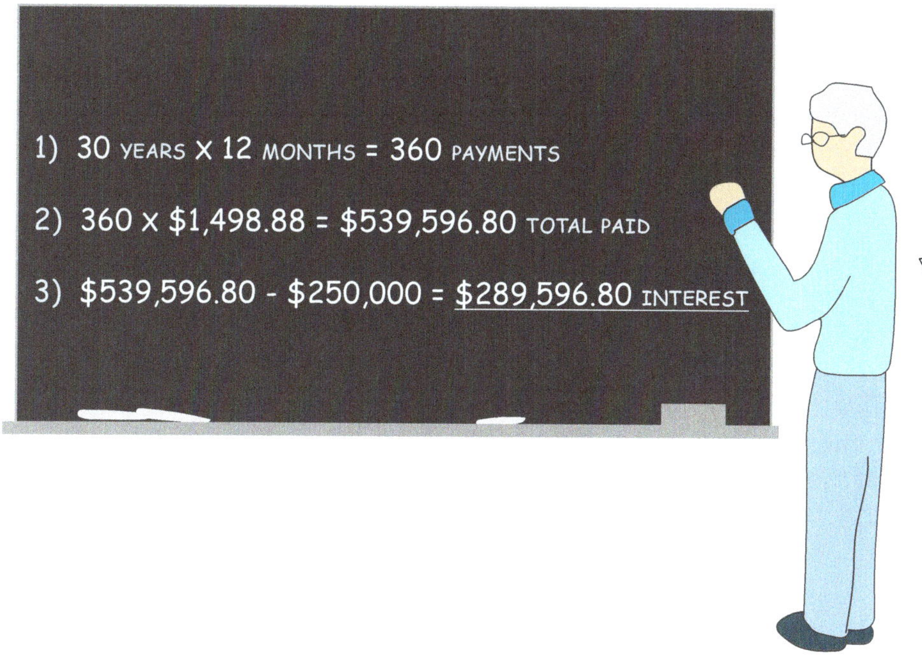

Step 1
Determine the total number of monthly payments you will make by multiplying the number of years by 12.

Step 2
Multiply the number of payments by the monthly payment. This will give you the total amount you will pay for the house.

Step 3
To find the interest, take the total amount paid and subtract the principal of the mortgage.

Interest on Top of the House

When you buy a house, you have to borrow a large amount of money. Because you have to borrow so much, you will pay a lot more interest than on other kinds of loans such as car loans or student loans. Depending on the terms of your mortgage, you may end up paying as much in interest as you do for the house.

A Couple of Ways to Reduce Interest

Buying a house involves paying interest, but the amount of interest you end up paying can be reduced in the following ways:

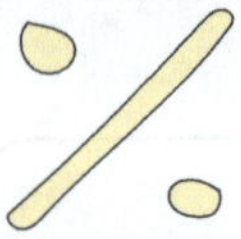

Lower Interest Rate

With good credit, you can get a lower interest rate, which can lower the amount of interest you pay.

Shorter Mortgage

Getting a shorter mortgage will cause your monthly payments to go up, but will greatly reduce the amount of interest you have to pay and save you money in the long run.

4. Now Do the Math ...

To compare the following mortgage terms, calculate the monthly payment and the total cost of interest for each of them.

A. Original House

Selling Price = $350,000.00
Interest Rate = 5.5%
Time = 30 years
Monthly Payment = ____________________
Total Amount Paid = ____________________
Total Cost of Interest = ____________________

B. Lower Interest Rate

Selling Price = $350,000.00
Interest Rate = 4%
Time = 30 years
Monthly Payment = ____________________
Total Amount Paid = ____________________
Total Cost of Interest = ____________________

C. Shorter Mortgage

Selling Price = $350,000.00
Interest Rate = 5.5%
Time = 15 years
Monthly Payment = ____________________
Total Amount Paid = ____________________
Total Cost of Interest = ____________________

5. What Do You Think?

A. When you look at your answers to the exercise on the previous page, which house has the lowest monthly payment?

B. Which house has the lowest amount of interest?

C. Which option reduces the interest the most, having a lower interest rate or a shorter mortgage?

D. Would you rather pay a lower monthly payment or pay a lower amount of interest? Explain why.

Why is There so Much Interest?

Depending on the details of the mortgage, the amount of interest can be more than the price of the house. In this section, you will explore the math behind interest, how it's calculated, and how it changes over time. You will get to see what happens to each monthly payment and be able to make what's called an "amortization table" to see how much interest you pay each month for the full length of the loan.

Using a Spreadsheet to Create an Amortization Schedule

The reason you end up paying a lot of interest is that every time you make a monthly payment, the bank will keep some of it as interest. Whatever is left over will go to pay off the principal of the loan. Spreadsheets can create an amortization table that will show how much interest you pay each month. In this example, you will look at a mortgage of $350,000 with an interest rate of 6% for 30 years.

Step 1

At the bottom of your spreadsheet, double-click the plus sign next to the Monthly Payment sheet.

	A	B	C	D	E	F
1						
2						
3						
	Monthly Payment		+			

Step 2

Rename the new sheet as Amortization Table and press enter.

	A	B	C	D	E	F
1						
2						
3						
	Monthly Payment		Amortization Table			

Step 3

Start in A1 and create the following headings.

	A	B	C	D	E	F
1	Month	Principal	Interest Rate	Monthly Payment	Amount Paid on Interest	Amount Paid on Principal
2						

Step 4

In A1, type the number 1 for the first month. In B2, type in your principal and in C2, type in your interest rate.

	A	B	C	D	E	F
1	Month	Principal	Interest Rate	Monthly Payment	Amount Paid on Interest	Amount Paid on Principal
2	1	$350,000.00	6%			

Step 5

Use the PMT function to find the monthly payment. In D2, type =pmt(.

	A	B	C	D	E	F
1	Month	Principal	Interest Rate	Monthly Payment	Amount Paid on Interest	Amount Paid on Principal
2	1	$350,000.00	6%	=PMT(		

Using a Spreadsheet to Create an Amortization Schedule

Step 6

First is the rate per period. Click on your Interest Rate in C2 and divide / it by 12. Then type a comma , .

	A	B	C	D	E	F
1	Month	Principal	Interest Rate	Monthly Payment	Amount Paid on Interest	Amount Paid on Principal
2	1	$350,000.00	6%	=PMT(C2/12,		

Step 7

Next is the total number of periods. Type in the number of years and multiply * it by 12. Then type a comma , .

	A	B	C	D	E	F
1	Month	Principal	Interest Rate	Monthly Payment	Amount Paid on Interest	Amount Paid on Principal
2	1	$350,000.00	6%	=PMT(C2/12,30*12,		

Step 8

Last is the principal. Since you are dealing with debt, it will be negative. Type a negative - sign and click on your Principal in B2. Then, close the parentheses) to finish the function.

	A	B	C	D	E	F
1	Month	Principal	Interest Rate	Monthly Payment	Amount Paid on Interest	Amount Paid on Principal
2	1	$350,000.00	6%	=PMT(C2/12,30*12,-B2)		

Step 9

Press enter and the spreadsheet will do the math showing that $2,098.43 is the monthly payment.

	A	B	C	D	E	F
1	Month	Principal	Interest Rate	Monthly Payment	Amount Paid on Interest	Amount Paid on Principal
2	1	$350,000.00	6%	$2,098.43		

Using a Spreadsheet to Create an Amortization Schedule

Step 10

In E2, press = , click on the Principal in B2, multiply * it by the Interest Rate in C2, and divide / it by 12. Then press tab.

	A	B	C	D	E	F
1	Month	Principal	Interest Rate	Monthly Payment	Amount Paid on Interest	Amount Paid on Principal
2	1	$350,000.00	6%	$2,098.43	=B2*C2/12	

Step 11

In F2, press =, click on the Monthly Payment in D2, and subtract – the Amount Paid on Interest in E2.

	A	B	C	D	E	F
1	Month	Principal	Interest Rate	Monthly Payment	Amount Paid on Interest	Amount Paid on Principal
2	1	$350,000.00	6%	$2,098.43	$1,750.00	=D2-E2

Step 12

Press enter and the spreadsheet will do the math showing that only $348.43 of your monthly payment went to pay off the loan.

	A	B	C	D	E	F
1	Month	Principal	Interest Rate	Monthly Payment	Amount Paid on Interest	Amount Paid on Principal
2	1	$350,000.00	6%	$2,098.43	$1,750.00	$348.43
3						

Step 13

In A3, type the number 2 for the second month.

	A	B	C	D	E	F
1	Month	Principal	Interest Rate	Monthly Payment	Amount Paid on Interest	Amount Paid on Principal
2	1	$350,000.00	6%	$2,098.43	$1,750.00	$348.43
3	2					

Step 14

In B3, press =, click on the Principal in B2, and subtract – the Amount Paid on Principal in F2. Then press tab.

	A	B	C	D	E	F
1	Month	Principal	Interest Rate	Monthly Payment	Amount Paid on Interest	Amount Paid on Principal
2	1	$350,000.00	6%	$2,098.43	$1,750.00	$348.43
3	2	=B2-F2				

Using a Spreadsheet to Create an Amortization Schedule

Step 15

The Interest Rate will stay the same. In C3, press = and click on the Interest Rate in C2. Then press tab.

	A	B	C	D	E	F
1	Month	Principal	Interest Rate	Monthly Payment	Amount Paid on Interest	Amount Paid on Principal
2	1	$350,000.00	6%	$2,098.43	$1,750.00	$348.43
3	2	$349,651.57	=C2			

Step 16

The monthly payment will also stay the same. In D3, press = and click on the Monthly Payment in D2. Then press tab.

	A	B	C	D	E	F
1	Month	Principal	Interest Rate	Monthly Payment	Amount Paid on Interest	Amount Paid on Principal
2	1	$350,000.00	6%	$2,098.43	$1,750.00	$348.43
3	2	$349,651.57	6%	=D2		

Step 17

In E3, press = , click on the Principal in B3, multiply * it by the Interest Rate in C3, and divide / it by 12 months. Then press tab.

	A	B	C	D	E	F
1	Month	Principal	Interest Rate	Monthly Payment	Amount Paid on Interest	Amount Paid on Principal
2	1	$350,000.00	6%	$2,098.43	$1,750.00	$348.43
3	2	$349,651.57	6%	$2,098.43	=B3*C3/12	

Step 18

To find how much of your payment will go towards the loan, select F3, press =, click on the Monthly Payment in D3, and subtract - the Amount Paid on Interest in E3.

	A	B	C	D	E	F
1	Month	Principal	Interest Rate	Monthly Payment	Amount Paid on Interest	Amount Paid on Principal
2	1	$350,000.00	6%	$2,098.43	$1,750.00	$348.43
3	2	$349,651.57	6%	$2,098.43	$1,748.26	=D3-E3

Using a Spreadsheet to Create an Amortization Schedule

Step 19

Press enter and the spreadsheet will do the math showing that you will pay $350.17 towards your loan in the second month.

	A	B	C	D	E	F
1	Month	Principal	Interest Rate	Monthly Payment	Amount Paid on Interest	Amount Paid on Principal
2	1	$350,000.00	6%	$2,098.43	$1,750.00	$348.43
3	2	$349,651.57	6%	$2,098.43	$1,748.26	$350.17
4						

Step 20

Select the bottom row.

	A	B	C	D	E	F
1	Month	Principal	Interest Rate	Monthly Payment	Amount Paid on Interest	Amount Paid on Principal
2	1	$350,000.00	6%	$2,098.43	$1,750.00	$348.43
3	2	$349,651.57	6%	$2,098.43	$1,748.26	$350.17

Step 21

Click on the fill handle and drag it down to the total number of months. To find the total months, multiply * the number of years by 12.

	A	B	C	D	E	F	
1	Month	Principal	Interest Rate	Monthly Payment	Amount Paid on Interest	Amount Paid on Principal	
2	1	$350,000.00	6%	$2,098.43	$1,750.00	$348.43	
3	2	$349,651.57	6%	$2,098.43	$1,748.26	$350.17	
360							
361							360

Step 22

Let go of the mouse and the rest of the spreadsheet will fill in.

	A	B	C	D	E	F
1	Month	Principal	Interest Rate	Monthly Payment	Amount Paid on Interest	Amount Paid on Principal
2	1	$350,000.00	6%	$2,098.43	$1,750.00	$348.43
3	2	$349,651.57	6%	$2,098.43	$1,748.26	$350.17
360	359	$4,165.59	6%	$2,098.43	$20.83	$2,077.60
361	360	$2,087.99	6%	$2,098.43	$10.44	$2,087.99

Step 23

Select the cell underneath the last entry in the interest column. In this case, it's cell E362. Type =sum(. Then, select everything in that column.

	A	B	C	D	E	F
1	Month	Principal	Interest Rate	Monthly Payment	Amount Paid on Interest	Amount Paid on Principal
2	1	$350,000.00	6%	$2,098.43	$1,750.00	$348.43
3	2	$349,651.57	6%	$2,098.43	$1,748.26	$350.17
360	359	$4,165.59	6%	$2,098.43	$20.83	$2,077.60
361	360	$2,087.99	6%	$2,098.43	$10.44	$2,087.99
362					=SUM(E2:E361)	

USING A SPREADSHEET TO CREATE AN AMORTIZATION SCHEDULE

STEP 24

Press enter and the spreadsheet will do the math showing that you will pay a total of $405,433.66 in interest over the life of the loan. Make sure to save your work.

	A	B	C	D	E	F
1	Month	Principal	Interest Rate	Monthly Payment	Amount Paid on Interest	Amount Paid on Principal
2	1	$350,000.00	6%	$2,098.43	$1,750.00	$348.43
3	2	$349,651.57	6%	$2,098.43	$1,748.26	$350.17
360	359	$4,165.59	6%	$2,098.43	$20.83	$2,077.60
361	360	$2,087.99	6%	$2,098.43	$10.44	$2,087.99
362					$405,433.66	

CONCLUSION

When you take out a loan, you will be required to pay a monthly payment each month until the loan is paid off. Part of each payment will go toward interest, and that interest will add up over time.

6. WHAT DO YOU THINK?

A. Look at the amortization table you just made. What was your "Amount Paid on Interest" in the following months:

Month 1 = ____________________

Month 12 = ____________________

Month 60 = ____________________

Month 120 = ____________________

Month 360 = ____________________

B. Do you pay more in interest at the beginning of your mortgage or at the end? Why do you think that is?

Buying a House

Since buying a house is one of the Garcias' top financial goals, they want to explore their options. They want to know how different down payments, interest rates, monthly payments, and lengths of mortgage will affect their financial situation. They want to buy a house right away, but they are willing to wait to find the right place and get the right mortgage. Making an informed decision will allow them to continue saving for their other important financial goals. Let's help the Garcias explore the different mortgage scenarios that they might encounter as they save up and prepare to buy a house!

Section 4C: Homework

1. Carlos and Susan have been saving a portion of their disposable income for a down payment for a house.
    a. If their monthly income is $3,789.10 and they save 10% of it and their total expenses are $2,854.00, what is their disposable income?
    b. If they have been saving 60% of their disposable income each month for a house, how much money have they been saving each month?
    c. They have been saving that much for 3 years now. How much money do they have to go towards a down payment for a house?

2. The first house they looked at was priced at $320,000 and required an 8% down payment.
    a. How much would the down payment be?
    b. Based on your answer to question number 1, can the Garcias afford this down payment?
    c. How much more money would they need?
    d. If they continue to save the same amount of money each month, how many months would they need to save in order to have enough to buy this house? *Round your answer to the nearest month.*
    e. How many years would that be? *Round your answer to the nearest year.*

3. They decide to shop around and find a condo that was selling for $160,000 which also required an 7% down payment.
    a. How much would the down payment be?
    b. Based on your answer to question number 1, can the Garcias afford this down payment?

4. Based on the Garcias' credit history, they qualify for an interest rate of 4.5% and have several mortgage options for the condo.
    a. After paying the down payment, what will the principal on their mortgage be?
    b. If they get a 30 year mortgage, what will their monthly payment be?
    c. If they get a 20 year mortgage, what will their monthly payment be?
    d. If they get a 15 year mortgage, what will their monthly payment be?

5. The Garcias are able to afford $1,100 a month.
    a. What is the shortest amount of time the Garcias can pay off their mortgage and still afford the monthly payment?
    b. Create an amortization schedule for the condo. Record your answers from the first month and the last month.

	A	B	C	D	E	F
1	Month	Principal	Interest Rate	Monthly Payment	Amount Paid on Interest	Amount Paid on Principal
2						

    c. What is the total amount of interest for the condo?

Section 4D: Planning a Vacation

In Sections 4B and 4C, you learned about making informed decisions when buying a car or a house. These are major purchases that fulfill many day-to-day needs, but financial planning can also include some fun. In this section, you will learn how to plan for a vacation.

Choosing a Location

Exploring Travel Costs

Updating Your Budget

Create a Savings Plan for the Vacation

Bon Voyage

In previous chapters, you looked at the importance of savings and at some of the ways you can reduce expenses and prioritize your financial goals. But what's the point of saving all that money if you can't have a little fun?! So far in this chapter you have investigated two of life's major financial decisions – a car and a house – but, in this section, you will treat yourself to a well-deserved vacation.

Taking a vacation can be an adventure, even if you stay close to home. Whether it's a road trip to see family, luxury hotels in a big city, or backpacking through the woods, it's nice to get away sometimes. What do you like about traveling? What is the best vacation you have taken? If you could go anywhere in the world, where would you go? Well you don't just have to imagine, because in this section you will look at the process of planning a trip and budgeting to make it a reality.

Essential Questions for Travel ...

1. Companions - Who will go with you?
2. Destination - Where will you go?
3. Duration - How long will you be gone?
4. Location - Where will you stay?
5. Dining - What will you eat?
6. Transportation - How will you get around?
7. Attractions - What would you like to do or see?
8. Miscellaneous - Do you have any other needs such as passports or language classes?

Section 4C: Vacation Planning Project

Part 1 - Research

Do some research about your destination to help you plan for your trip. Then answer the following questions and make sure to record the websites for any information you collect on the Internet.

1. Who will go with you? *Pick at least one other person.*
2. Where will you go? *Check one of the following countries:*

□ Australia	□ Brazil	□ Costa Rica	□ Finland	□ India
□ Ivory Coast	□ Malaysia	□ Russia	□ South Africa	□ Turkey

3. Pick a city in that country and print a map of where you plan to go.
4. What is the culture like? *Do some research about the culture, politics, history, and religion of your destination. List five facts about the country and make sure to document the sources for your information.*
5. How long will you be gone? *Pick somewhere between one week and one month.*
6. Where will you stay? *Look on-line and find a hotel or hostel in the city you plan to visit. Write the name of the place, the price per night to stay there, and the website you used to find your information.*
7. What would you like to see or do? *List at least three attractions you will visit or activities you will do during your vacation. Include the price for each.*
8. What will you eat? Do some research about your destination and list several restaurants in the area and their prices.
9. How will you get around? Decide whether you will rent a car, get taxis, or use public transportation. Then record the prices of your choice of transportation.
10. Do you need anything else? Some destinations require a passport, language classes, immunizations etc. Make a list any of these needs and their costs.

Part 2 - Make a Plan

Once you do some research on your vacation, it's time to make a plan. Going on a vacation usually requires saving money, so we will need to return to our budgeting skills.

11. Make a list of each of your expenses for your group.

12. Organize your expenses into the following categories and create a spreadsheet. Record your answers below.

	A	B
1	**Expense**	**Amount**
2	Plane Tickets	
3	Food	
4	Transportation	
5	Accommodations (hotels)	
6	Attractions/Activities	
7	Misc	
8		

13. Create a pie chart for your expenses.

14. What is the total cost of your trip?

15. How many months do you plan to save for your trip?

16. Given that length of time, how much money will you have to save each month?

17. Refer back to your budget project from Chapter 1. What was your total income and disposable income?

18. What percent of your total income will go towards saving for your vacation each month?

19. What percent of your disposable income will go towards saving for your vacation each month?

20. Why do you think your answers to problems 18 and 19 are different?

Part 3 - Present

You now know more about where you want to go and have a plan to get there. Now it's time to share your adventure with others. Give a 3-5 minute presentation to the class.

CHAPTER 5: BUSINESS MATH

Section 5A: Algebra Review

In Chapters 1-4 of this book, you learned how to manage your personal finances using percentages and spreadsheets. In Chapter 5-7 of this book, you will learn how to open and operate a small business. Success in business involves knowing how to price your products and services. In this section, you will learn some algebra skills so you can solve problems in the business world.

Algebra Vocabulary

Variables

Combining Like Terms

Solving Equations

Dealing with Uncertainty

Life is full of uncertainty. Finances are no exception. Making informed decisions about your personal or professional life requires tools to navigate the unknown. Algebra is a tool that uses the information you know to figure out what you don't know. It plays a key role in making business decisions, and in pricing products to ensure companies are profitable. After all, businesses that aren't profitable aren't businesses for long.

Building Logical Thinking Skills

Critical thinking is discussed a lot, especially in education. At its core, critical thinking is about making clear, reasonable decisions, which you've been practicing in this book. Developing the skills to think critically requires learning about different aspects of a problem and questioning your assumptions.

Common Sense

Life is full of common sense problems. It is how most day-to-day decisions are made. Common sense is a great place to start when building logic.

Creating a System

Common sense situations can be broken down to create a system that will work for similar situations.

Complex Problems

Once there is a system in place, it can be used to solve more complex problems where common sense no longer works.

Parts of an Algebra Problem

Algebra brings the known and unknown together to solve problems. Every algebra problem has a combination of the following parts:

123

Constants

The information you already know about a situation. Constants are represented by numbers. They are called constants because their value doesn't change.

ABC

Variables

The information you don't know about a situation. Variables are represented by letters of the alphabet. They are called variables because their value can change.

1. Vocabulary Check ...

Complete the table below by determining which descriptions are constants and which are variables.

Description	Constant	Variable
A. There are 7 days in a week.		
B. Susan goes grocery shopping weekly and she always buys apples. The number of apples she buys is based on their price that week.		
C. Carlos brings home tips each night, which depend on the number of customers that come to the restaurant.		
D. Susan has a full time job that pays a salary. She always receives $1,052.08 for each paycheck.		

2. What Do You Think?

A. What is an example of a constant in your life?

B. What is an example of a variable in your life?

Ways to Write Multiplication

Since algebra involves using the letter "x" as a variable, it can be confusing to use "x" as a symbol for multiplication. Here are other, clearer ways to write multiplication.

WITH AN "X"

WITH A DOT

WITH PARENTHESES

Variables Act as Abbreviations

Since variables represent unknown quantities of something, they act as abbreviations for that thing. It would be impractical to write the word "apple" or draw an apple every time you need to make a calculation, so you can use a single letter, "a," to represent the number of apples instead. The examples below show how variables are a way of representing something without having to write out the entire word.

Ways to Write the Price for Apples

$0.25(number of apples)

$0.25(apples)

$0.25()

$0.25(a)

$0.25a

Like Terms

When there is more than one of the same thing, such as apples, you can use a single expression. Just as you might say 1 apple + 1 apple = 2 apples, algebra can be used to express the same thing as:
$1a + 1a = 2a$.

1a + 1a = 2a

Omitting the Number "1" Before a Variable

Traditionally, when there is only 1 thing, such as 1 apple, the number is omitted in algebra. By definition, an apple is 1 apple.

$$1a = a$$

Working with Different Variables

Only apples can go with apples and only bananas can go with bananas. In algebra, you can only add or subtract like terms that have the same variables.

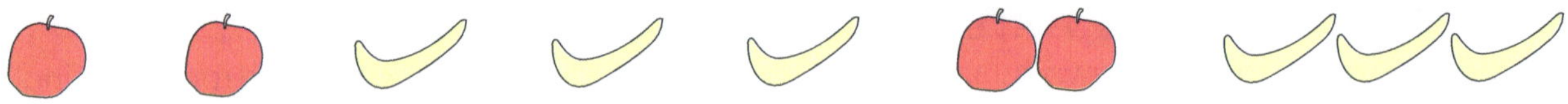

$$a + a + b + b + b = 2a + 3b$$

Combining Like Terms

Now that you have established the concept of like terms, you can use it anytime you see the same variable repeated. The example below shows you how to identify and combine like terms.

The Problem

Combine like terms in the following problem.

$$2x + 9y + 11 + x - 3y - 2$$

Step 1

Rearrange the problem so that the terms with the same variables (letters) and the constants (numbers without variables) are next to each other.

$$2x + 9y + 11 + x - 3y - 2$$
$$2x + x + 9y - 3y + 11 - 2$$

Step 2

If a variable doesn't have a number in front of it, write a 1 in front of it.

$$2x + x + 9y - 3y + 11 - 2$$
$$2x + \underline{1}x + 9y - 3y + 11 - 2$$

Step 3

Add or subtract like terms.

$$2x + 1x + 9y - 3y + 11 - 2$$
$$3x + 6y + 9$$

3. Now Do the Math ...

Combine like terms in the following problems.

A. $7a + 9a - 10$

B. $12y + 5 - y + 12$

C. $6n + 9c + 10n - n + 5$

Types of Algebra Problems

Two basic categories of problems exist in algebra: expressions and equations. The difference between these two is very important since it will determine what kind of work you need to do.

$x - 5 + 8$

Expression

A problem that doesn't have an equal sign. You can simplify an expression by combining like terms.

$x - 5 = 8$

Equation

A problem that has an equals sign. You can solve an equation by isolating the variable to find its value.

4. Vocabulary Check ...

Complete the table below by determining which are expressions and which are equations.

Problem	Expression	Equation
$7y + 14 - 3y$		
$15x + 2 = 3x - 8$		
$5 + b = 9$		
$18d - 20 + 2$		

Susan's Trip to the Store

Life is full of common sense problems. Most people use algebra every day and may not even realize it. Susan went to the store with $5 in her pocket. When she left, she had an apple and $2. How much did the apple cost? The answer may be clear to you before doing the math, but we can break a problem like this into steps to find its logic. That logic can then be applied to more complex problems.

Breaking It Down with Algebra

Algebra is your tool to decode real life situations so you can make informed decisions. In the following example, you will see the process of thinking that applies to all algebra problems you will encounter.

Step 1

To help visualize the situation, you can draw a scale. Equations are like a scale. There are 2 sides that must stay in balance. If one side changes, the other must change accordingly.

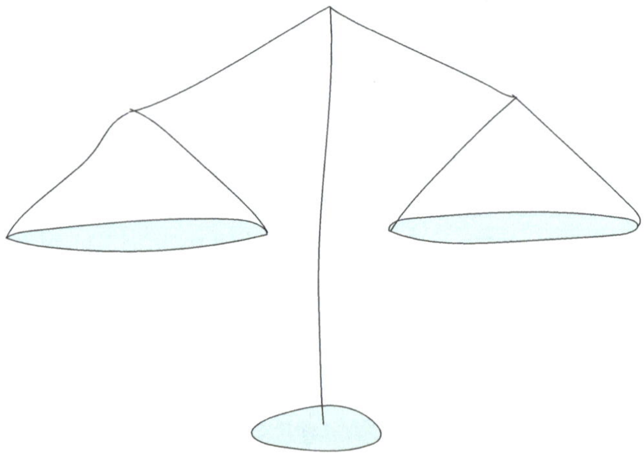

Step 2

In Susan's problem, one side of the scale will represent what Susan had before going to the store. On the other side will be what she had when she left.

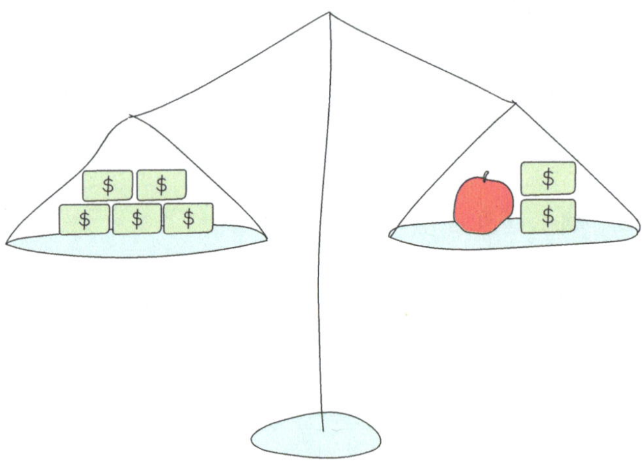

Step 3

You can write this visualization as an equation using the variable "a" for the apple.

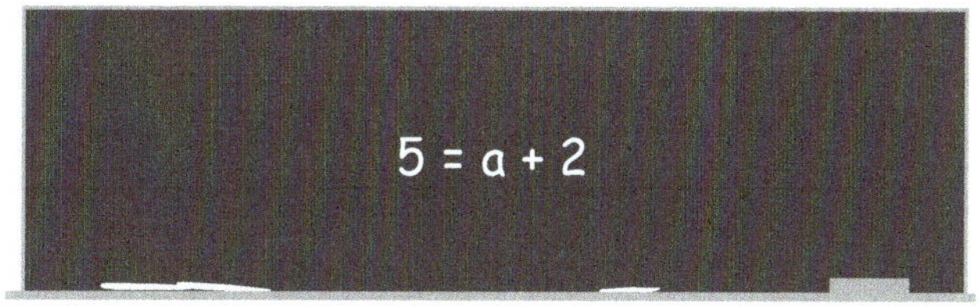

Step 4

In order to solve the problem, you need to get the apple by itself. If you remove $2 from that side of the equation, you must do the same to the other side in order to keep the balance.

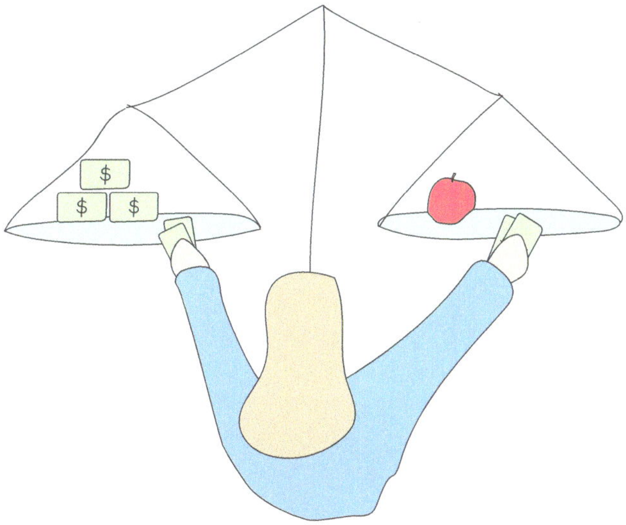

Step 5

To show the previous step using algebra, you can subtract 2 from both sides of the equation, which shows that the apple costs $3. In other words, the solution is $3.

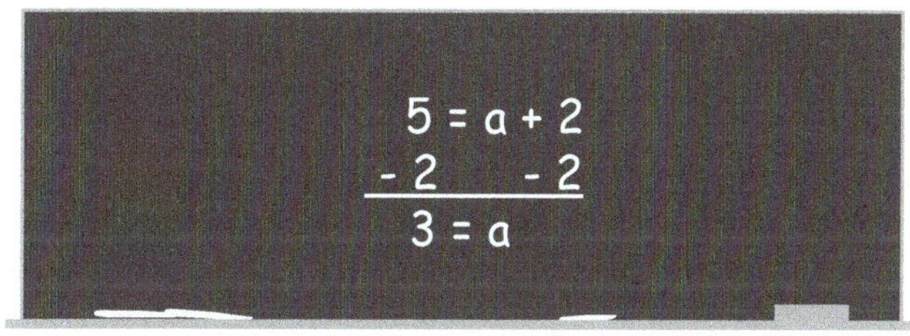

Conclusion

Susan paid $3 for the apple. Algebra can help you solve real world problems in a structured way that you can apply to other situations. Although the solution to this example problem was $3 and could be found through common sense, that approach is limited to simple situations.

5. What Do You Think?

A. What is a situation in your life in which you used algebra, but didn't realize it?

B. Write the situation you identified as an algebra problem.

Carlos' Trip to the Store

Carlos likes to go to a used DVD store where he can trade in his old movies for new ones. He took 2 DVDs to the store and had $8 in his pocket. When he left, he had 3 DVDs and $4 in his pocket. How much did a DVD cost at this store?

Breaking It Down with Algebra

Algebra is your tool to answer Carlos' question about how much DVDs cost. Assume that all DVDs cost the same at the store.

Step 1

Set up a scale where one side of the scale represents what Carlos had before going to the store. The other side will represent what he had when he left.

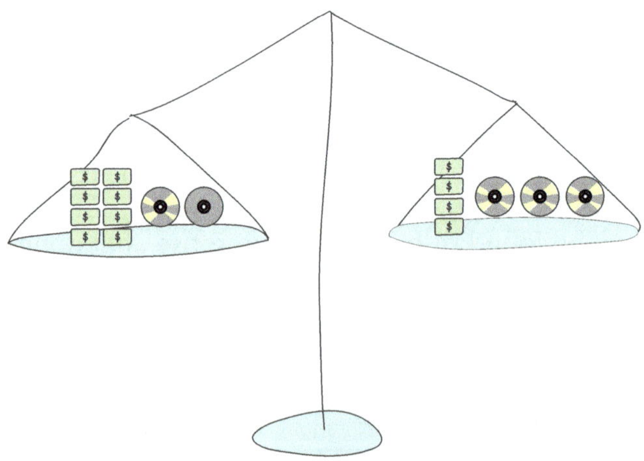

Step 2

Use your scale to create an equation. In this example, you will use "d" as the variable to represent the number of DVDs.

$$8 + 2d = 4 + 3d$$

Step 3

Since Carlos can trade an old DVD for a new one, take away the same number of DVDs from both sides. In this case, both sides have 2 DVDs in common.

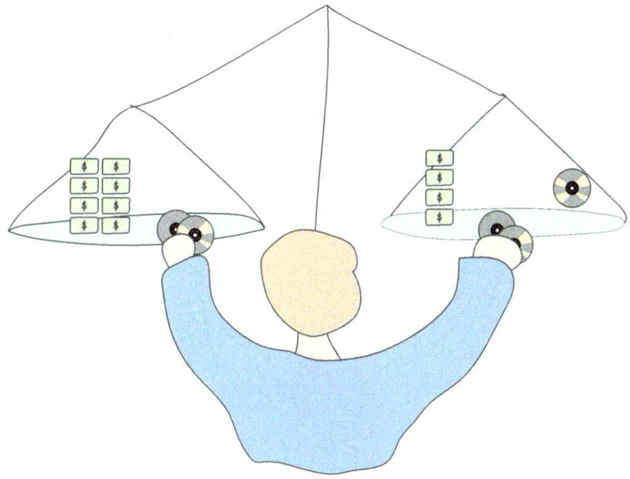

Step 4

To represent the previous step using algebra, you can subtract "2d" from both sides.

$$\begin{aligned} 8 + 2d &= 4 + 3d \\ -2d &\quad\ -2d \\ \hline 8 &= 4 + d \end{aligned}$$

Step 5

In order to solve the rest of the problem, you will need to get the remaining DVD by itself. You can take away $4 from both sides of the equation.

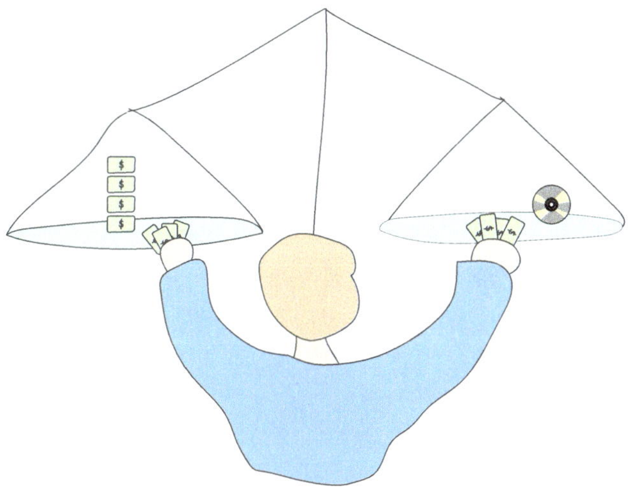

Step 6

To represent the previous step using algebra, you can subtract 4 from both sides.

$$\begin{aligned} 8 &= 4 + d \\ -4 &\quad -4 \\ \hline 4 &= d \end{aligned}$$

Conclusion

Each DVD at the store costs $4. In this example, the algebra confirmed real life experience.

Uncle Rob's Trip to the Store

Uncle Rob just moved into a new apartment and he wants to decorate. He goes to the store with $20 and leaves with 3 lamps and $2 left. How much does each lamp cost?

Breaking It Down with Algebra

Algebra is useful because the process is the same whether your problem is simple or complicated.

Step 1

Set up a scale where one side of the scale represents what Uncle Rob had before going to the store. The other side represents what he had when he left.

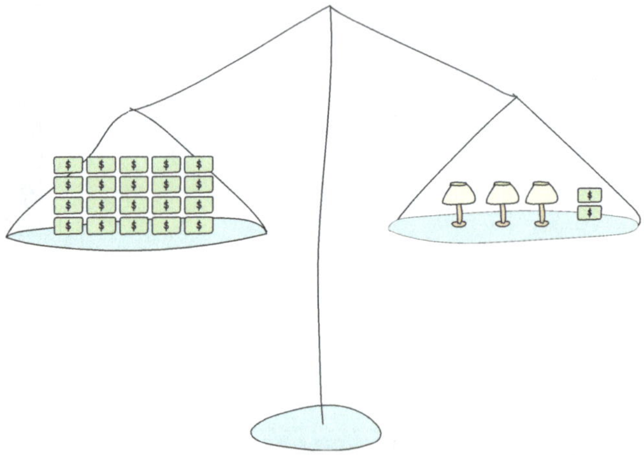

Step 2

Use your scale to create an equation. In this example, you will use "L" as the variable for lamps.

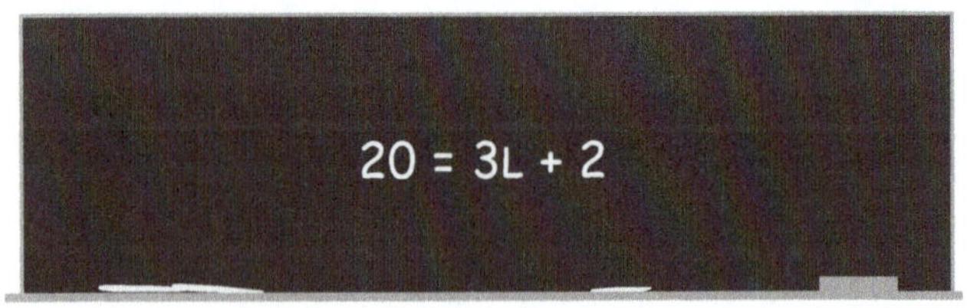

Step 3

You will need to get the lamps by themselves. You can take $2 from both sides.

Step 4
To represent that situation using algebra, subtract 2 from both sides.

$$\begin{array}{rcl} 20 & = & 3L + 2 \\ -2 & & \quad -2 \\ \hline 18 & = & 3L \end{array}$$

Step 5
Since there are 3 lamps, you will need to divide each side into 3 equal groups.

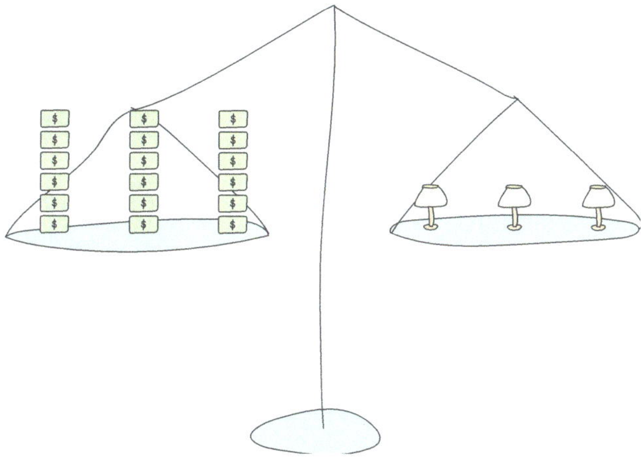

Step 6
To represent that situation using algebra, divide both sides by 3 since there are 3 lamps.

$$\frac{18}{3} = \frac{3L}{3}$$

$$6 = L$$

Conclusion
Uncle Rob paid $6 for each lamp. Algebra allowed you to analyze a more complicated situation using the same approach as in the previous problems. As the situations become more complicated, algebra becomes increasingly useful to avoid using guesswork to solve problems.

Solving Equations

Now that you have established the concepts of solving equations, you can use them anytime you see an equals sign. The example below summarizes the procedures for solving equations.

The Problem

Solve for x in the following equation.

$$5x + 2 = 10 + 3x - 4$$

Combine Like Terms

Like terms are on the same side of the equals sign.

$$5x + 2 = 10 + 3x - 4$$
$$5x + 2 = 6 + 3x$$

Move Variables to One Side

Move variable terms to the same side. Choose a variable term to cancel. Perform the opposite operation to both sides.

$$\begin{array}{r} 5x + 2 = 6 + 3x \\ \underline{-3x \qquad\quad -3x} \\ 2x + 2 = 6 \end{array}$$

Move Constants to the Other Side

Move constant terms to the other side of the equation. Perform the opposite operation to both sides.

$$\begin{array}{r} 2x + 2 = 6 \\ \underline{-2 \quad -2} \\ 2x \qquad = 4 \end{array}$$

Divide by the Coefficient

Once all variable terms are on one side and the constant terms are on the other side, divide both sides by the coefficient of the variable.

$$\frac{2x}{2} = \frac{4}{2}$$
$$x = 2$$

6. Now Do the Math ...

Solve each equation:

A. $6 + 2x = 26$

B. $5a + 2 = 22$

C. $2x + 4 = 25 - x$

D. $5x + 11 = 99 + 3x$

E. $x - 4 = 7.50$

F. $64 = 4p - 20$

G. $90 - 2y = 3y$

H. $3c + 30 = 5c + 2$

Penny's Birthday Party

Penny's birthday party is full of algebra, from the cake recipe to the presents. In this homework, you will explore the algebra of Penny's birthday party.

Section 5A: Homework

1. It's Penny's 6th birthday and Carlos wants to bake her a cake. The recipe calls for flour. Before making the cake, he had 10 cups of flour. After making it he had 7 cups. How much flour is in the cake?
   a. What are the constants in the problem?
   b. What is the variable?
   c. Write an equation to describe the problem.
   d. Solve the equation.

2. Susan bought a pack of 20 birthday candles for $11.95. How much does each candle cost?
   a. What are the constants in the problem?
   b. What is the variable?
   c. Write an equation to describe the problem.
   d. Solve the equation. *Round your answer to the nearest hundredth.*

3. Susan got a set of 12 birthday hats and 8 people showed up to the party. How many hats went unused?
    a. What are the constants in the problem?
    b. What is the variable?
    c. Write an equation to describe the problem.
    d. Solve the equation.

4. When Carlos went to the store he had $25 in his pocket. He bought a $3 birthday card and 2 rolls of wrapping paper. He left the store with $16 in his pocket. How much did each roll of wrapping paper cost?
    a. What are the constants in the problem?
    b. What is the variable?
    c. Write an equation to describe the problem.
    d. Solve the equation.

5. Carlos decided to make tacos for the party. He made 32 tacos and 10 people showed up. At the end of the party, there were 2 tacos left. How many tacos did each person eat on average?
    a. What are the constants in the problem?
    b. What is the variable?
    c. Write an equation to describe the problem.
    d. Solve the equation.

6. Uncle Rob got Penny a toy cash register. Before going to buy it, he had $40 in his wallet. The cash register cost $18.99 and he filled it with 10 pennies, 10 nickels 20 dimes, 2 quarters and some dollar bills. When he gave the present to Penny he had $12.91 left in his pocket. How many dollar bills are in the cash register?
    a. What are the constants in the problem?
    b. What is the variable?
    c. Write an equation to describe the problem.
    d. Solve the equation.

7. When Penny started playing with the cash register Uncle Rob gave her, she put one of each coin and a dollar bill in her piggy bank. How much was left in her cash register?
    a. What are the constants in the problem?
    b. What is the variable?
    c. Write an equation to describe the problem.
    d. Solve the equation.

8. Describe a situation in your life where you could use algebra.
    a. Give a brief description of the situation.
    b. What are the constants?
    c. What is the variable?
    d. Write an equation to describe your situation.
    e. Solve your equation.

Section 5B: Setting Prices

In Section 5A, you learned how to solve an equation using algebra. Now it's time to put that skill to work in business. In this section, you will learn how to price your products to make a profit. You will also learn about different spending habits, so you can better understand your customers.

Understanding Your Customers

Spending Habits

Unit and Fixed Costs

Break-Even Analysis

Pie in the Sky or a Great Business Idea?

Successful businesses have one thing in common: they start with a good idea. There are many ways to come up with a good idea for a business and in this section, you will use the skills you've been developing to come up with your own idea for a business. Later, you'll help the Garcias get started with theirs. Whether or not you already have an idea for a business, this section will give you an opportunity to learn about what goes into starting a business from an idea, including tools and techniques to help you develop an idea. The first thing to do is identify a need or want in the community or economy.

Components of a Good Business Idea

Coming up with business ideas can be a fun and creative process. Some of the factors that go into successful, sustainable businesses are personal, financial, and community enrichment.

Personal Enjoyment

When work is something you enjoy and are good at, you will have the drive and passion to keep going when challenges arise.

Meets a Need or Want in the Community

Work that meets wants or needs in the community is more likely to withstand economic slowdowns. Creating value in the community will attract and keep loyal customers.

Profitability

In order to survive as a business, you need to make money. Your customers need to be able to afford and be willing to pay for your products or services.

Meet Susan's Cousin, Jill

Jill is a college student and needs to make some money this summer. She has many business ideas. Let's look at three of them to see if they are good ideas.

Jill's First Idea

Jill's friends were complaining about waiting on hold for tech support for their computers. Jill wonders if she could charge people to call tech support companies for them. The problem is that Jill doesn't like talking on the phone.

Jill's Second Idea

Jill loves cats and wants to open a business where she would charge people to come and look after their cats.

Jill's Third Idea

Jill grew up in Santa Fe and knows a lot about the history and culture. She is outgoing and loves meeting new people. She wants to open a business to be a private guide for tourists.

1. What Do You Think?

A. Out of Jill's ideas, which one(s) do you think involve doing something she enjoys?

B. Which one(s) meet a need or want in the community?

C. Which one(s) do you think people are most likely to pay for?

D. Overall, which of Jill's ideas is the best to pursue? Explain why.

Getting Paid for Your Services

When you work for someone else, you know how much to charge for products and services. When you work for yourself, you need to figure out how to price your products and services in order to make money. Product pricing is an important step in starting any business.

Pricing Your Products and Services

There are some things you need to know before you set prices for your products and services. In this section, you will learn about setting prices based on your own spending habits, your customers, and your break-even point.

Know Yourself

When setting your prices, it helps to know your own relationship to making and spending money so you can make informed decisions on behalf of the business.

Know Your Customers

It's also important to know your customers. Knowing what your customers respond to when looking at prices is helpful.

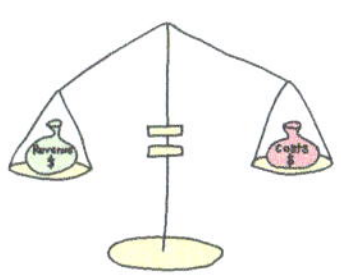

Find Your Break-Even Point

The break-even point is the minimum amount you can charge in order to recoup what you spend to make and deliver your product.

How Do You Want to Be Paid?

When you run your own business, you have to think about how you want to be paid. There are a few ways this can happen.

Be Paid Based on Time

You will put a lot of time into starting and running a business, so you might decide to pay yourself based on how much time you invest.

Be Paid Based on Results

Your business will only be successful if you see results from all your hard work. Since results are the key to a sustainable business, you might decide to pay yourself based on the results of your hard work.

2. What Do You Think?

A. What are the pros and cons of getting paid based on time?

B. What are the pros and cons of getting paid based on results?

C. How could you get paid based on both?

What Motivates you?

Motivation is essential to success. Ideally, your business endeavor earns money and fulfills a dream, but you might value one of these things over the other. Be honest with yourself and think about what really matters to you.

Money First

If you decide that money is the priority, then decisions you make will be based on what is most profitable.

Dreams First

If you decide that dreams are the priority, then decisions you make will be based on your vision for the business.

3. What Do You Think?

A. What are the pros and cons of putting money first?

B. What are the pros and cons of putting dreams first?

C. How can you put both first?

Making the Most of Your Money

In business as in life, there is often a trade-off between quantity and quality. In business, finding the right balance between quantity and quality is important for success.

Quantity

If your customers prefer products that are inexpensive, lower prices will help you sell a larger quantity of products.

Quality

If your customers prefer high quality products, you can charge more and sell fewer items.

4. What Do You Think?

A. What are the pros and cons of spending money based on quantity?

B. What are the pros and cons of spending money based on quality?

C. Do you think your customers prefer quantity or quality? Why?

Price and Perception

For your customers, affordability is relative. What might seem inexpensive for one could be expensive for another. Your goal is to align the price of your products with the perceptions of your customers. The rule is, your product is worth what people will pay for it. The examples below show how different prices affect whether a house has a price that customers might consider in the affordable range.

Cheap

If the Garcias' list their home at $30,000 it would be considered very cheap. Some buyers might be interested, but others might think there is something wrong with the house. Furthermore, the Garcias would not make any profit if they sold at this price.

Expensive

If the Garcias' list their home at $3,000,000 it would be considered very expensive. Very few people could afford to buy this house at that price, but the Garcias would make a lot of profit if they could sell at this high price.

5. What Do You Think?

A. What are the pros and cons of pricing to appear cheap?

B. What are the pros and cons of pricing to appear expensive?

C. What would be a price of a house that would seem affordable?

Finding the Balance

You can use algebra as a tool to find the balance between costs and revenue. At a minimum, you have to make enough revenue to cover your costs. You can't sustain a business that doesn't cover its costs, and revenue must exceed costs in order to make a profit.

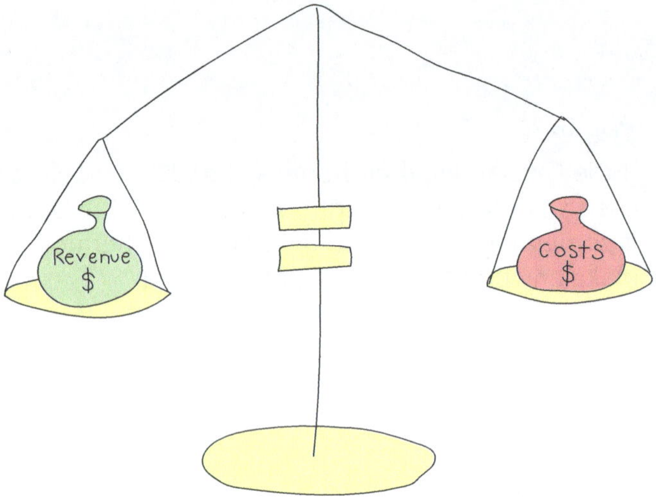

Break-Even Analysis

Finding the break-even point tells you the minimum amount you must charge to recoup the costs of making and delivering the product or service. After you know that amount, you can increase your prices based on your customers' spending habits and your business's financial goals. The following is a list of vocabulary needed to do a break-even analysis.

Unit
A single product or service sold.

Number of Units Sold
The total number of products or services sold.

Unit Cost
The amount of money it costs to produce one product or service.

Fixed Costs
The amount of money you spend no matter how many products or services you sell. This could include rent, utilities, advertising, etc.

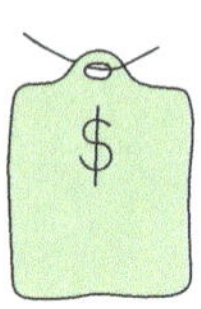

Selling Price
The price you charge for a single product or service.

What Is the Unit Cost of a Taco?

The Garcias are thinking about opening a taco truck. In order to make sure they don't lose money on their tacos, they need to know how much each taco costs to produce. Here is a list of all their ingredients.

Ingredient	Amount Needed	Unit Cost
\$2.15 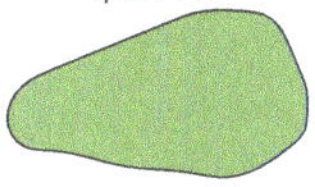	Makes 5 tacos 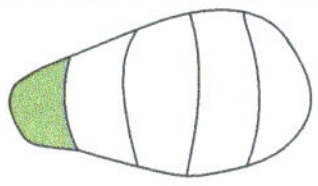	\$2.15 ÷ 5 tacos = \$0.43 per taco
\$3.99 	Makes 10 tacos 	\$3.99 ÷ 10 tacos = \$0.40 per taco
\$1.20 	Makes 160 tacos 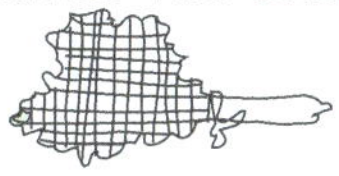	\$1.20 ÷ 160 tacos = \$0.01 per taco
\$0.22 	Makes 4 tacos 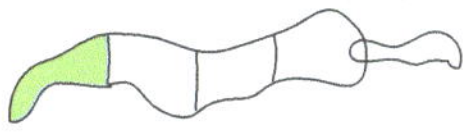	\$0.22÷ 4 tacos = \$0.06 per taco
\$0.49 	Makes 3 tacos 	\$0.49 ÷ 3 tacos = \$0.16 per taco
\$5.95 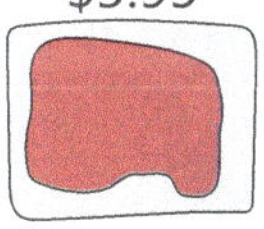	Makes 6 tacos 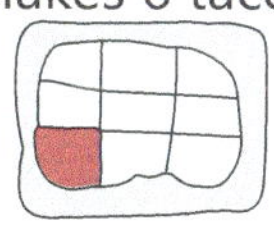	\$5.95 ÷ 6 tacos = \$0.99 per taco
\$2.99 	Makes 25 tacos 	\$2.99 ÷ 25 tacos = \$0.12 per taco
\$6.99 	Makes 30 tacos 	\$6.99 ÷ 30 tacos = \$0.23 per taco
\$0.68 	Makes 2 tacos 	\$0.68 ÷ 2 tacos = \$0.34 per taco

Unit Cost of a Taco = \$2.74

Fixed Costs

Some expenses occur no matter how many products you sell. These expenses can include rent, employee salaries, gas, and utilities. When pricing your products it's important to include these costs so you know how much revenue you have to generate in order to cover them.

Break-Even Formula

Once you know your unit and fixed costs, you can use the break-even formula to help you determine how much to charge or how many products you need to sell to stay in business.

SELLING PRICE (NUMBER OF UNITS SOLD) = UNIT COST (NUMBER OF UNITS SOLD) + FIXED COSTS

Finding the Number of Units Sold

Find the number of tacos the Garcias need to sell if they have a unit cost of \$2.74 and fixed costs of \$500, and they want to set the selling price at \$3.50 per taco.

Step 1

Write down the break-even formula and fill in what you know.

SELLING PRICE (NUMBER OF UNITS SOLD) = UNIT COST (NUMBER OF UNITS SOLD) + FIXED COSTS

\$3.50 (x) = \$2.74 (x) + 500

Step 2

Complete any multiplication.

$$3.50(x) = 2.47(x) + 500$$
$$3.50x = 2.47x + 500$$

Step 3

Since you have variables on both sides, cancel one of them out by perform the opposite operation to both sides.

$$\begin{array}{rcl} 3.50x & = & 2.47x + 500 \\ \underline{-2.47x} & & \underline{-2.47x} \\ 1.03x & = & 500 \end{array}$$

Step 4

When you have a number in front of the variable, divide both sides by that number.

$$\frac{1.03x}{1.03} = \frac{500}{1.03}$$

x = 485 TACOS

Finding the Selling Price

You can also use the break-even formula to find a selling price . Find the selling price needed to break-even if you can sell 400 tacos, have a unit cost of $2.74, and have fixed costs of $500.

Step 1

Write down the break-even formula and fill in what you know.

SELLING PRICE (NUMBER OF UNITS SOLD) = UNIT COST (NUMBER OF UNITS SOLD) + FIXED COSTS

x (400) = $2.74 (400) + 500

Step 2

Complete any multiplication.

x(400) = 2.47(400) + 500

400x = 988 + 500

Step 3

When you have like terms on the same side, combine them.

400x = 988 + 500

400x = 1,488

Step 4

When you have a number in front of the variable, divide both sides by that number.

$$\frac{400x}{400} = \frac{1{,}488}{400}$$

x = 3.72 SELLING PRICE OF A TACO

6. Now Do the Math ...

A. Find the selling price needed to break even for an artist who makes handmade bowls if she can sell 20 bowls, each bowl costs $4.50 to make, and her fixed costs are $55.

B. She needs to charge more than her break-even point in order to make money. If her clients prefer to buy based on quality, what do you think she should charge for her bowls?

C. How many cups of coffee must a coffee shop sell to break even if they charge $3.85, it costs $1.12 to make each cup of coffee and they have fixed expenses of $2,750? *Round your answer to the nearest whole number.*

The Food Truck

Carlos enjoyed making tacos for Penny's birthday party. He was a culinary arts major in college, because he loves cooking. He cooks at his job, but doesn't have the freedom to innovate. He decides he wants to open a taco truck.

Section 5B: Homework

1. Uncle Rob is willing to pay for the down payment on a truck. One of Uncle Rob's financial goals was giving gifts to his family and friends. He saves part of his disposable income for this goal.
    a. If Uncle Rob makes $4,825.00 per month, saves 10% of it and has fixed expenses of $2,480.40, what is his disposable income?
    b. If he saves 30% of his disposable income for gifts, how much does he save each month?
    c. He has been saving that much for 2 years. How much does he have for gifts?

2. Carlos found a retrofitted taco truck for $60,000. It requires a 20% down payment.
    a. How much is the down payment?
    b. Can Uncle Rob afford to cover the down payment?

3. The loan on the truck comes with a 5.75% interest rate.
    a. After Uncle Rob makes the down payment, what will the principal be on the loan?
    b. If Carlos got a 5 year loan, how much would the monthly payment be? *Refer to section 4B for a review on how to calculate monthly payments.*

4. The gas mileage on the truck is 15 miles per gallon. Carlos needs to drive the truck about 75 miles per month.
    a. How many gallons of gas must he purchase a month?

b. If the price of gas is $3.15 per gallon, how much will he spend on gas?

5. What are Carlos' fixed monthly costs?

6. If Carlos buys conventional ingredients, the unit price of a taco is $2.74.
   a. How many tacos must he sell each month to break even if he charges $4.50 per taco? *Round your answer to the nearest taco.*
   b. How many tacos must he sell each month to break even if he charges $3.75 per taco? *Round your answer to the nearest taco.*

7. If Carlos buys organic ingredients, the unit price will go up to $3.45 per taco.
   a. How many tacos must he sell each month to break even if he charges $4.50 per taco? *Round your answer to the nearest taco.*
   b. How many tacos must he sell each month to break even if he charges $3.75 per taco? *Round your answer to the nearest taco.*

8. Carlos interviewed some other taco truck owners to learn about their pricing choices. He learned he can expect to get about 750 sales a month.
   a. If he wants to buy conventional ingredients with a unit cost of $2.74, how much must he charge to break even if he gets 750 sales each month?
   b. If he wants to buy organic ingredients with a unit cost of $3.45, how much must he charge to break even if he gets 750 sales each month?

NOW IT'S TIME TO COME UP WITH YOUR OWN BUSINESS IDEA.

You will be working with your own business idea for the remainder of this book. To come up with an idea, you have two options.

- Option 1: If you already have a business idea, or an area of interest, you will develop your own idea.
- Option 2: If you don't have an idea, pick a small business you either work for or would want to work for in the future and base your idea off that business. Understanding the business you work for will make you a better employee and can lead to future promotions.

9. Answer the following questions about your business.
   a. What kind of business is it?
   b. What products and services will it sell?
   c. Where will your business be located?
   d. What will you call your business?

Section 5C: Sales

In Section 5B, you learned how to price your products and services. Many customers respond to sales and enjoy the satisfaction of saving money. In this section, you will learn how to price products for a sale. You will also consider the pros and cons of sales so you can use them effectively.

Sales Vocabulary

Supply and Demand

Sales Formula

Percent Decrease

Saving Money

There are two ways people think about saving money. When you decide not to spend money and put it in a savings account, you are saving money. When you go shopping and buy something on sale, you are saving money. Sometimes, businesses will set higher prices so they can put them on sale. In those cases, you might be paying the intended price, but it seems like a discount and a good deal.

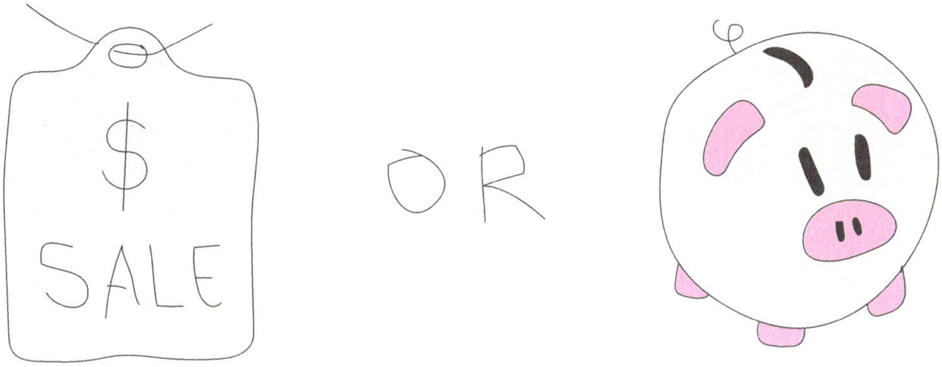

Why Have Sales?

Sales encourage customers to buy more. If a product isn't selling well, customers may not want it, or the price may be too high, or both. Sales are also a way to keep the supply of products and the demand for products in balance.

Supply

The availability of products or services.

Demand

The desire of people to buy products and services.

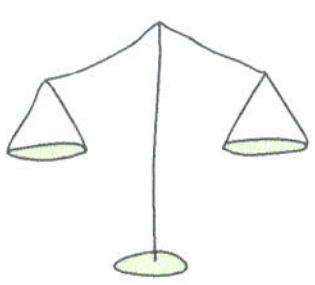

Keeping the Balance

Sales can offset weak demand for products and services, because a lower price can attract more customers. Sales are one way to keep the balance between supply and demand.

Balancing the Scales

It's important to keep supply and demand in balance so there isn't too much of one or the other. Being able to raise or lower prices is a good way to keep the balance.

Low Supply and High Demand

When there is not enough of a product and there is high demand for that product, the price of the product will increase.

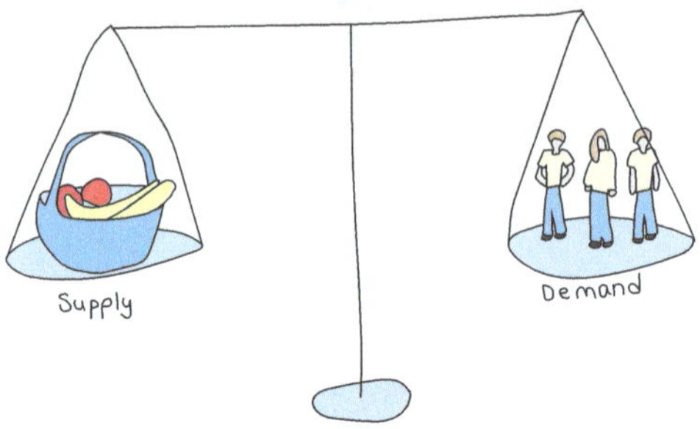

Balanced Supply and Demand

When there is a balance between the availability of a product and the demand for that product, there is stable product pricing. This situation is known as price equilibrium.

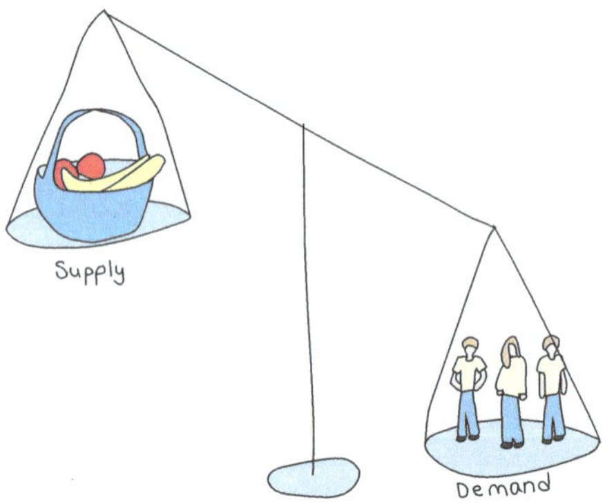

High Supply and Low Demand

When there is too much of a product and there is low demand for that product, the price of the product will decrease.

1. What Do You Think?

If price equilibrium is the goal, which of the three situations above do you think will benefit the most from providing sales? Why?

2. Now Do the Math ...

A. If you charge $6.00 for a taco, you will only be able to sell 30 tacos a day. How much revenue will you receive in a day?

B. If you charge $1.50 for a taco, you will be able to sell 300 tacos a day. How much revenue will you receive in a day?

C. If you charge $3.00 for a taco, you will be able to sell 200 tacos a day. How much revenue will you receive in a day?

3. What Do You Think?

Which price in the exercise above will produce the most revenue?

Sales

Another way to price products is to put them on sale. This gives customers the perception of getting a good deal and saving money. As an example, look at pricing a taco if it's put on sale in the following problem.

4. Now Do the Math ...

Suppose you charge $6.00 for a taco but you put it on sale for 50% off. This means you will actually charge $3.00 a taco. If this sale attracts more customers and you sell 350 tacos in a day, how much revenue will you receive?

Sales Vocabulary

To put products on sale, start with the original price and mark it down based on a percentage, and charge customers at the sale price.

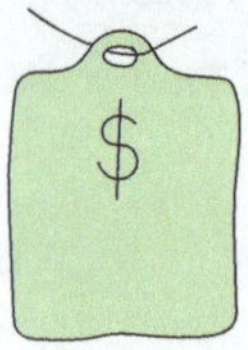

Original Price

The price of the product before it goes on sale.

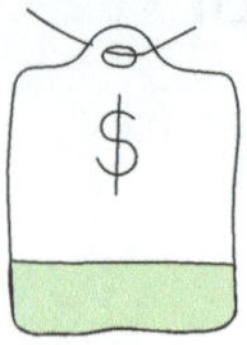

Percent Discount

A percentage of the original price that customers will save.

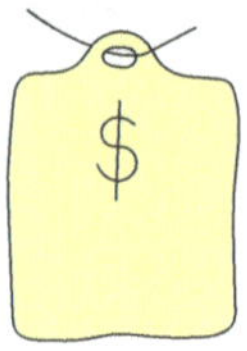

Sale Price

The price customers will have to pay when the product is on sale.

Sales Formula

The sales formula is a way of calculating the sale price of a product based on the percent discount off the original price. Find the sale price by subtracting the discount amount from the original price.

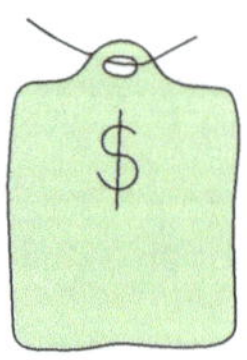

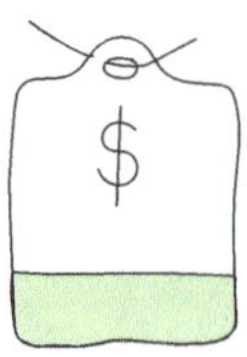

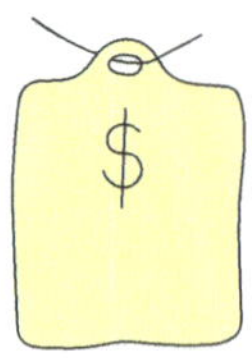

$$\text{Original Price} - \text{Percent Discount}\left(\text{Original Price}\right) = \text{Sale Price}$$

5. What Do You Think?

Which price in the sales formula will always be higher, the original price or the sale price?

Finding the Sale Price

Use the sales formula to find the sale price of a product that has an original price of $7.50 and a percent discount of 30%.

Step 1

Write down the sales formula and fill in what you know. Use "x" for the unknown.

Original Price	-	Percent Discount	(	Original Price	)	=	Sale Price
7.50	-	0.30	(	7.50	)	=	x

Step 2

Complete any multiplication.

$$7.50 - 0.30(7.50) = x$$
$$7.50 - 2.25 = x$$

Step 3

When you have like terms on the same side, add or subtract them.

$$7.50 - 2.25 = x$$
$$5.25 = x$$

6. Now Do the Math ...

A. Find the sale price of an item that originally costs $40 and is on sale for 20% off.

B. Find the sale price of an item that originally costs $4.75 that is marked down 60%.

C. Find the sale price of an item that originally costs $399 that is discounted 25%.

Finding the Percent Discount

Use the sales formula to find the percent discount of a product that has an original price of $11.99 and a sale price of $8.49.

Step 1

Write down the sales formula and fill in what you know. Use "x" for the unknown.

$$\text{Original Price} - \text{Percent Discount}(\text{Original Price}) = \text{Sale Price}$$

$$11.99 - x(11.99) = 8.49$$

Step 2

Complete any multiplication.

$$11.99 - x(11.99) = 8.49$$

$$11.99 - 11.99x = 8.49$$

Step 3

When you have constants on both sides of the equals sign, cancel one of them out by doing the opposite operation to both sides.

$$\begin{aligned} 11.99 - 11.99x &= 8.49 \\ -11.99 \qquad\qquad &\;\; -11.99 \\ \hline -11.99x &= -3.50 \end{aligned}$$

Step 4

If you have a number in front of the variable, divide both sides by that number.

$$\frac{-11.99x}{-11.99} = \frac{-3.50}{-11.99}$$

$$x = 0.29$$

Step 5

Since you are finding a percent, multiply your answer by 100 to turn it into a percent.

$$x = 0.29$$

$$0.29(100) = 29\%$$

7. Now Do the Math ...

A. Find the percent discount on an item that originally costs $220 and is on sale for $165.

B. Find the percent discount on an item that is on sale for $8.50 and originally cost $12.75. *Round to the nearest whole percent.*

Finding the Original Price

Use the sale formula to find the original price of a product that has a sale price of \$14.25 and a percent discount of 40%.

Step 1
Write down the sales formula and fill in what you know. Use "x" for the unknown.

$$\text{Original Price} - \text{Percent Discount}\left(\text{Original Price}\right) = \text{Sale Price}$$
$$x - 0.40\,(\;x\;) = 14.25$$

Step 2
Complete any multiplication.

$$x - 0.40(x) = 14.25$$
$$1x - 0.40x = 14.25$$

Step 3
If you have like terms on the same side of the equals sign, combine them.

$$1x - 0.40x = 14.25$$
$$0.60x = 14.25$$

Step 4
If you have a number in front of the variable, divide both sides by that number.

$$\frac{0.60x}{0.60} = \frac{14.25}{0.60}$$
$$x = 23.75$$

8. Now Do the Math ...

A. Find the original price of an item that has been discounted 40% and has a sale price of \$13.50.

B. Find the original price of an item that is on sale for \$82.96 that has been marked down 15%.

C. Find the original price of an item that is 35% off and on sale for \$225.90. *Round to the nearest hundredth.*

Finding the Best Deal

Finding the best deal means knowing the math behind how prices are calculated. In this homework, you will explore different pricing options to find the best deal and determine sale prices.

Section 5C: Homework

1. Carlos needs to buy 8 pounds of tomatoes for the week.
    a. The first store charges \$2.89 per pound, which are on sale for 30% off. What is the sale price? *Round your answer to the nearest hundredth.*
    b. A second store charges \$1.19 per pound and has a sale for 15% off. What is the sale price? *Round your answer to the nearest hundredth.*
    c. A third store charges \$3.25 per pound and has a sale for 50% off. What is the sale price? *Round your answer to the nearest hundredth.*
    d. Which store offers the best deal?

2. Carlos also needs to buy lettuce.
    a. The first store charges \$0.89 with a 5% discount. What is the sale price? *Round your answer to the nearest hundredth.*
    b. The second store charges \$2.05 per pound with a 20% discount. What is the sale price? *Round your answer to the nearest hundredth.*
    c. The third store charges \$1.79 per pound with a 15% discount. What is the sale price? *Round your answer to the nearest hundredth.*

   d. Which store offers the best deal?

3. Carlos needs to buy 600 tortillas.
   a. If he buys tortillas at the store, he can buy packs of 30 tortillas. How many packs does he need to buy?
   b. If each pack costs $3.95, how much would he spend?
   c. The store offers a sale for 40% off. With the sale, how much would he spend?

4. Carlos went to school with someone who works at a tortilla company. He decides to see if they have a better deal.
   a. The company charges $0.08 per tortilla. How much would Carlos have to pay if he bought 600 tortillas?
   b. The company also offers a bulk deal. If Carlos bought 1,000 tortillas, they would mark them 50% off. How much would he pay with the bulk deal?
   c. Which is the best tortilla option for Carlos?

5. Carlos needs green chili. He likes to buy it as fresh as possible and goes to a local farm.
   a. The farm charges $3.25 per pound and Carlos needs 8 pounds. How much does he have to pay?
   b. The farm also offers a discount if Carlos decides to become a member. They would only charge him $2.15 per pound. What percent discount would they give him? *Round your answer to the nearest whole percent.*

6. Carlos is planning to charge $3.75 for his tacos. If he sells 500 tacos, how much revenue would he receive?

7. He wants to provide a sale to attract customers. When he marks the $3.75 tacos on sale for 30% off, he is able to sell 700 tacos.
   a. What is his sale price? *Round your answer to the nearest hundredth.*
   b. How much will he make?
   c. How does this compare to your answer to problem 6?

Section 5D: Wholesale and Resale

In Section 5C, you learned how to mark products on sale to attract customers. There are other price change calculations that happen before customers enter the store. In this section, you will learn about the relationship between the companies that create products and the companies that sell them.

Wholesale

Resale

Markups

Trade Discounts

The Middle Man

Customers usually don't go to a factory to buy products. Factories aren't usually designed to provide customer service or a comfortable shopping experience. Instead, they sell their products to stores who, in turn, sell those products to customers. In this section, you will learn how prices are determined between factories and stores.

Types of Businesses

There are many different kinds of businesses which serve different purposes and serve different groups of people. Most businesses fall within one of the following three categories.

Wholesale

A company that designs and produces products and then sells those products to retail stores.

Resale

A store or website that buys products from wholesale businesses and then resells them to customers.

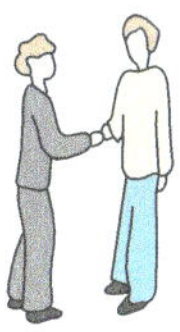

Service

A company that offers services to customers instead of products. Examples of those who provide services include therapists, accountants, and lawyers.

1. What Do You Think?

Which of the three categories above best describes your business idea?

The Wholesale/Resale Process

There are several steps that happen in order to make products available for purchase. These are key elements of the supply and demand chain that connects product producers to their customers.

Production
The wholesale company produces a product.

Retail
The store buys the product at the wholesale price.

Customer
The store sells the product to customers at the retail price.

Two Ways Whole and Resale Businesses Work Together

Both product producers and resellers need to make a profit when selling products, so there are two main ways retail stores interact with wholesale companies.

Markups

Markups happen when the wholesale company sets the wholesale price and then the retailer marks up the price.

Trade Discounts

Trade discounts happen when the wholesale company wants to set the retail price (the price customers will pay) and gives the retailer a discount. Trade discounts are markdowns.

Types of Prices

The price a retailer pays a factory for products will be different than the price customers will pay. Marking up prices keeps stores in business and allows them to be profitable.

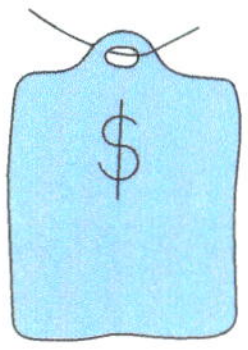

Wholesale Price

The price the store has to pay for the product.

Percent Markup

An increase in a product's price based on a percentage of the wholesale price.

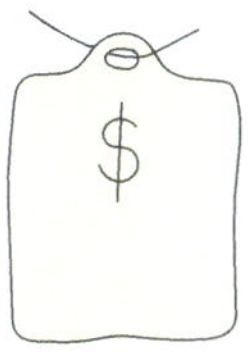

Retail Price

The price customers pay for the product.

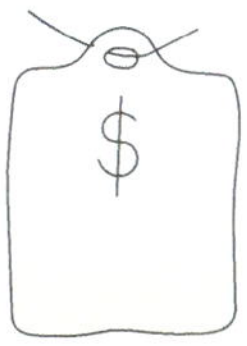

Percent Discount

An decrease in a product's price based on a percentage of the retail price.

Markup Formula

When the factory sets the wholesale price of a product, the retail store can use the markup formula to determine what to charge its customers.

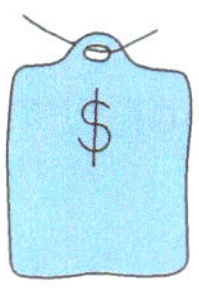

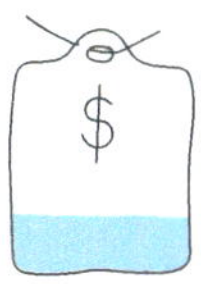

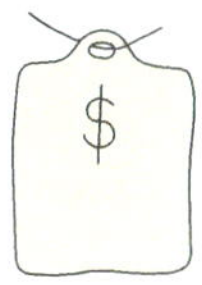

Wholesale Price + Percent Markup (Wholesale Price) = Retail Price

2. What Do You Think?

Which price in the markup formula will always be higher, the wholesale price or the retail price?

Using the Markup Formula

Use the markup formula to find the retail price of a product that has a wholesale price of $12.35 and a percent markup of 55%.

Step 1

Write down the sales formula and fill in what you know. Use "x" for the unknown.

WHOLESALE PRICE + PERCENT MARKUP (WHOLESALE PRICE) = RETAIL PRICE

$12.35 + 0.55\,(12.35) = x$

Step 2

Complete any multiplication.

$12.35 + 0.55(12.35) = x$

$12.35 + 6.79 = x$

Step 3

If you have like terms on the same side of the equals sign, combine them.

$12.35 + 6.79 = x$

$19.14 = x$

3. Now Do the Math ...

A. Find the retail price of an item that has a wholesale price of $6.40 and is marked up 40%.

B. Find the retail price of an item that is purchased from a wholesaler for $240.50 and is marked up 28.5%. *Round to the nearest hundredth.*

C. Find the retail price of an item that will be marked up 70% on a wholesale price of $39.50.

Trade Discount Formula

Sometimes companies that produce products want to control the price customers will pay for those products. When they set the retail price, they offer retailers a trade discount.

Retail Price − Percent Discount (Retail Price) = Wholesale Price

Using the Trade Discount Formula

Use the discount formula to find the wholesale price of a product that has a list price of $24.95 and a percent discount of 40%.

Step 1
Write down the sales formula and fill in what you know. Use "x" for the unknown.

Retail Price − Percent Discount (Retail Price) = Wholesale Price

24.95 − 0.40 (24.95) = x

Step 2
Complete any multiplication.

24.95 - 0.40(24.95) = x
24.95 - 9.98 = x

Step 3
If you have like terms on the same side of the equals sign, combine them.

24.95 - 9.98 = x
14.97 = x

4. Now Do the Math ...

A. Find the wholesale price of an item that has a retail price of $19.95 and a discount of 60%.

B. Find the wholesale price of an item that has a 25% discount on a retail price of $299.99. *Round to the nearest hundredth.*

Selling Souvenirs

The Garcias want to start selling souvenirs as part of the branding for their company. They also want to determine how much to mark up products. In this homework, you will help the Garcias mark up their products.

Section 5D: Homework

1. The Garcias want to get T-Shirts made with their logo to sell to customers. A company offers a wholesale price of $2.50 per T-Shirt. Carlos wants to mark it up by 40%. What is the retail price?

2. A different T-Shirt company makes more attractive shirts, but charges $4.25 per shirt wholesale. Carlos wants to mark them up 45%. What is the retail price?

3. Susan suggests they sell mugs with the logo as well. A mug company charges $2.30 per mug wholesale. They want to mark it up 20%.
   a. What will the retail price be?
   b. How much money will they make from each mug sale?

4. Carlos also wants to sell baseball caps. They want the retail price to be $14.95 and to have a 30% mark up. How much can they spend wholesale getting the cap. *Round your answer to the nearest hundredth.*

5. The piggy bank sits next to Carlos when he makes tacos, and customers find it cute. Penny thinks they should sell piggy bank key chains. A wholesale company offers $1.20. The Garcias want to mark it up 50%. How much would they sell the piggy key chains for?

6. Carlos wants to sell sodas to go with the tacos. He can purchase sodas wholesale for $0.50 a can. He can sell them to customers for $2.50 a can. What percent markup does he have?

7. A potato chip company sets the retail price at $2.15 per bag and offers a discount of 45%. How much will Carlos pay wholesale for the chips? *Round your answer to the nearest hundredth.*

CHAPTER 6: FINANCIAL STATEMENTS

6A Balance Sheets

6B Income Statements

6C Tax Preparation

6D Tax Project

Section 6A: Balance Sheets

In Chapter 5, you learned how to price products and work with discounts and markups. These skills help you with the day-to-day operations of your business. You will also have to document your company's activities to analyze the health of your business and provide proper documentation to tax authorities. In this section, you will learn how to make a balance sheet, which gives you a picture of the health of your business.

Types of Assets

Types of Liabilities

Types of Equity

Create a Balance Sheet in a Spreadsheet

Your Financial Position

Knowing your financial position is a good way to understand the financial health of your business. The balance sheet is an important financial document that summarizes the financial information of a business so that you, investors, or a lender can make decisions about whether current business strategies are working. Along with other financial documents, a balance sheet can inform a business owner about opportunities for improvement or expansion.

The Balance Sheet

There are three parts to a balance sheet.

Assets

Assets are financial resources that have value, whether tangible or intangible. If they can be owned or controlled and can produce value, they are assets.

Liabilities

Liabilities are the financial obligations of a business. If a business borrows money or has expenses it must pay, it has liabilities.

Equity

Equity is the difference between assets and liabilities. If a business owns more than it owes, it has equity. If a business owes more than it owns, it has negative equity.

The Balance Sheet Formula

The fundamental accounting equation is essential to understanding how a business balances its assets, liabilities, and equity.

1. Now Do the Math ...

Use the balance sheet formula above to solve the following problems. For a review of solving equations, refer to Appendix B.

A. Find the assets of a business if it has liabilities of \$20,000 and equity of \$7,000.

B. Find the liabilities of a business if it has assets of \$65,000 and equity of \$22,000.

C. Find the equity of a business if it has liabilities of \$35,000 and assets of \$52,000.

2. What Do You Think?

Explain what the relationship is between assets, liabilities, and equity. Why do you think the fundamental accounting equation is so useful in business?

3. The Balance Sheet and Your Budget ...

A. Make a list of your assets. Assets include the value of personal possessions and money in the bank or credit union.

B. List all your liabilities. Liabilities include all loans and credit card balances.

C. Use the balance sheet formula to find your equity.

Types of Assets

There are different kinds of assets that will show up on the balance sheet.

Cash

Cash includes money a business has on hand or money deposited in a bank or credit union.

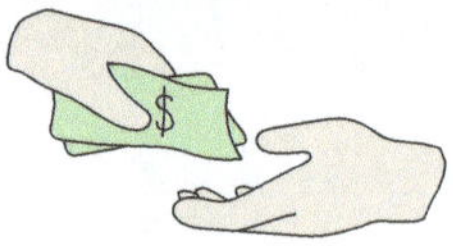

Accounts Receivable

Money that customers owe a business for products or services. Customers usually receive the product or service and an invoice that specifies the date the bill is to be paid.

Inventory

Products that a business has on hand that have not yet been sold.

Prepaid Expenses

Expenses that are paid in advance and count as assets. Their value decreases over time as the business receives the good or service for which it has prepaid. An example of this is insurance, whose payments are often paid upfront and whose value is received over time.

Other Assets

Assets that do not fall into one of the other specific categories of assets are lumped together and listed as "other assets."

Fixed Assets at Cost

Fixed assets are property, buildings, equipment (including vehicles), and furniture that a business owns and does not intend to sell within one year. Collectively, fixed assets can be referred to as "plant."

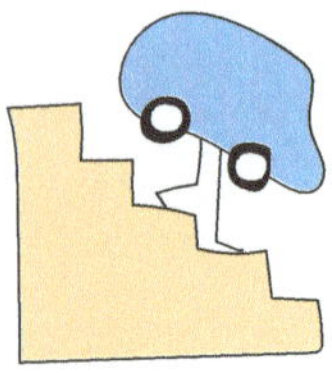

Depreciation

Some assets depreciate over time. These decreased values are represented on the balance sheet over time. It is important for businesses to plan for the replacement of assets that depreciate, including vehicles and other equipment.

4. Vocabulary Check ...

Complete the chart below by indicating which category each of the following items belongs to.

Item	Cash	Accounts Receivable	Inventory	Prepaid Expenses	Other Assets	Fixed Assets at Cost	Accumulated Depreciation
A. Tortillas			✓				
B. Trademark for the truck's logo							
C. Insurance for the truck							
D. A grill that has been owned for 3 years							
E. An unpaid birthday party order							
F. Money in the bank account							
G. A credit card reader purchased recently							
H. Napkins							
I. Change in the cash register							

Types of Liabilities

There are different kinds of liabilities that will show up on the balance sheet.

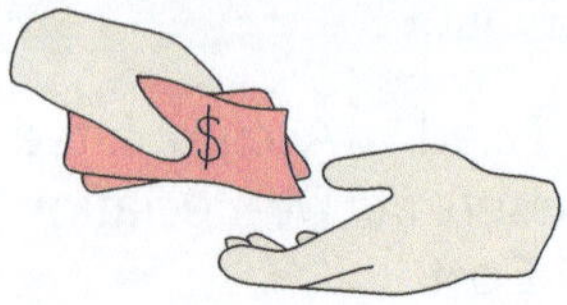

Accounts Payable

Money that a business owes for products or services it receives.

Accrued Expenses

An expense that is accounted for in the balance sheet before it is paid. Accrued expenses are the opposite of prepaid expenses and include such expenses as interest from a loan the business has taken out.

Current Portion of Debt

The amount of debt that the business must pay within the next year. It only includes the portion of long-term debt that will be actually be paid within the next year.

Income Taxes Payable

The amount of taxes that must be paid within one year. Accounting for this throughout the year avoids the surprise of large expenses at the end of the year, and might be required, depending on the details of your business finances.

Long Term Debt

Long-term debt is all debt that a business has that will not be paid off within one year. Often, large loans cannot be paid off within one year and are categorized as long-term debt.

5. Vocabulary Check ...

Complete the chart below by indicating in which category each of the following items belongs.

Item	Accounts Payable	Accrued Expenses	Current Portion of Debt	Income Taxes Payable	Long-term debt
A. Monthly payments for the next year on a new computer			✓		
B. Money set aside to pay taxes at the end of the year					
C. An employee bonus that will be paid at the end of the year					
D. An order for tortillas that has not been paid					
E. A loan for the truck that will take 3 years to pay off					
F. A personal loan from Uncle Rob that will be paid back over 10 years					

Types of Equity

There are different kinds of equity that will show up on your balance sheet.

Retained Earnings

The portion of profit that stays in the company to fund future purchases and projects.

Owner's Equity

The portion of equity that goes to the owner.

6. Vocabulary Check ...

Complete the chart below by indicating in which category each of the following items belongs.

Item	Retained Earnings	Owner's Equity
A. Carlos keeps $2,500 from the company's earnings for his own expenses.		
B. The taco truck will need to stay in business during the winter months when sales tend to slow down. Carlos plans to keep $5,000 in the company to keep the truck open.		

7. What Do You Think?

When you open your company, do you plan to keep most of the money in the company or take most of it out to pay yourself? Explain why.

MAKING A BALANCE SHEET

Use a spreadsheet to make a balance sheet for Carlos' taco truck.

STEP 1
Start by opening a blank spreadsheet.

	A	B	C	D
1				
2				
3				
	Sheet 1	+		

STEP 2
Rename it to Balance Sheet and press enter.

	A	B	C	D
1				
2				
3				
	Balance Sheet	+		

STEP 3
Start in A1 and create the following headings.

	A	B	C	D
1	Assets		Liabilities and Equity	
2	Cash		Accounts Payable	
3	Accounts Receivable		Long-Term Liabilities	
4	Inventory			
5	Current Assets		Liabilities	
6				
7	Taco Truck		Retained Earnings	
8	Fixed Assets		Owner's Equity	
9				
10	Total Assets		Total Liabilities & Equity	

STEP 4
Fill in the information you know.

	A	B	C	D
1	Assets		Liabilities and Equity	
2	Cash	$2,000.00	Accounts Payable	$50.00
3	Accounts Receivable	$300.00	Long-Term Liabilities	$48,000.00
4	Inventory	$700.00		
5	Current Assets		Liabilities	
6				
7	Taco Truck	$60,000.00	Retained Earnings	$5,000.00
8	Fixed Assets		Owner's Equity	
9				
10	Total Assets		Total Liabilities & Equity	

Making a Balance Sheet

Step 5

To find Current Assets, select cell B5 and type =sum(. Then select all of the assets in B2 to B4.

	A	B	C	D
1	Assets		Liabilities and Equity	
2	Cash	$2,000.00	Accounts Payable	$50.00
3	Accounts Receivable	$300.00	Long-Term Liabilities	$48,000.00
4	Inventory	$700.00		
5	Current Assets	=sum(B2:B4)	Liabilities	

Step 6

To find the Liabilities, select cell D5 and type =sum(. Then select all of the assets in D2 to D3.

	A	B	C	D
1	Assets		Liabilities and Equity	
2	Cash	$2,000.00	Accounts Payable	$50.00
3	Accounts Receivable	$300.00	Long-Term Liabilities	$48,000.00
4	Inventory	$700.00		
5	Current Assets	$3,000.00	Liabilities	=sum(D2:D3)

Step 7

To find the Fixed Assets, select cell B8 and type equals = and click on the taco truck in B7.

	A	B	C	D
7	Taco Truck	$60,000.00	Retained Earnings	$5,000.00
8	Fixed Assets	=B7	Owner's Equity	

Step 8

To find the Total Assets, select cell B10 and type equals = and add the current assets in B5 plus the fixed assets in B7.

	A	B	C	D
1	Assets		Liabilities and Equity	
2	Cash	$2,000.00	Accounts Payable	$50.00
3	Accounts Receivable	$300.00	Long-Term Liabilities	$48,000.00
4	Inventory	$700.00		
5	Current Assets	$3,000.00	Liabilities	
6				
7	Taco Truck	$60,000.00	Retained Earnings	$5,000.00
8	Fixed Assets	$60,000.00	Owner's Equity	
9				
10	Total Assets	=B5+B7	Total Liabilities & Equity	

Making a Balance Sheet

Step 9

To find Owner's Equity, select cell D8 and press equals =. Then click on the Total Assets in B10, subtract the Liabilities in D5 and subtract the Retained Earnings in D7.

	A	B	C	D
1	Assets		Liabilities and Equity	
2	Cash	$2,000.00	Accounts Payable	$50.00
3	Accounts Receivable	$300.00	Long-Term Liabilities	$48,000.00
4	Inventory	$700.00		
5	Current Assets	$3,000.00	Liabilities	$48,050.00
6				
7	Taco Truck	$60,000.00	Retained Earnings	$5,000.00
8	Fixed Assets	$60,000.00	Owner's Equity	=B10-D5-D7
9				
10	Total Assets	$63,000.00	Total Liabilities & Equity	

Step 10

To find Total Liabilities & Equity select cell D10 and press equals =. Click on the liabilities in D5 and add the Retained Earnings in D7 and add the Owners Equity in D8.

	A	B	C	D
1	Assets		Liabilities and Equity	
2	Cash	$2,000.00	Accounts Payable	$50.00
3	Accounts Receivable	$300.00	Long-Term Liabilities	$48,000.00
4	Inventory	$700.00		
5	Current Assets	$3,000.00	Liabilities	$48,050.00
6				
7	Taco Truck	$60,000.00	Retained Earnings	$5,000.00
8	Fixed Assets	$60,000.00	Owner's Equity	$9,950.00
9				
10	Total Assets	$63,000.00	Total Liabilities & Equity	=D5+D7+D8

Conclusion

The Total Assets equal the Total Liabilities plus Equity. Why is this the case? Recall the fundamental accounting equation: Assets = Liabilities + Equity. What does the ratio of assets to liabilities tell you about the financial health of this business?

Garcia Tacos' Balance Sheet

An important part of staying in business is knowing what your balance sheet looks like. In this section, you will help the Garcias create balance sheets for their blossoming taco truck business.

Section 6A: Homework

1. Carlos signed up for an auto loan on his taco truck. The truck cost $60,000 and Uncle Rob paid the 20% down payment.
   a. What was the principal of the loan?
   b. If he has an interest rate of 5.75% and a 5 year car loan, what is his monthly payment?
   c. Create a loan repayment schedule found in section 2C for his taco truck.

	A	B	C	D	E	F
1	Month	Principal	Rate	Monthly Payment	Amount Paid on Interest	Amount Paid on Principal
2						

2. Look at the loan repayment schedule from problem number 1.
   a. How much does Carlos own on the truck in the third month?
   b. Use that amount for the long-term liabilities and create a balance sheet for Carlos. Assume that he has $2,800 in cash, $350 in accounts receivable, $900 in inventory, the taco truck is worth $60,000, there are no accounts payable, and he plans to keep $1,500 in retained earnings. Record your answers below.

	A	B	C	D
1	Assets		Liabilities and Equity	
2	Cash		Accounts Payable	
3	Accounts Receivable		Long-Term Liabilities	
4	Inventory			
5	Current Assets		Liabilities	
6				
7	Taco Truck		Retained Earnings	
8	Fixed Assets		Owner's Equity	
9				
10	Total Assets		Total Liabilities & Equity	

3. Look at the loan repayment schedule again from problem number 1.
   a. How much does Carlos own on the truck in the 10th month?
   b. Use that amount for the long-term liabilities and create a balance sheet for Carlos. Assume that he has $1,750 in cash, $40 in accounts receivable, $1,200 in inventory, the taco truck is worth $60,000, no accounts payable, and he plans to keep $2,000 in retained earnings. Record your answers below.

	A	B	C	D
1	Assets		Liabilities and Equity	
2	Cash		Accounts Payable	
3	Accounts Receivable		Long-Term Liabilities	
4	Inventory			
5	Current Assets		Liabilities	
6				
7	Taco Truck		Retained Earnings	
8	Fixed Assets		Owner's Equity	
9				
10	Total Assets		Total Liabilities & Equity	

Section 6B: Income Statements

In Section 6A, you learned how to make a Balance Sheet. Another important financial document is called the income statement, which shows the relationship between the money you receive from sales and the costs that go into producing your products. In order to have a successful, sustainable business, you have to have income greater than expenses.

Revenue

Cost of Goods Sold

Net Income

Create an Income Statement with a Spreadsheet

Net Income

Net income is how much money the company keeps after paying all expenses. The Income Statement is a financial document that shows how much income a business has and what it's spending it on. The Income Statement is known by several other names, including the Profit & Loss Statement and the Earnings Statement. The last line of the Income Statement is Net Income (Profit), which is why it's often referred to as "the bottom line."

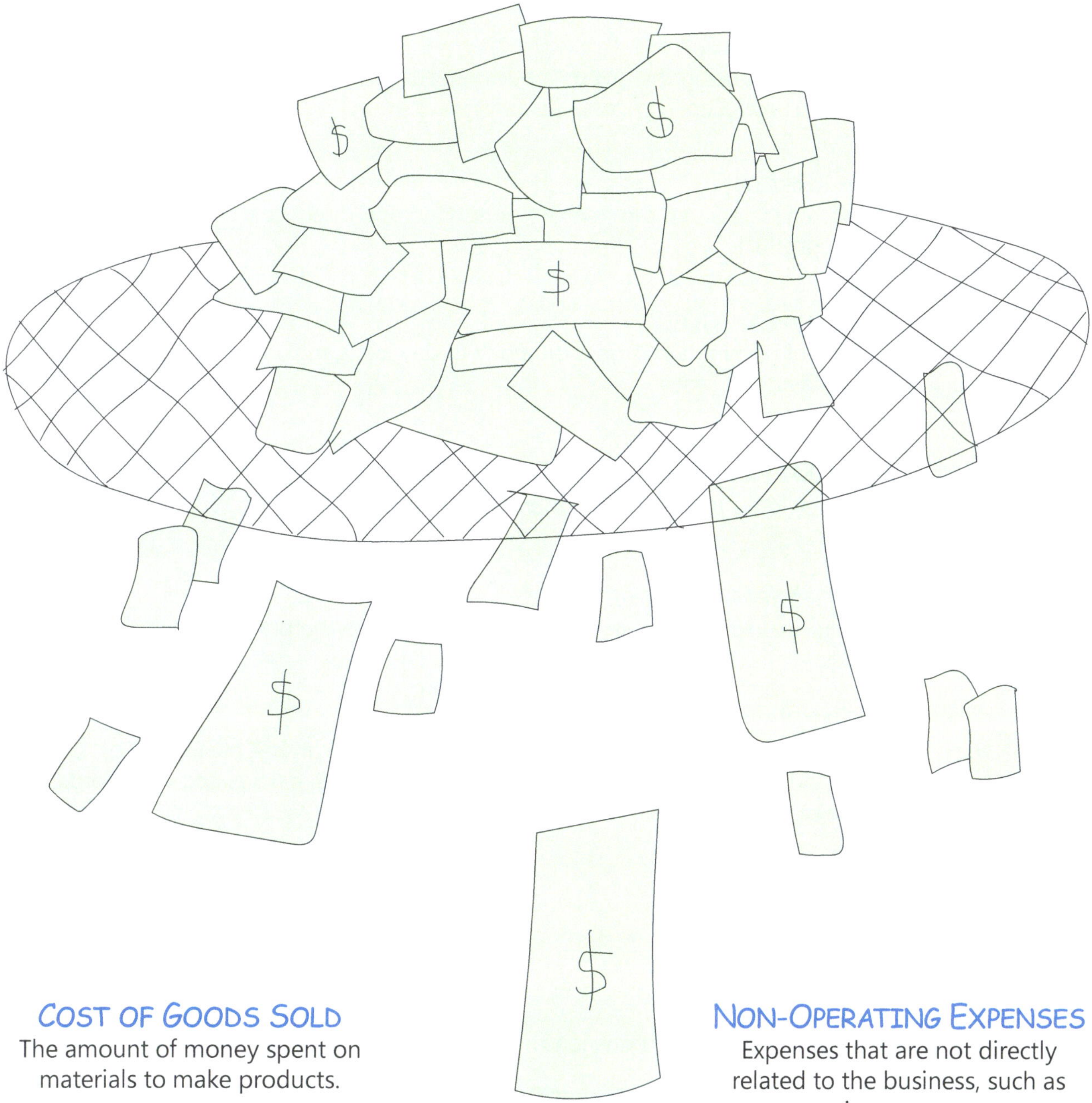

Cost of Goods Sold

The amount of money spent on materials to make products.

Non-Operating Expenses

Expenses that are not directly related to the business, such as insurance.

Operating Expenses

Money spent on rent, utilities, and employee salaries.

Types of Income and Expenses

The money that goes into and out of a business can be categorized.

Revenue

The money a business takes in as a result of engaging in business activities.

Cost of Goods Sold

The cost of producing the goods a business sells, including materials and labor used in the production process.

Gross Margin

The difference between the revenue generated and direct costs of producing and selling a product.

Operating Expenses

The costs of running a business on a day to day basis, including Cost of Goods Sold, salaries, and rent.

Operating Income

The money left after paying all Operating Expenses.

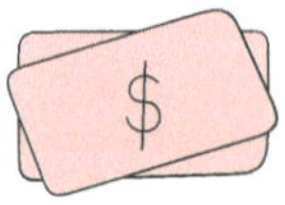

Non-Operating Expenses

The costs incurred by activities not directly related to the primary operations of a business.

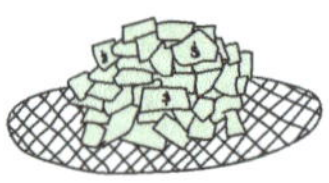

Net Income (Profit)

The money left after paying for everything needed to run the business: Cost of Goods Sold, Operating Expenses, and Non-Operating Expenses. In other words, revenue minus expenses.

Gross Margin Formula

To find Gross Margin, find the difference between the Cost of Goods Sold and the Revenue.

Operating Income Formula

To find Operating Income, find the difference between the Gross Margin and Operating Expenses.

Net Income Formula

To find Net Income, find the difference between the Operating Income and Non-Operating Expenses.

1. Now Do the Math ...

A. What is the Gross Margin of a company that has Revenue of $55,000 and Cost of Goods Sold of $33,750?

B. If that same company also has $3,800 in Operating Expenses, what is its Operating Income?

C. Find the Net Income of a company with Operating Income of $15,000 and Non-Operating Expenses of $2,300.

D. Find the Net Income of a company with Operating Income of $32,700 and Non-Operating Expenses of $1,700.

Make an Income Statement with a Spreadsheet

Use a spreadsheet to create an Income Statement for a business with $18,500 in Revenue, $11,000 in Cost of Goods Sold, Operating Expenses of $3,000, and Non-Operating Expenses of $500.

Step 1

Open a new spreadsheet and create the following headings.

	A	B
1	Revenue	
2	Cost of Goods Sold	
3	Gross Margin	
4	% of Revenue	
5	Operating Expenses	
6	% of Revenue	
7	Operating Income	
8	% of Revenue	
9	Non-Operating Expenses	
10	Net Income	
11	% of Revenue	

Step 2

Underline rows 2, 4, 6, 8, and 9. Double underline row 11 to show the final total.

	A	B
1	Revenue	
2	Cost of Goods Sold	
3	Gross Margin	
4	% of Revenue	
5	Operating Expenses	
6	% of Revenue	
7	Operating Income	
8	% of Revenue	
9	Non-Operating Expenses	
10	Net Income	
11	% of Revenue	

Step 3

Type in the Revenue, Cost of Goods Sold, Operating Expenses, and Non-Operating Expenses.

	A	B
1	Revenue	$18,500.00
2	Cost of Goods Sold	$11,000.00
3	Gross Margin	
4	% of Revenue	
5	Operating Expenses	$3,000.00
6	% of Revenue	
7	Operating Income	
8	% of Revenue	
9	Non-Operating Expenses	$500.00
10	Net Income	
11	% of Revenue	

Make an Income Statement with a Spreadsheet

Step 4

To find the Gross Margin, select cell B3 and type =. Then click on the Revenue in B1 and subtract the Cost of Goods Sold in B2. Press enter.

	A	B
1	Revenue	$18,500.00
2	Cost of Goods Sold	$11,000.00
3	Gross Margin	=B1-B2
4	% of Revenue	
5	Operating Expenses	$3,000.00
6	% of Revenue	
7	Operating Income	
8	% of Revenue	
9	Non-Operating Expenses	$500.00
10	Net Income	
11	% of Revenue	

Step 5

To find the Percent (%) of Revenue, select cell B4 and type =. Then click on the Gross Margin in B3 and divide it by the Revenue in B1. Press enter and then press % to turn it into a percentage.

	A	B
1	Revenue	$18,500.00
2	Cost of Goods Sold	$11,000.00
3	Gross Margin	$7,500.00
4	% of Revenue	=B3/B1
5	Operating Expenses	$3,000.00
6	% of Revenue	
7	Operating Income	
8	% of Revenue	
9	Non-Operating Expenses	$500.00
10	Net Income	
11	% of Revenue	

Step 6

To find the Net Income as a percentage of Revenue, select cell B6 and type =. Then click on the Operating Expenses in B5 and divide by the Revenue in B1. Press enter and then press % to turn it into a percentage.

	A	B
1	Revenue	$18,500.00
2	Cost of Goods Sold	$11,000.00
3	Gross Margin	$7,500.00
4	% of Revenue	41%
5	Operating Expenses	$3,000.00
6	% of Revenue	=B5/B1
7	Operating Income	
8	% of Revenue	
9	Non-Operating Expenses	$500.00
10	Net Income	
11	% of Revenue	

Make an Income Statement with a Spreadsheet

Step 7

To find the Operating Income, select cell B7 and type =. Then click on the Gross Margin in B3 and subtract the Operating Expenses in B5. Press enter.

	A	B
1	Revenue	$18,500.00
2	Cost of Goods Sold	$11,000.00
3	Gross Margin	$7,500.00
4	% of Revenue	41%
5	Operating Expenses	$3,000.00
6	% of Revenue	16%
7	Operating Income	=B3-B5
8	% of Revenue	
9	Non-Operating Expenses	$500.00
10	Net Income	
11	% of Revenue	

Step 8

To find Percent of Revenue, select cell B8 and type =. Then click on the Operating Income in B7 and divide by the Revenue in B1. Press enter and click on % to turn it into a percentage.

	A	B
1	Revenue	$18,500.00
2	Cost of Goods Sold	$11,000.00
3	Gross Margin	$7,500.00
4	% of Revenue	41%
5	Operating Expenses	$3,000.00
6	% of Revenue	16%
7	Operating Income	$4,500.00
8	% of Revenue	=B7/B1
9	Non-Operating Expenses	$500.00
10	Net Income	
11	% of Revenue	

Step 9

To find the Net Income, select cell B10 and type =. Then click on the Operating Income in B7 and subtract the Non-Operating Expenses in B9. Press enter.

	A	B
1	Revenue	$18,500.00
2	Cost of Goods Sold	$11,000.00
3	Gross Margin	$7,500.00
4	% of Revenue	41%
5	Operating Expenses	$3,000.00
6	% of Revenue	16%
7	Operating Income	$4,500.00
8	% of Revenue	24%
9	Non-Operating Expenses	$500.00
10	Net Income	=B7-B9
11	% of Revenue	

Make an Income Statement with a Spreadsheet

Step 10

To find the Percent of Revenue, select cell B11 and type =. Then click on the Net Income in B10 and divide the Revenue in B1. Press enter and click on % to turn it into a percentage.

	A	B
1	Revenue	$18,500.00
2	Cost of Goods Sold	$11,000.00
3	Gross Margin	$7,500.00
4	% of Revenue	41%
5	Operating Expenses	$3,000.00
6	% of Revenue	16%
7	Operating Income	$4,500.00
8	% of Revenue	24%
9	Non-Operating Expenses	$500.00
10	Net Income	$4,000.00
11	% of Revenue	=B10/B1

Conclusion

Even though this company made $18,500 in Revenue, its Net Income was $4,000. In business, as well as in personal finance, it is not about how much you make, but how much of that you get to keep.

2. Now Do the Math ...

Create an Income Statement with the following information:
Revenue = $5,480.00
Cost of Goods Sold = $750.00
Operating Expenses = $2,900.00
Non-operating expenses = $1,400.00

	A	B
1	Revenue	
2	Cost of Goods Sold	
3	Gross Margin	
4	% of Revenue	
5	Operating Expenses	
6	% of Revenue	
7	Operating Income	
8	% of Revenue	
9	Non-Operating Expenses	
10	Net Income	
11	% of Revenue	

The Garcia's Income Statement

The income statement is another important part of a healthy business. In this homework, you will help the Garcias create income statements that reflect how their business might change over time.

Section 6B: Homework

1. Carlos made $2,800 in revenue from sales last month and his cost of goods sold were $950. What was his gross margin?

2. Create an income statement for Carlos if his sales were $2,800, cost of goods sold was $950, his operating expenses were $1,100 and he had no non-operating expenses. Record your results below

	A	B
1	Revenue	
2	Cost of Goods Sold	
3	Gross Margin	
4	% of Revenue	
5	Operating Expenses	

6	% of Revenue	
7	Operating Income	
8	% of Revenue	
9	Non-Operating Expenses	
10	Net Income	
11	% of Revenue	

3. Create an income statement for Carlos a few month later if his sales were $1,750, cost of goods sold was $1,050, his operating expenses were $700 and his non-operating expenses were $120. Record your results below.

	A	B
1	Revenue	
2	Cost of Goods Sold	
3	Gross Margin	
4	% of Revenue	
5	Operating Expenses	
6	% of Revenue	
7	Operating Income	
8	% of Revenue	
9	Non-Operating Expenses	
10	Net Income	
11	% of Revenue	

SECTION 6C: TAX PREPARATION

In Section 6B, you learned how to make an Income Statement. The Income Statement, the Cash Flow Statement, and the Cash Flow Statement comprise the three required documents for publicly-traded companies (companies whose stock you can buy). Since the purpose of this book is to learn about small businesses, Cash Flow Statements are not addressed directly. Instead, 6C focuses on taxes, which are a part of everyday life and every business, large and small alike.

PAYROLL TAXES

FEDERAL INCOME TAXES

STATE INCOME TAXES

FILING TAXES

Taxes

Taxes are everywhere. Taxes are a government's way of paying for the public expenditures that it deems necessary. Taxes pay for all sorts of things, including roads, parks, public school lunches and many other things. Understanding how much you will pay in taxes is an important part of personal budgeting and running a successful business. This section will give you an overview of taxes and some of the ways they are calculated, but is not a substitute for professional advice from a tax preparer or certified public accountant.

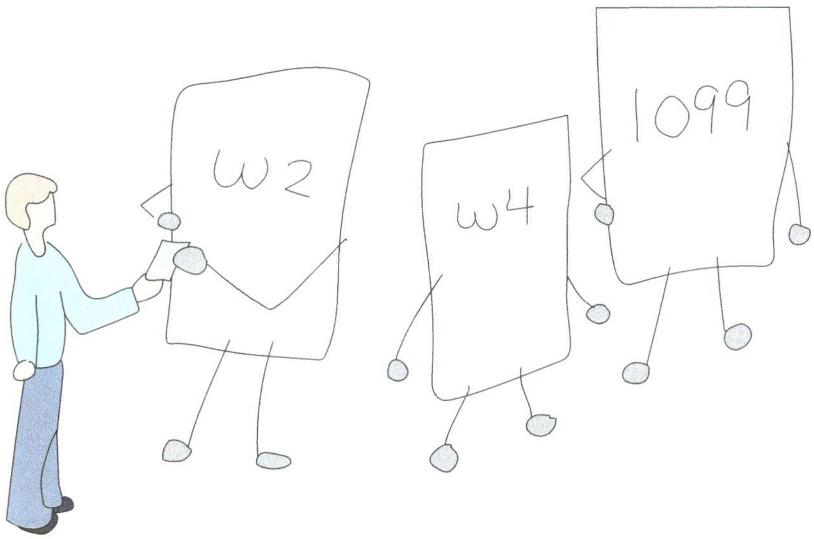

1. What Do You Think?

What are two other examples of things that taxes pay for? Use the Internet to help you. Share your findings with your classmates.

Payroll Taxes

Payroll taxes fund Social Security and Medicare, and are often referred to collectively as FICA (Federal Insurance Contributions Act) taxes. Payroll taxes are paid by both the employee and the employer. They are based on an employee's earnings, hence the term payroll taxes.

Social Security

Social Security, as you learned in 3B, is a government program designed to provide some income security for the elderly, widow(er)s, and individuals with disabilities.

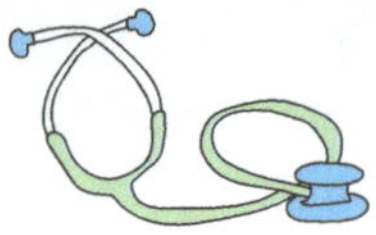

Medicare

Medicare, as you learned in 3D, is a government program designed to provide health insurance for the elderly and individuals with disabilities.

If You Are an Employee ...

Payroll (FICA) taxes consist of payments made to Social Security (6.2% on income up to $118,500) and Medicare (1.45%). Together, these taxes are 7.65% of gross pay and your employer matches that contribution, meaning the total tax paid on an employee's pay is 15.3% (half paid by the employee and half by the employer).

You Pay
7.65% in payroll taxes

Your Employer Pays
7.65% in payroll taxes

If You Are Self-Employed ...

For self-employed individuals, the equivalent of FICA is referred to as SECA (Self Employed Contributions Act). Self-employed individuals are responsible for both parts of the payroll tax (15.3% of gross pay) since they are both the employer and the employee. Keep this in mind when you think about your business and pricing strategies.

You Pay
15.3% in payroll taxes

If You Are a Student Worker ...

Student workers enrolled at least half-time (6+ credits) and working part-time as student workers are exempt from payroll (FICA) taxes. (Off-campus earnings are taxed regularly.)

You Pay
0% in payroll taxes

Calculating Payroll Taxes

When you get a job offer, remember that you are being offered the gross pay. Calculate your payroll taxes (contributions to FICA) as part of calculating your actual take-home pay (net income).

The Problem

Calculate pay after payroll taxes for a given gross pay.

GROSS PAY OF $1,460

Step 1

Determine the tax rate (7.65% combined FICA rate) and convert to a decimal.

7.65% -> 0.0765 DECIMAL

Step 2

Multiply the gross pay by the tax rate as a decimal to calculate the amount of tax paid.

GROSS PAY X TAX RATE = TAX PAID
$1,460 x 0.0765 = $111.69

Step 3

Subtract the tax paid from the gross pay to calculate after-tax amount.

GROSS PAY - TAX PAID = AFTER-TAX AMOUNT
$1,460 - $111.69 = $1348.31

Step 4

Calculate pay after payroll taxes by calculating tax paid and subtracting it from gross pay.

EMPLOYER MATCHES THIS CONTRIBUTION AND PAYS AN ADDITIONAL $111.69, MAKING THE TOTAL PAYROLL TAX PAID:
$111.69 x 2 = $223.38

2. Now Do the Math ...

A. Calculate payroll taxes and pay after payroll taxes for an employee with a gross pay of $865. *Round your answers to the nearest hundredth.*

payroll taxes = ______________________________

pay after payroll taxes = ______________________

B. Calculate payroll taxes and pay after payroll taxes for an employee with a gross pay of $1,525. *Round your answers to the nearest hundredth.*

payroll taxes = ______________________________

pay after payroll taxes = ______________________

C. Calculate payroll taxes and pay after payroll taxes for a self-employed individual with a gross pay of $2,342. *Round your answers to the nearest hundredth.*

payroll taxes = ______________________________

pay after payroll taxes = ______________________

Income Taxes

In addition to payroll taxes, your employers deduct state and federal income taxes from your paycheck. These income tax payments are estimates, which is why you might get a tax refund or owe more money in taxes when you file your tax return. Income tax rates vary based on income, with tax rates increasing as income increases. Remember that every year, April 15 is the deadline to file your income tax return electronically or have your envelope postmarked if filing by mail.

Federal Income Taxes

Federal income taxes are collected by the Internal Revenue Service (IRS) to generate revenue for the federal government budget. Healthcare (Medicaid and Medicare), military spending, and government assistance programs make up the majority of federal government spending.

State Income Taxes

In New Mexico, state income taxes are collected by the Taxation and Revenue Department (TRD) to generate revenue for the state government budget, though state income taxes generate less state budget revenue than many other revenue sources. Health and Human Services and education make up the majority of state government spending.

Filing Status for Income Taxes

There are several different filing statuses for income taxes, depending on whether you are single, married, or support dependents. There are many nuances to taxes, so be sure to visit IRS.gov or a qualified professional if you need help determining your specific filing status. Definitions of marriage, divorce, and legal separation are based on state law, not federal laws. Here are general descriptions for the most common filing statuses:

Single

Single individuals file their own tax returns and cannot be claimed by anyone else as a dependent. Unmarried, divorced, and legally separated individuals who do not support dependents generally file as Single.

Head of Household

Individuals who are not married and support dependents generally file as Head of Household.

Married Filing Jointly

Married couples can choose to file their taxes jointly. Choosing this option depends on the income of both individuals and other factors that influence tax owed.

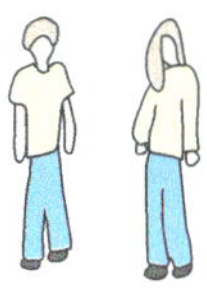

Married Filing Separately

Married couples can choose to file their taxes separately. Choosing this option depends on the income of both individuals and other factors that influence tax owed.

Types of Tax Reductions

There are several ways to reduce taxable income or income tax owed.

Standard Deductions

The standard deduction reduces taxable income. The amount and availability of the standard deduction depends on income and filing status.

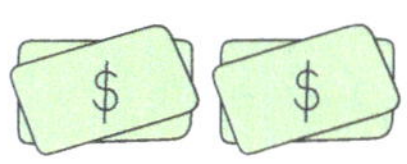

Itemized Deductions

Itemized deductions reduce taxable income. If allowable deductions are greater than the standard deduction, itemize (list all deductions). Mortgage interest, certain business expenses, and charitable gifts are examples of deductions that can be itemized. Certain situations require itemizing.

Exemptions

Tax exemptions reduce taxable income. You get one exemption for yourself, your spouse, and any dependents.

Credits

Credits reduce tax owed, not taxable income. Taxes already paid throughout the year count as credits toward the final tax owed. A portion of qualifying retirement savings contributions is an example of a tax credit. Tax professionals can advise you as to tax credits that apply to your specific tax situation.

Types of Income

Income tax is based on the portion of income that can be taxed.

Gross Income

Total income before accounting for any deductions. Gambling winnings are taxable and must be included as a source of income. Generally, scholarships are also considered income and count toward gross income.

Adjusted Gross Income (AGI)

Gross income minus certain adjustments, including allowable contributions to retirement savings, half of any self-employment tax paid, as well as college tuition, fees, and student loan interest.

Taxable Income

An individual's income that is subject to taxes. Generally, this is an individual's adjusted gross income, minus exemptions and deductions.

Calculating Your Taxable Income

The specifics of your tax situation are unique to you and can be complicated. However, the general formula for calculating taxable income is shown below:

Taxable Income	=	Gross Income	−	Deductions	−	Exemptions
The amount of income that can be taxed	is	total income	minus	allowable reductions to gross income	minus	allowable reductions to gross income.

3. Now Do the Math ...

Uncle Rob wants to know whether he will owe money or get a refund when he files his taxes, so first he needs to calculate his taxable income. Uncle Rob earned $48,250 in gross income for the year. He has no children and is not married, so he can claim one exemption of $4,000. He can also take the standard deduction, which is $6,300 for his filing status of Single.

Find Uncle Rob's taxable income.

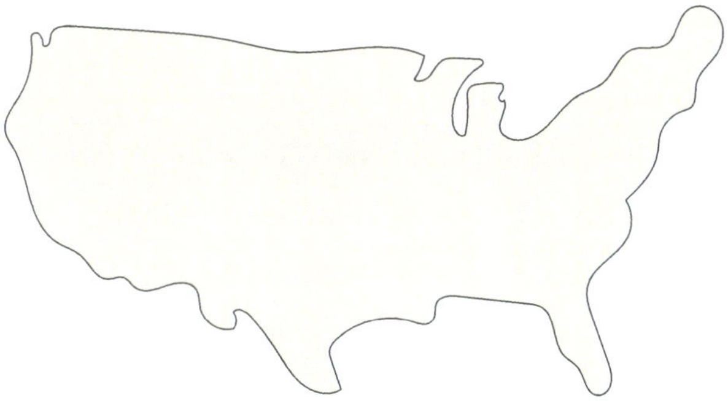

Calculating Federal Income Taxes

Once you have calculated your taxable income and your filing status, you can locate your tax bracket in the corresponding table. Then, use the tax formula for your tax bracket to determine how much federal tax you will owe for the year. The specific income amounts for tax brackets change periodically, as do the specific dollar amount for exemptions and deductions.

Federal: Single		
Taxable Income	Tax Bracket	Tax Formula
$0 to $9,225	10%	= 10%*(your taxable income)
$9,226 to $37,450	15%	= $922.50 + 15%*(your taxable income - $9,225)
$37,451 to $90,750	25%	= $5,156.25 + 25%*(your taxable income - $37,450)
$90,751 to $189,300	28%	= $18,481.25 + 28%*(your taxable income - $90,750)
$189,301 to $411,500	33%	= $46,075.25 + 33%*(your taxable income - $189,300)
$411,501 to $413,200	35%	= $119,401.25 + 35%*(your taxable income - $411,500)
Above $413,200	39.6%	= $119,996.25 + 39.6%*(your taxable income - $413,200)

Federal: Head of Household		
Taxable Income	Tax Bracket	Tax Formula
$0 to $13,150	10%	= 10%*(your taxable income)
$13,151 to $50,200	15%	= $1,315 + 15%*(your taxable income - $13,150)
$50,201 to $129,600	25%	= $6,872.50 + 25%*(your taxable income - $50,200)
$129,601 to $209,850	28%	= $26,772.50 + 28%*(your taxable income - $129,600)
$209,851 to $411,500	33%	= $49,242.50 + 33%*(your taxable income - $209,850)
$411,501 to $439,000	35%	= $115,787 + 35%*(your taxable income - $411,500)
Above $439,000	39.6%	= $125,412 + 39.6%*(your taxable income - $439,000)

Federal: Married Filing Jointly		
Taxable Income	Tax Bracket	Tax Formula
$0 to $18,450	10%	= 10%*(your taxable income)
$18,451 to $74,900	15%	= $1,845 + 15%*(your taxable income - $18,450)
$74,901 to $151,200	25%	= $10,312.50 + 25%*(your taxable income - $74,900)
$151,201 to $230,450	28%	= $29,387.50 + 28%*(your taxable income - $151,200)
$230,451 to $411,500	33%	= $51,577.50 + 33%*(your taxable income - $230,450)
$411,501 to $464,850	35%	= $111,324 + 35%*(your taxable income - $411,500)
Above $464,850	39.6%	= $129,996.50 + 39.6%*(your taxable income - $464,850)

Federal: Married Filing Separately		
Taxable Income	Tax Bracket	Tax Formula
$0 to $9,225	10%	= 10%*(your taxable income)
$9,226 to $37,450	15%	= $922.50 + 15%*(your taxable income - $9,225)
$37,451 to $75,600	25%	= $5,156.25 + 25%*(your taxable income - $37,450)
$75,601 to $115,225	28%	= $14,693.75 + 28%*(your taxable income - $75,600)
$115,226 to $205,750	33%	= $25,788.75 + 33%*(your taxable income - $115,225)
$205,751 to $232,425	35%	= $55,662 + 35%*(your taxable income - $205,750)
Above $232,425	39.6%	= $64,998.25 + 39.6%*(your taxable income - $232,425)

4. Now Do the Math ...

Based on Uncle Rob's taxable income from example 3 on page 306, find the federal tax owed by locating the correct tax bracket for his taxable income and using the corresponding formula.

Calculating State Income Taxes

Once you have calculated your taxable income and your filing status, you can locate your tax bracket in the corresponding table. Then, use the tax formula for your tax bracket to determine how much state tax you will owe for the year. The specific income amounts for tax brackets change periodically, as do the specific dollar amount for exemptions and deductions.

State: Single		
Taxable Income	Tax Bracket	Tax Formula
$0 to $5,500	1.7%	= 1.7%*(your taxable income)
$5,501 to $11,000	3.2%	= $93.50 + 3.2%*(your taxable income - $5,500)
$11,001 to $16,000	4.7%	= $269.50 + 4.7%*(your taxable income - $11,000)
Above $16,000	4.9%	= $504.50 + 4.9%*(your taxable income - $16,000)

State: Head of Household or Married Filing Jointly		
Taxable Income	Tax Bracket	Tax Formula
$0 to $8,000	1.7%	= 1.7%*(your taxable income)
$8,001 to $16,000	3.2%	= $136 + 3.2%*(your taxable income - $8,000)
$16,001 to $24,000	4.7%	= $392 + 4.7%*(your taxable income - $16,000)
Above $24,000	4.9%	= $768 + 4.9%*(your taxable income - $24,000)

State: Married Filing Separately		
Taxable Income	Tax Bracket	Tax Formula
$0 to $4,000	1.7%	= 1.7%*(your taxable income)
$4,001 to $8,000	3.2%	= $68 + 3.2%*(your taxable income - $4,000)
$8,001 to $12,000	4.7%	= $196 + 4.7%*(your taxable income - $8,000)
Above $12,000	4.9%	= $384 + 4.9%*(your taxable income - $12,000)

5. Now Do the Math ...

Based on Uncle Rob's taxable income from example 3 on page 306, find the state tax owed by locating the correct tax bracket for his taxable income and using the corresponding formula.

Refunds

Whether you receive a tax refund or owe money when you file your taxes depends on your tax bill and how much you have paid in taxes throughout the year.

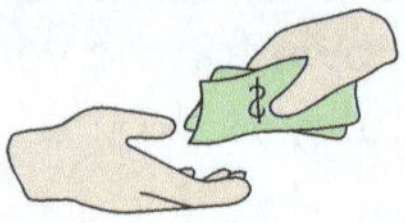

Tax Refunds

If you have paid more in taxes than you owe for the year, then you are entitled to a refund. Contributions you make throughout the year are credits toward your tax bill.

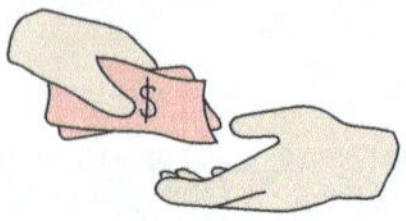

Taxes Owed

If you owe more in taxes than you have paid during the year, then you will owe money when you file your tax return.

6. Now Do the Math ...

A. Uncle Rob paid $6,038.75 in federal tax withholding from his paycheck throughout the year. Based on your results from page 308, will Uncle Rob receive a federal tax refund or will he owe money? How much?

B. Uncle Rob paid $1,262.50 in state tax withholding from his paycheck throughout the year. Based on your results from page 309, will Uncle Rob receive a state tax refund or will he owe money? How much?

7. What Do You Think?

A. Uncle Rob was in the 25% tax bracket for his federal taxes, but did he pay 25% of his taxable income in federal taxes? Why or why not?

B. What percentage of his taxable income did he pay in federal taxes? This is known as the effective tax rate.

List of Tax Forms

There are many different tax forms. Understanding what the different tax forms are will help you understand the filing process.

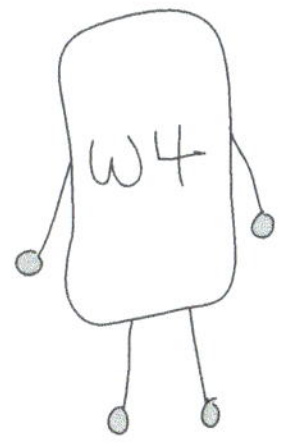

W-4

A W-4 is a form that employees fill out when they are hired to help employers determine the amount of tax withholding for an employee. Accurate completion of this form reduces the likelihood of owing taxes or paying too much in taxes when filing a tax return.

W-2

A W-2 is issued to employees by January 31 of each year. It details all compensation (wages, tips, etc.) and all withholdings for an employee during the tax year.

1099

1099-MISC is issued for independent contractors who are paid more than $600 per year. Independent contractors do not have income tax withheld, which means they often owe taxes when they file tax returns. There are other 1099 forms, including statements of interest earned and tuition paid. A 1099 is issued by January 31 of each year.

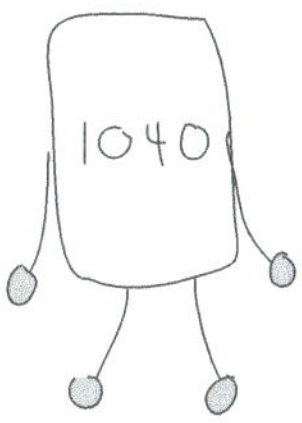

1040

A Form 1040 is the form used to file federal income taxes. There are different versions of this form, depending on the complexity of your tax situation. A 1040 is due to the IRS by April 15.

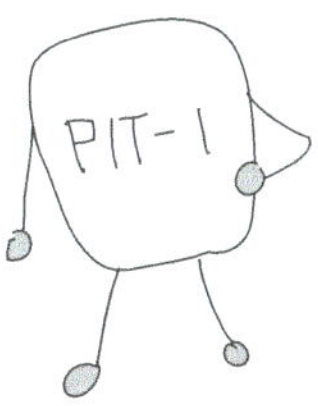

PIT-1

Form PIT-1 is the form used to file New Mexico state income taxes. PIT stands for Personal Income Tax. There are other PIT forms, depending on the complexity of your tax situation. A PIT-1 is due by April 15 to TRD.

Extension

You can file an extension if you need more time to file your taxes, but you must still pay any tax owed by the April 15 deadline. Failure to pay any tax owed by the deadline will result in a penalty.

Paying Taxes

The Garcias know that every time they earn or spend money, they pay taxes. What they don't know is how much they have to pay. Help the Garcias figure out how much they will pay in taxes.

Section 6C: Homework

1. Susan makes $1,052.08 each pay check. She pays 7.65% in payroll taxes.
    a. What are her payroll taxes for each pay check?
    b. What is her take home pay for each pay check?
    c. If she gets paid twice a month, what is her take home pay for one month?

2. At Carlos' last job, he made $912.26 each pay check. He pays 7.65% in payroll taxes.
    a. What are his payroll taxes?
    b. What is his take home pay for each pay check?
    c. If he gets paid twice a month, what is his take home pay for one month?

3. When Carlos opened the taco truck, he stopped working at his old job. His net income from his business was $6,250. Since he is self-employed he must pay 15.3% in payroll taxes.
    a. What are his payroll taxes?
    b. What was his take home pay?

4. In the last year Susan received 26 paychecks of $1,052.08. Carlos received 14 paychecks of $912.26 and he also earned $6,250 from his business. How much was their gross income?

5. The Garcias opened an IRA for their retirement savings and put $216 into the account each month. How much did they save for retirement in the last year?

6. Retirement savings are subtracted from the gross income to get the adjusted gross income. What is the Garcias' adjusted gross income?

7. The Garcias will take a standard deduction of $6,300 and 3 exemptions of $4,000 each. What is their taxable income?

8. Calculate the Garcias' federal income taxes assuming they are married filing jointly.

9. Calculate the Garcias' state income taxes assuming they are married filing jointly.

Section 6D: Tax Project

In Section 6C, you learned about different taxes and how to calculate and file them. Taxes can be very complicated, but the availability of computer software and tax prep professionals helps to make the process manageable. In this section, you will explore Susan's business endeavors and help her figure out what she's making and what her tax situation looks like.

Business Expenses

Revenue and Net Income

Sales and Gross Receipts Taxes

Average Pay Per Hour

Susan Joins a Craft Fair

Susan earned a degree in Fashion Design, but she hasn't made anything in a while. When she sees an advertisement for a craft show, she decides to sign up and pursue her talents. In this section, you will explore her expenses, time, and profit. You will also calculate her taxes for the show.

Batik Dresses and Handbags

Susan plans to make 30 handmade dresses and 20 matching handbags. She wants to do batik, which is a technique that involves hand-painting designs on fabric with beeswax, dyeing the fabric another color, and then melting off the wax to leave beautiful designs in the fabric.

Supplies

Susan needs to buy the following supplies to make 30 dresses and 20 handbags.

Fabric

Susan buys green fabric for the dresses that costs $6.99 per yard and blue fabric for the handbags that costs $4.85 per yard.

Pattern

Susan buys a $11.95 pattern set for the dresses and handbags which. It calls for 3 yards of fabric for each dress and 1.375 yards for each handbag.

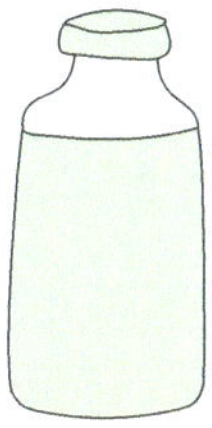

Fabric Dye

Susan needs to purchase bottles of fabric dye. Each bottle costs $3.88. One bottle of green dye will make 5 dresses and one bottle of blue dye will make 10 handbags.

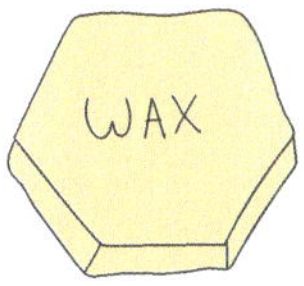

Beeswax

She also needs a block of beeswax that costs $24.

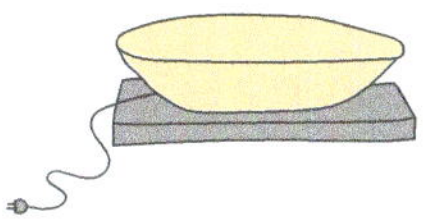

Wax Melting Pot

She will need an electric pot to melt the wax as she does the batik work. This costs $48.33.

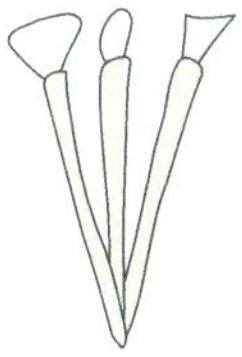

Brushes

She will need a pack of brushes that costs $7.99.

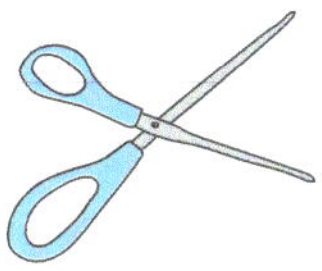

Scissors

She will need a sharp pair of scissors to cut the fabric. Good scissors are $14.50.

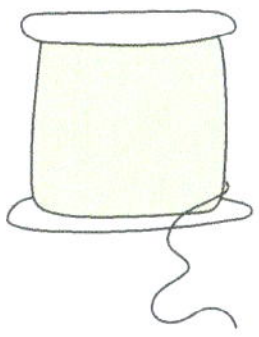

Thread

She will need thread for sewing. Each spool costs $2. The dresses require 4 spools each, and the handbags require 1 spool each.

Check Out

After 45 minutes of shopping, Susan checks out.

Making the Dresses and Handbags

Susan must get to work if she wants to finish her products in time for the big craft fair.

Cutting the Fabric

The first step is to cut out the fabric. It takes 15 minutes to cut out the pieces for each dress, and it takes 10 minutes to cut out the pieces for each handbag.

Painting Patterns with Beeswax

Once the fabric pieces are cut, she will need to paint designs with beeswax. Each dress takes 50 minutes to paint, and each hand bag takes 20 minutes.

Dyeing the Fabric

The next step is to dye the fabric. It takes 30 minutes to dye everything.

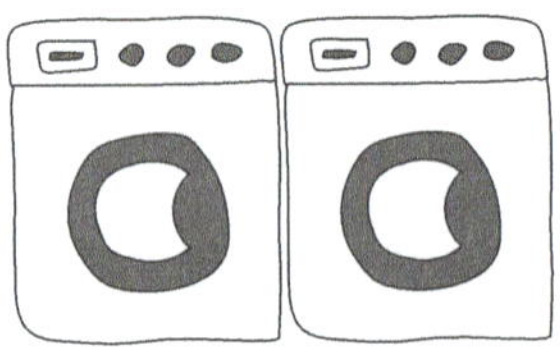

Washing Out the Dye

She must wash out the dye. One load of laundry takes 2 hours to wash and dry, and she will need 3 loads to clean everything.

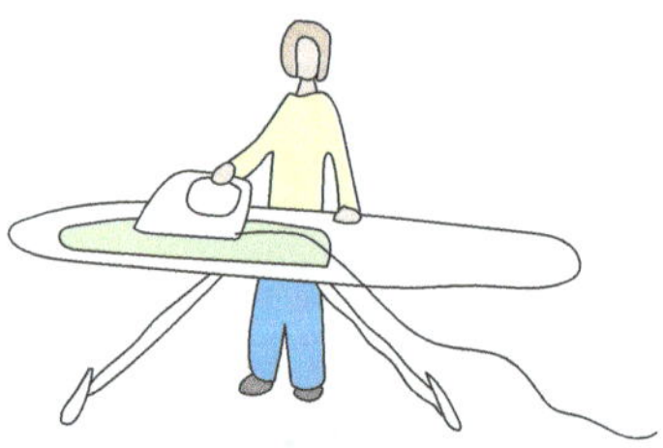

Melting the Wax

Once the fabric has been dyed and washed, she can remove the beeswax with an iron. Each dress takes 5 minutes to iron and each handbag takes 2 minutes.

Sewing the Dresses and Handbags

Lastly, Susan will have to sew everything. She already has a sewing machine, so each dress will take 2 hours to sew and each handbag will take 1.5 hours.

Travel and Accommodation

Once she gets to the craft fair, Susan has to set up her space and get ready for customers.

Trip to the Store

Susan must travel 8 miles from her home to get to the local craft store. The drive takes 5 minutes.

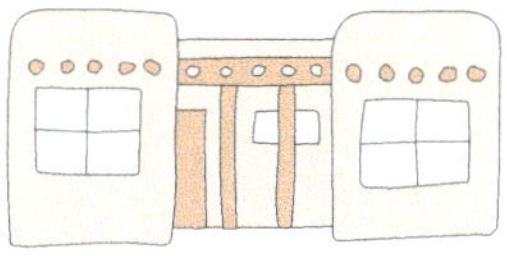

Going Home After Shopping

After shopping, Susan drives back home, another 8 miles that takes her 5 minutes.

Traveling to the Fair

The craft fair is in Truth or Consequences (T or C), so to get there Susan must travel 210 miles, taking about 3 hours.

Hotel

The craft fair lasts 3 days, so she will have to stay overnight for 2 nights. The hotel costs $88 each night.

Eating Out

The hotel where Susan is staying has a free continental breakfast, but she will have to buy lunch and dinner for 3 full days. On average, lunches cost $11.85 and dinners cost $14.32.

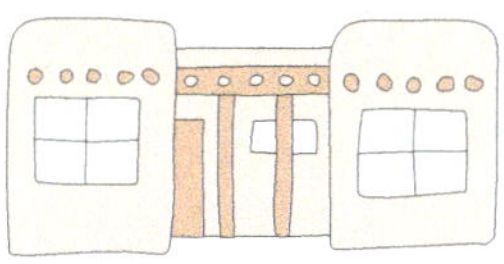

Driving Home After the Fair

Finally, Susan drives back home, traveling 210 miles in about 3 hours.

Working at the Fair

Once she gets to the craft fair, Susan has to set up her space and get ready for customers.

Set-Up

Susan spends 3 hours setting up her space.

Running the Booth

The fair lasts 3 days and she needs to be there from 10 a.m. to 4 p.m. each day.

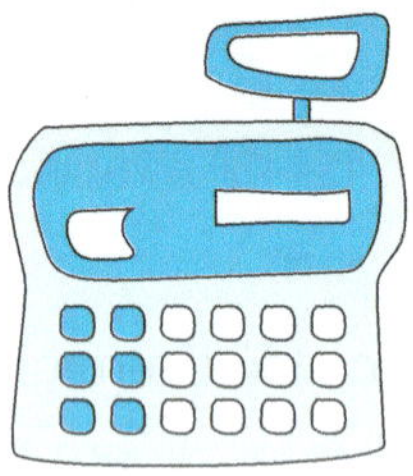

Sales

During the fair, Susan sells 28 dresses and 5 handbags. Her dresses were priced at $100 each and her handbags were $35 each.

Space Rental

In order to have a booth at the fair, Susan has to pay a $125 registration fee. She also has to pay 20% of all of her sales to the craft fair.

Take Down

At the end of the fair, Susan spends 2 hours packing up her stuff and taking down her tent.

Section 6D: Homework

1. Susan was able to sell dresses and handbags at the show.
   a. How much revenue did Susan receive in sales at her show?
   b. If gross receipts tax is 8.1875% on all sales, how much will she pay in gross receipts tax on her sales?
   c. Subtracting the tax she has to pay from her revenue, how much of her revenue does Susan get to keep?

2. How much did Susan pay to rent the space at the craft fair?

3. Susan had to buy supplies to make the dresses and handbags.
   a. What were Susan's expenses for craft supplies?
   b. If the sales tax in her town is 8.1875%, how much did she pay in sales tax?
   c. Including tax, how much did Susan spend on craft supplies?

4. Susan had to travel to the store as well as the craft fair.
   a. How many miles did Susan travel?
   b. If Susan's truck gets 18 miles per gallon, how many gallons of gas did she use round-trip?
   c. If gas is $2.85, how much did the trip cost her in gas?
   d. For tax purposes, Susan can claim a deduction of $0.50 for every mile she travels for her craft business. What will her mileage deduction be from this trip?
   e. Will her tax deduction cover the cost of gas?

5. What were Susan's total travel expenses, including gas, hotel, and food?

6. What were Susan's total expenses?

7. Although Susan made money at the show, some of that money will be used to cover her expenses.
   a. What was Susan's net income?
   b. If Susan's net income from her craft business is more than $400 per year, she will have to pay payroll taxes to the IRS at the self-employed rate of 15.3%. How much would that be?
   c. Subtracting payroll taxes from what she earned at the craft fair, how much did she make?

8. How many hours, including travel, shopping and making her products, did Susan work?

9. On average, how much did Susan make per hour?

10. What are some ways Susan's efforts could have been more profitable? List at least 3 suggestions.

Chapter 7: Business Plans

7A Exective Summary

7B Operational Plan

7C Marketing Plan

7D Financial Plan

Section 7A: Executive Summary

In Chapters 5 and 6, you learned how to price products and read financial statements. Now it's time to put it all together. In Chapter 7, you will write a Business Plan. Section 7A starts the process with an Executive Summary which gives an overview of your business and its goals.

Choose a Business Name

Design a Logo

Write a Business Description

Complete a SWOT Analysis

Making the Leap

When you work for someone else, your job description, hours, and pay are determined for you. You know how you will be compensated for your work. When you open your own business, there are no guarantees. You may need to do a variety of tasks and work long hours without knowing how much you will make. Writing a business plan is a way to reduce uncertainty, focus your attention, and communicate your ideas to others.

The Business Plan

The role of a Business Plan is to clarify the goals of a business. It is a necessary part of applying for loans or attracting investors. Generally, Business Plans have the following components:

Executive Summary

The Executive Summary gives an overview of your business. It describes what your business does, who it serves, and how it plans to make money. It will be the first document potential investors read and needs to catch their attention, so they will want to keep reading. It is best to keep it short and to the point.

Operational Plan

The Operational Plan describes the day-to-day activities needed to keep your business open and running. It lists the roles of employees and their pay. It also describes your legal identity as a company.

Marketing Plan

The Marketing Plan focuses on your customers and how to reach them. It includes your marketing strategy and product pricing. It also looks at your competitors and how you plan to compete.

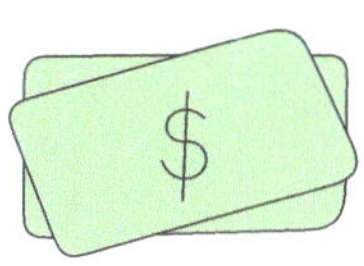

Financial Plan

The Financial Plan describes how your company will make money. It includes business projections, a break-even analysis, and financial documents. Potential investors or loan officers consider your financial plan in determining whether supporting your company is worth the risk.

The Cover Sheet

The Cover Sheet is the first page of your business plan. It sets the tone for what's to come and includes your business name and logo.

Business Name

The name of your business expresses what your business does and its personality. Great names are memorable and clear.

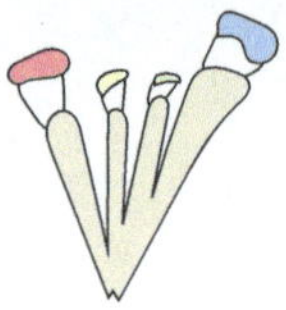

Logo

A logo is an image that accompanies your business name as part of a brand. It expresses your company's personality. The best logos are simple and colorful, and look good in different sizes.

Make Sure Your Name Is Not Already Taken

The last thing you want is to start a business only to find out someone else has the same name as you. Before settling on your business name, make sure to do some research to make sure no one has already registered or trademarked it.

Trademark Search

You can do an online trademark search to see if anyone else has registered the name or something similar with the United States Patent and Trademark Office (uspto.gov).

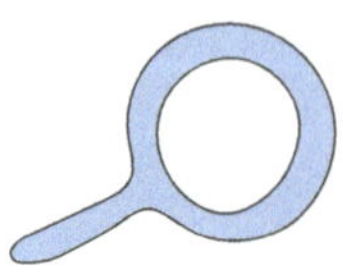

Website Search

It is also prudent to see if anyone has a website with your name or something similar. Search your business' name to see if anything comes up.

Secretary of State

You can visit the New Mexico Secretary of State's website (sos.state.nm.us) to look at a listing of the current businesses registered in the state.

1. Describe Your Company ...

A. What is your company's name? *Make sure it's not already in use.*

B. What will your logo look like? Draw a picture below.

C. What products or services will your company provide?

D. Where will your business be located? Do you need a store front, a factory, or an office, or can you work from home? Will you have one location or several?

E. Who are your customers? Describe their demographics (characteristics of age, gender, buying power), interests, and spending habits.

F. Why will customers want to buy your products and services? What makes you different from your competition?

G. How will your business make money from the activities it engages in?

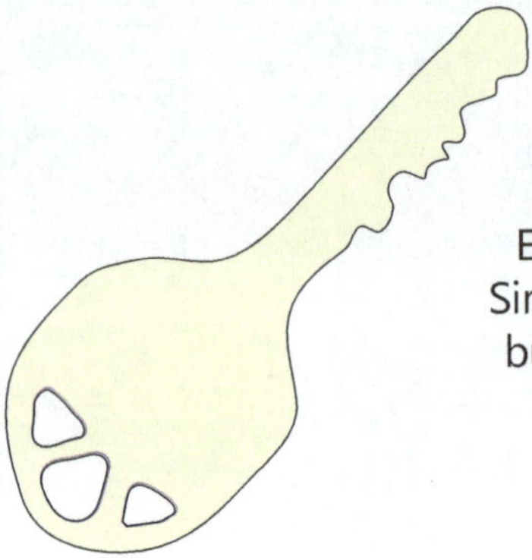

The Key to Success

Everyone is different and will approach obstacles in unique ways. Similarly, every business is unique. The key is to know yourself and your business. The more you know, the better able you are to make decisions and move your business forward.

SWOT Analysis

Many business plans include an evaluation of Strengths, Weaknesses, Opportunities, and Threats (SWOT analysis). This analysis is an examination of the internal and external factors that are favorable or unfavorable for business. Taking the time to think about these qualities in yourself and your business will help you problem solve and be prepared for challenges that may arise in the process of starting your business. When you start a business, knowing yourself is an important part of success.

Strengths

Everyone has strengths. These are personality traits, skills, and natural abilities that will bring value to your company. Every business idea has strengths: What is your business really good at?

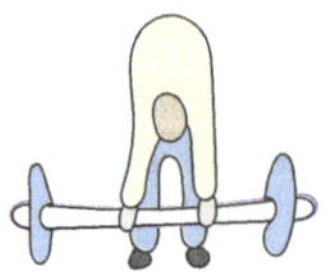

Weaknesses

Everyone has weaknesses. Knowing your weaknesses will motivate you to improve in those areas or collaborate with others who have the skills you need. Every business has weaknesses: How can you improve your business?

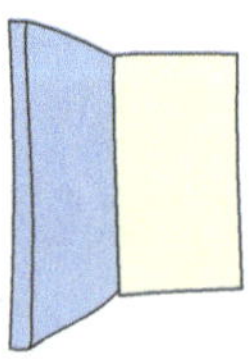

Opportunities

Opportunities in business include personal connections, new customers, and helpful resources that you can take advantage of.

Threats

A business can be fragile to start, and it can take a while to become established. Many factors can threaten your business and being aware of them helps you avoid them and be resilient when they arise.

2. Complete a SWOT Analysis ...

A. What are the strengths of your business?

B. How will the business take advantage of these strengths?

C. What are the weaknesses of your business?

D. What are some ways the business can manage these weaknesses?

E. What are the opportunities for your business?

F. How can the business best take advantage of these opportunities?

G. What are the threats to your business?

H. What measures will the business take to protect itself from these threats?

Challenges of Opening a Business

There are many challenges that can arise when opening a business. Below are some of the most common challenges a new business faces.

Competitors

Even if you have a great business idea, chances are you aren't the only one. It is important to know whom you're up against and how to compete with them.

Time

Opening a business requires time and energy. While juggling your current job, a family, and the demands of everyday life, it can be challenging to find the time needed to get your company off the ground. Many small business owners work on nights and weekends in the early stages of developing their companies.

Money

Starting a business also requires money. Some businesses require more than others, but every business needs some starting capital. Being able to afford initial costs may mean sacrificing in other areas. Budgeting is helpful. You can pursue investors right away, but most banks and credit unions only make loans after you've been in business for 2 years.

Family

Opening a business often requires a sacrifice of time and money in the hopes that it will pay off later. Until it pays off, it can put stress on your family. Stability and support will be helpful, especially in the early stages of a business.

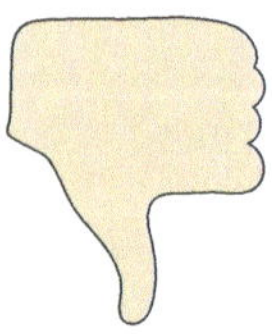

Naysayers

When you start a business, you won't have results right away. In the beginning you will have ideas, but ideas won't gain the support of everyone. Don't let their doubt deter you; consider the criticism of naysayers, and use it to strengthen your business plan.

Personal Fears and Doubts

In addition to external challenges, personal fears and doubts can also be challenging. There are no guarantees in entrepreneurship, and other people may or may not be supportive. The fear of failure can prevent people from moving forward. Learning about yourself is an important step to opening a business.

3. How Do You Face Challenges?

A. Are there businesses that are similar to yours? How are you going to compete with them?

B. Who are the naysayers in your life? What do they say?

C. How much time will you need to start your business? How will you create that time in your life?

D. How much money do you think you will need to start your business? What are you willing to sacrifice in order to start your business?

E. Do you have support from friends and family? Are any of them partners or investors? How will your family support you as you start your company?

F. What are some of your personal fears and doubts about going into business? How will you overcome them?

Executive Summary

Carlos wants to get a loan from a local bank, so he puts together an executive summary as part of a business plan.

Company Description

Garcia Tacos is a food truck that sells handmade tacos using only local and organic ingredients. The truck is located on the Santa Fe plaza from 11am to 2pm. It primarily sells tacos to state employees and tourists. Customers choose Garcia Tacos for the fresh and health ingredients.

Strengths

Garcia Tacos' greatest strength is its ingredients. Carlos Garcia, owner of the company, has many personal contacts with local farmers. This allows him to get discounts on local organic produce. Carlos is also an excellent cook and makes tasty, innovative tacos that keep customers coming back for more.

Weaknesses

The main weakness of the food truck is customer service. Carlos cannot afford to hire an assistant. He must take orders and cook at the same time, which prevents him from giving his customers the attention they expect.

Opportunities

Garcia Tacos is gaining a reputation for its tasty and healthy food. A local newspaper is interested in doing a story on the food truck. The publicity would mean increased sales.

Threats

Another food truck started parking next to Garcia Tacos. It sells fajitas and takes some of Carlos' business. To keep up with the competition, Carlos plans on painting a new sign on his truck. He is also considering adding other items to his menu.

Section 7A: Homework

Part 1 - The Garcia Tacos' Executive Summary

Read Carlos' executive summary for his taco truck. Pretend you work for a bank and you decide which businesses will receive loans.

a. Based on his executive summary, would you lend money to his food truck? Why or why not?

b. What questions would you ask Carlos before lending him money?

Part 2 - Your Business

Write your own executive summary. Make sure to include your business name, logo, a business description and a SWOT analysis.

Part 3 - Analyze a Classmate's Plan

Trade your executive summary with one of your classmates. Again, pretend you work for a bank and get to decide if this business will receive a loan or not.

a. Based on their executive summary, would you lend money to this company? Why or why not?

b. What questions would you ask the owner before lending them money?

Section 7B: Operational Plan

In Section 7A, you wrote an Executive Summary, which is an overview of your business. Now it's time to get into the details. In this section, you will write an Operational Plan to explore the day-to-day activities that keep your business running.

Product Description

SMART Goals

Paying Employees

Types of Businesses

How Does it Work?

The way to turn a great idea into a reality is planning and action. An operational plan gives you a step-by-step guide to make your vision come to life.

The Operational Plan

The Operational Plan describes the logistical side of your business. It talks about your products, services, employees, and legal structure.

Products and Services

Every business has something to sell. The Operational Plan describes the products and services you will be providing. It highlights their main features and how production will take place.

Goals

The purpose of opening a company is to reach goals. These goals could be financial, or they could focus on quality and customer service. Clearly defining your goals makes reaching them more likely.

Employees

Most companies require employees to carry out key functions in their business. Your Operational Plan will describe the types of employees needed and how they will be paid.

Legal Structure

There are different kinds of businesses and each has different legal liabilities and tax reporting methods. You will list the type of your business in your Operational Plan.

WHAT ARE YOU SELLING?

Your Operational Plan includes a detailed description of your products and services. Describe what you are selling and why it is of benefit to your customers.

1. PRODUCT/SERVICE DESCRIPTION ...

A. What will you sell? What are the key features?

B. How are your products produced and services delivered?

C. How much does it cost to produce 1 item?

D. Is shipping required? If so, how much does shipping cost?

E. Who will buy your products and services?

F. How much will they pay for them?

SMART Goals

The Operational Plan includes your company's goals and the plan to achieve them. Well-defined business goals are Specific, Measurable, Achievable, Realistic, and Timely, and are often referred to as SMART goals. SMART goals have been used in business since the 1980s.

Specific

The results and process are clearly defined and unambiguous. You will know when you've reached your goal.

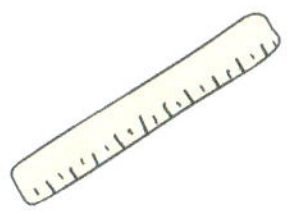

Measurable

The process can be measured and progress can be tracked. You will know how close you are to your goal.

Achievable

The goal is something you can achieve at the current stage of your business. Choosing intermediate goals can be helpful in outlining a path to achieve long-term goals.

Realistic

The goal is realistic based on what resources and opportunities are available to your business.

Timely

The time-line for achieving the goal must be clear. You will know how long it will take to achieve the goal.

2. Which Goals Are SMART?

Complete the chart below by checking off the characteristics of each goal.

	Specific	Measurable	Achievable	Realistic	Timely
A. Katherine has a flower shop. She wants to sell flowers to a lot more customers and plans to do this soon.					
B. A graphic designer currently works with 10 clients a month. Within the next six months, he wants to double that number.					
C. A computer programmer plans to advertise his new app using social media. He wants to get 3 million downloads within a few weeks of its release.					

Who Will You Hire?

Most companies need to hire employees to help run the business. Each company will be unique in its needs, so take some time to think about what roles your company will require. Also, consider how you plan to compensate them for their work.

Ways to Pay Employees

There are different ways to compensate employees for their work. Below are the most common ways. Recall that employers must pay payroll taxes and income tax estimates for hourly and salaried employees based on the employee's W-4.

Hourly Wages

For jobs where the hours worked have a fixed schedule, or where the number of hours worked varies, employees are often paid on an hourly basis. You are not required by law to provide many benefits to part-time employees, but you will have to pay overtime for any hours exceeding 40 hours per week.

Salaries

For jobs that require a long-term commitment and high skills, employees are often paid salaries, which are fixed amounts for a year. Salaried employees sometimes work more than 40 hours in order to get the job done. Salaries often include benefits such as health insurance, vacation time, and sick leave.

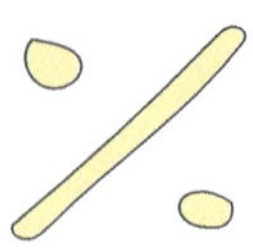

Commissions

One way to encourage high performance is to pay employees a commission. This is common in sales positions, such as car sales, real estate, and retail stores. Employees are paid a lower hourly rate or a salary and then keep a percentage of sales.

Contracts

Employees hired for a short-term project or service can be hired as independent contractors. Based on a contract agreement, you can pay independent contractors an hourly rate or agreed-upon amount in exchange for work.

3. Employee Chart

Complete the following table for the employees needed in your business.

Job Title	Job Description	Payment Type	Payment Amount

Types of Small Businesses

There are different legal structures for a business, which come with different tax reporting procedures. Here are the structures for small businesses:

Sole Proprietorship

This form of business is owned by one person, who receives all the profits, has complete control over the business, is the only employee, and is personally responsible for all debts or lawsuits against the business. Generally, income is reported by the individual on personal tax returns.

Partnership

A partnership is similar to a sole proprietorship, but involves more than one owner. The owners are personally responsible for all debts or lawsuits against the business. Generally, income is reported by the individuals on their personal tax returns.

Limited Liability Company (LLC)

A limited liability company (LLC) separates the personal finances of the owner(s) from those of the business. Profits can stay within the company or be distributed to the owner(s). The company is responsible for debts and lawsuits, but not the individual owner(s). LLCs can be owned by one person or more than one person.

Nonprofit Organization

Nonprofit organizations are similar to LLCs, in that those who work for the organization are paid an hourly rate or a salary, but the profits are kept within the business for further projects and are not distributed to owners.

The Operational Plan

In addition to the executive summary that he presented, Carlos needs to have an operational plan to show how he makes money. Showing the bank how the taco truck operates on a daily basis will help them determine if the taco truck is a good investment.

Products and Services

Garcia Tacos makes tacos with local organic ingredients. Carlos, the owner, makes a variety of tacos including steak, chicken and shrimp. His tacos sell for $3.75 each and cost him $2.15 to make. He sells the tacos to state employees and tourists during the lunch hour.

Goals

Carlos Garcia's goal is to increase sales by 10% in the next 3 months. He plans to do this by increasing his marketing efforts and painting a new sign on his truck

Employees

Currently Carlos is the only person working in the company. He cooks the food and sells it to customers. With a business loan, Carlos plans to hire an employee to take orders and sell the tacos to the customers. He would pay the employee $11 an hour.

Legal Structure

Garcia Tacos is a sole proprietorship with Carlos Garcia as the owner.

Section 7B: Homework

Part 1 - The Garcia Tacos' Operational Plan

Read Carlos' operational plan for the taco truck. Pretend you work for a bank and you decide which businesses will receive loans.

a. Based on his operational plan, would you lend money to his food truck? Why or why not?

b. What questions would you ask Carlos before lending him money?

Part 2 - Your Business

Write your own operational plan. Make sure to include your business name, logo, a business description and a SWOT analysis.

Part 3 - Analyze a Classmate's Plan

Trade your operational plan with one of your classmates. Again, pretend you work for a bank and get to decide if this business will receive a loan or not.

a. Based on their operational plan, would you lend money to this company? Why or why not?

b. What questions would you ask the owner before lending them money?

Section 7C: Marketing Plan

In Section 7B, you learned how to write an Operational Plan, which describes how a company operates. In Section 7C, you will learn about marketing and attracting customers to your business. You will compare your business to competitors to find your key strengths and learn how to advertise those strengths to customers.

Target Markets

Marketing Strategies

Customer Service

Create an Advertisement

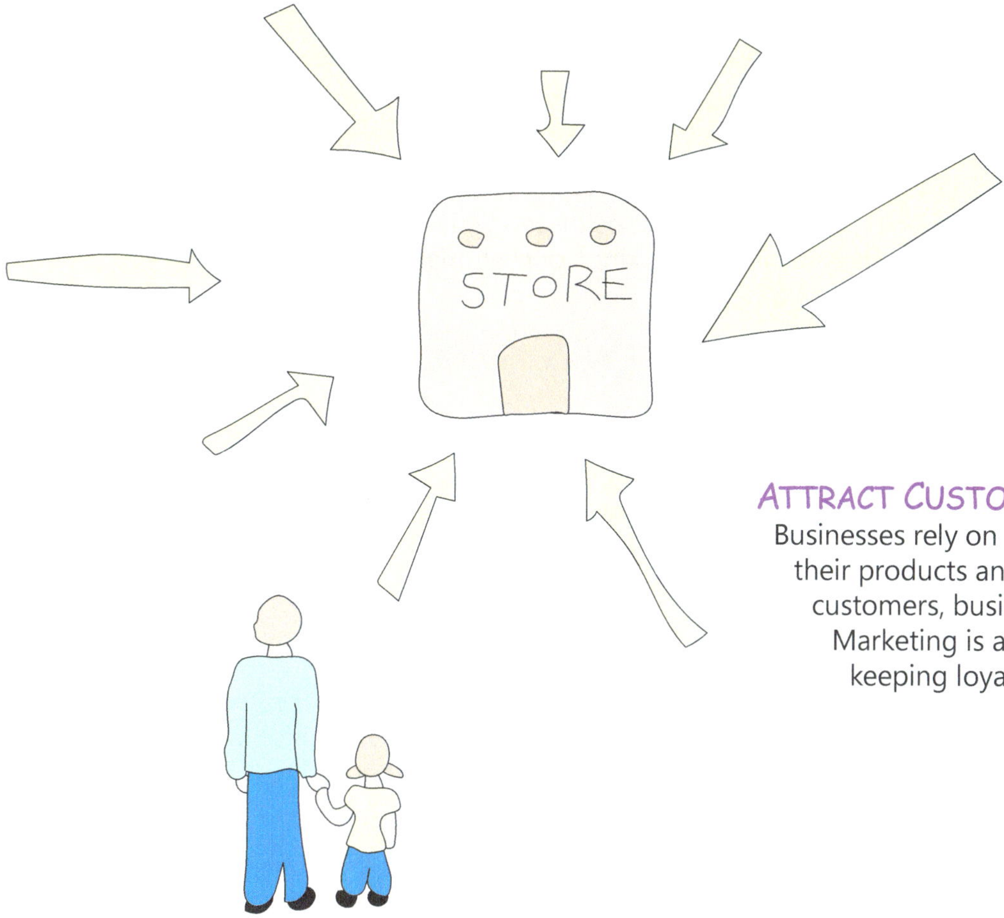

Attract Customers

Businesses rely on customers to buy their products and services. Without customers, businesses don't survive. Marketing is about attracting and keeping loyal customers.

1. What Do You Think?

A. What is an example of an advertisement that made you want to buy a product? Why?

B. What is an example of an advertisement that made you not want to buy a product? Why?

Marketing Principals

Although there are many ways to spread the word about your company, it is important to first consider your audience, why they want to buy your product, and what makes you unique.

Know Your Audience

There are many different groups of people and each has unique tastes and preferences. Knowing which kinds of customers you want will help you focus your marketing strategy.

Solve a Problem for Them

Once you know your customers, find out about their lives. What motivates them? What challenges do they face? What do they want? Do they have needs that aren't being met? Then figure out how your company will improve their lives and help to solve their problems.

Know What Makes You Unique

When you go into business, you will have competition. You need to figure out what makes your company unique so you can communicate to your customers why your company is a better fit for them.

2. What Do You Think?

A. Describe your audience.

B. What is a problem they face?

C. How will your product or service solve their problem and improve the quality of their lives?

D. What makes your product or service different from your competition?

Spread the Word

Once you identify your audience and why they want to do business with you, it's time to spread the word. This can be done through paid advertising. It can also be done through word of mouth. When customers do this it's free and effective.

Maintain Customer Loyalty

When establishing your business, keep in mind that people talk. A happy customer will keep doing business with you, but an unhappy customer will not only stop doing business with you, he will tell others about his experience and might write bad reviews online, potentially causing you to lose business. It is easier and more affordable to keep the customers you already have happy, than to get new ones.

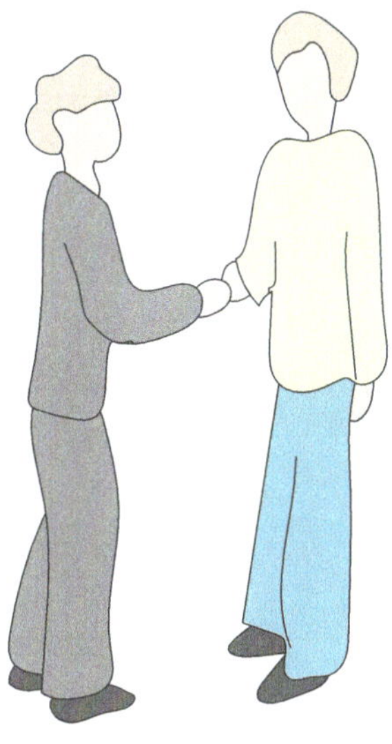

The Pros and Cons of Competition

One of the challenges that comes up when opening a business is competition. Although a threat, it can provide some benefits and make your company stronger.

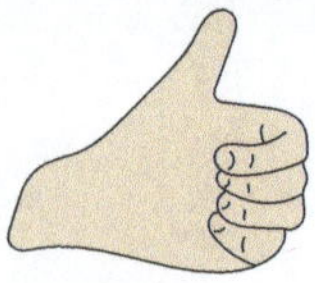

Pros

- Competition motivates you to continue to learn and grow.
- The fact that there is competition shows that there is a demand for your kind of business.
- When you have more business than you can handle, you can refer your customers to a cooperative competitor and vice versa.

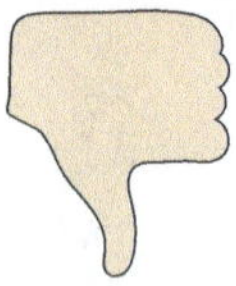

Cons

- Competition can take away customers from your business.
- Competition can force you to lower your prices.

Create a Competitor Analysis Chart

Business plans often include a competitor analysis chart that helps you compare your business to your competition. You are likely to be better than your competition in some areas and worse in others. This is normal and gives you a perspective about strengths and weaknesses. Knowing the key areas where you are better will help you market your products more effectively and attract the right customers. Here is a sample chart for the food truck.

Factor	Garcia Tacos' Truck	Southside Food Truck	Importance to Customers
Quality	Carlos has a degree in culinary arts and makes innovative and tasty tacos. He only uses local and organic ingredients.	The Southside Truck offers regular tacos and uses conventional ingredients. They taste good but are not innovative.	Medium importance
Customer Service	Carlos works by himself and has a hard time talking with customers while making tacos.	The Southside Truck has two employees and provides quick, friendly customer service.	High importance
Hours	Carlos' truck is only open during lunch hours.	The Southside Truck is open all day.	Low importance
Location	Carlos' truck is parked downtown where there is great foot traffic.	The Southside Truck is located in a neighborhood and is hard to find. Unless you know it's there, you won't look for it.	High importance

3. Now Your Turn ...

Create a competitor analysis chart for your business. Pick some factors that affect your business and fill in the chart below.

Factor	Your Company	Your Competition	Importance to Customers

Types of Advertising

There are many different types of advertising. All of them go back to the core principals of knowing your audience and why they want your products or services.

Social Media

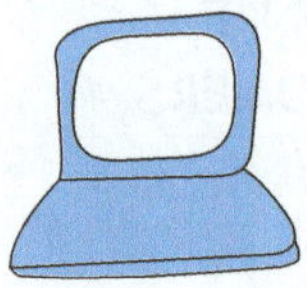

You can post videos, pictures, and text for free on social media sites, and you can pay to advertise or be promoted. It tends to attract a younger audience and can keep an ongoing relationship with customers. The downside is that your posts must be constantly updated, which takes time and energy, and customer feedback is public.

Radio

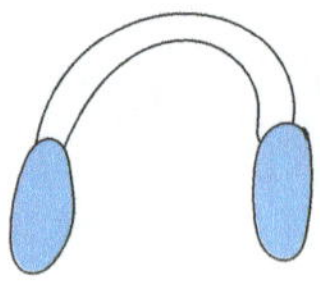

Advertising on the radio allows you to target your audience by choosing the type of station and time of day. You can repeat the same ad multiple times, potentially attracting diverse customers. The downside is that people listen to the radio for entertainment and news, not for the ads. Some listeners change the station or turn down the volume.

TV

Advertising on television is an expensive option, but it allows you to use both audio and visual communication. You can target your audience by choosing the station and time of day. Ads generally run repeatedly. As with radio, people may choose to change the channel or put your ad on mute.

Flyers

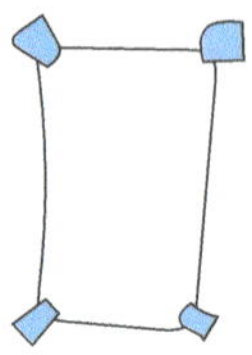

Flyers are relatively inexpensive and can be distributed around town. You can include coupons and promotional information, but many people ignore flyers or throw them away, creating trash.

Magazine/Newspaper

Advertising in newspapers and magazines can range from very expensive to inexpensive because you have a wide range of options about the size of the ad and whether it's in color or black and white. You can also target your audience by the publication you choose.

Billboards

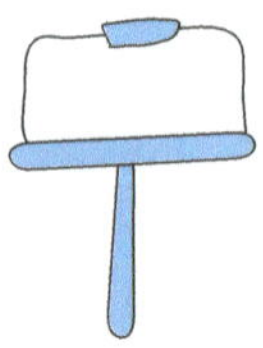

Using a billboard is dependent on the location. Everyone who drives in that area will see it, so you can reach a large and diverse audience. The downside is that billboards are expensive and can only contain a small amount of information, because people going by won't be able to read a lot of text.

4. Create a Marketing Budget ...

A. Choose a type of advertising from the list on the previous page and do some research. How much would it cost to run an ad for your business?

B. How many times will you run the ad in the first year of your business?

C. What will the total cost of advertising be for your first year?

5. What Do You Think?

A. How many customers do you think you will get from your ad?

B. Do you think it is a worthwhile expense? Why or why not?

Garcia Tacos' Marketing Plan

Marketing is an important part of attracting customers, especially as a new business. Garcia Tacos wants to get the word out about their great product and increase revenue by utilizing a marketing plan.

Products and Services

Garcia Tacos targets state employees and tourists. The truck is parked on the plaza during the lunch hour. The people who buy his tacos are hungry, want food that tastes good and is reasonably priced. They want food that can be prepared quickly and be eaten on the go. Many of the state employees who buy from Garcia Tacos become regular customers because they enjoy the taste of the food.

Competition

Garcia Tacos has several competitors. There are 3 other food trucks on the plaza. One sells Middle Eastern food. Another sells Indian food and one sells fajitas. The fajitas truck has stolen 25% of Carlos' business.

Advertising

Carlos plans to put an ad in the local newspaper. He also created an online fan page and uploaded pictures of the taco truck and the food available. Carlos is working on developing a website for the business which will provide hours and location details.

Section 7C: Homework

Part 1 - The Garcia Tacos' Marketing Plan

Read Carlos' marketing plan for his taco truck. Pretend you work for a bank and you decide which businesses will receive loans.

a. Based on his marketing plan, would you lend money to his food truck? Why or why not?

b. What questions would you ask Carlos before lending him money?

Part 2 - Your Business

Write your own marketing plan. Make sure to include your business name, logo, a business description and a SWOT analysis.

Part 3 - Analyze a Classmate's Plan

Trade your marketing plan with one of your classmates. Again, pretend you work for a bank and get to decide if this business will receive a loan or not.

a. Based on their marketing plan, would you lend money to this company? Why or why not?

b. What questions would you ask the owner before lending them money?

Section 7D: Financial Plan

In Section 7C, you created a Marketing Plan to attract customers to your business. Marketing is important because it can generate sales and work like an investment in your business. In this section, you will learn how to put all the information and documents for your business into one place and make a Financial Plan.

Will You Make Any Money?

No one can predict the future, but math is a powerful tool to check the facts. Using math to look at different scenarios can inform you about what's possible for your business. Making financial projections increases the chances that a bank will lend you the money you need to get started.

The Financial Plan

The last section of your business plan tells your potential investors or loan officers how you plan to make money at your business.

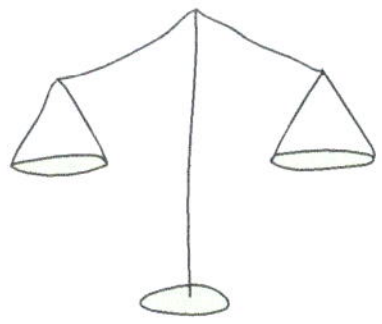

Break-Even Analysis

In Section 5B, you learned the break-even formula. Financial plans include the formula to show the minimum product pricing in order to break even.

Balance Sheet

In Section 6A, you learned how to make a Balance Sheet. Financial Plans include a Balance Sheet for your business.

Financial Projections

Although it is impossible to know how much money a business will make in the future, financial projections provide educated guesses based on similar businesses and current circumstances.

The Health of a Business

You can have a great business idea to make innovative and high quality products and offer excellent services, but if you spend more than you earn, your business won't be healthy. If you operate under a loss for too long, your company will fail.

Successful Business | Break-Even Business | Unsuccessful Business

1. What Do You Think?

A. How much money do you think you can make from your business in the first year?

B. How much do you think you can make after 3 years?

Financial Projections

When you make projections about your business, you will be combining facts with guesswork. Since it's impossible to know what the future holds, there are different projects that can simulate different business realities..

Liberal Projections

Liberal projections are the most optimistic. They assume your company will grow quickly, make a lot of money, and spend little. This is the best-case scenario, but it's rare for business to be successful right away. Usually it takes time to become established.

Moderate Projections

Moderate projections are still optimistic. They assume your company will grow and you will make money. The only difference is that moderate projections predict growth.

Conservative Projections

Conservative projections assume that growth will happen very slowly. Because they predict little to no growth or profit, they tend to favor less risky business ventures and decisions.

2. What Do You Think?

A. What kind of financial projections are you most likely to make?

B. What are the pros and cons to the kind of projection you will make?

Start-Up Costs

Starting a business requires money. Some companies will need more capital than others. The Financial Plan will list the specific costs required to start up your business.

Rent

Your business may need to rent a space, such as a store front, an office, or a factory.

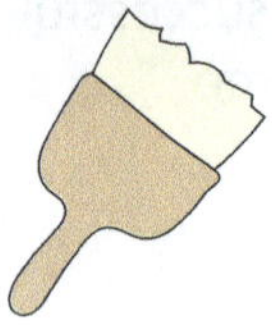

Space Renovations

Some spaces may need repairs or decorations before you can open your business. These renovations will cost money.

Equipment or Machinery

You may need to buy equipment to make or sell your products.

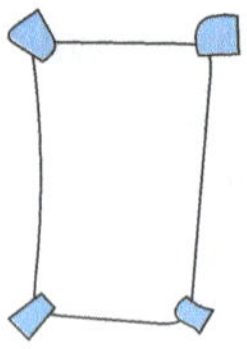

Advertising

Most businesses need to advertise to attract new customers to their business.

Business Licenses

Setting up your business will require filing paperwork and registering with local, state, and federal governments.

Trademarks, Copyrights, or Patents

Your company may need to buy a trademark to protect your company's name or logo. If you are creating art or print documents to sell, you may need to purchase a copyright. And if you are inventing a new product, you'll need a patent.

Inventory

You will need enough products on-hand to sell and have access to inventory for delivery.

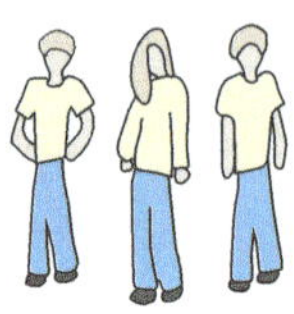

Employees

You will need to pay your employees.

Raising Start-Up Capital

Starting a business can be expensive and it's rare to be able to afford all of the costs on your own. Below are some of the more common ways to raise money for your business.

Business Loans

You can apply for a business loan with your bank or credit union. You will need to provide business documents, including your Business Plan, Balance Sheets, and Income Statements. Most financial institutions won't lend money to a business until it has been in business for two years.

Investors

You can get an investor who will pay for your start-up costs, but who will then own part of your business. Depending on the terms of your agreement, you can pay your investor back plus interest and gain full ownership.

Crowdfunding

You can use crowdfunding websites to promote your idea and receive contributions from supporters, some of whom you might not even know.

Personal Savings

If you plan ahead, you can save money each month to help you open a business in the future.

Family Contributions

Many companies get financial help from their family and friends when they start. Make sure people know the risks involved before committing money.

3. What Do You Think?

A. How do you plan to raise money for your business?

B. How will you convince people to lend or give you money?

Break-Even Formula

In Section 5B, you learned how to use the break-even formula. Financial Plans include a break-even point to show how many products you must sell and how much you will need to charge for each product in order to break even. In order to be profitable, you will have to charge or sell more than the break-even point.

$$\text{Selling Price}\left(\text{Number of Units Sold}\right) = \text{Unit Cost}\left(\text{Number of Units Sold}\right) + \text{Start-Up Costs}$$

4. Your Break-Even Point ...

A. What are your start-up costs?

B. How much will your selling price be?

C. What is your unit cost to produce your product?

D. Use the break-even formula to determine the number of products you must sell in order to break even.

The Balance Sheet

Financial plans also include a balance sheet to show the relationship between what the business owns and what it owes.

5. Your Balance Sheet ...

Refer to Section 6A to help you make a Balance Sheet for your business. Record your answers below.

	A	B	C	D
1	Assets		Liabilities and Equity	
2	Cash		Accounts Payable	
3	Accounts Receivable		Long-Term Liabilities	
4	Inventory			
5	Current Assets		Liabilities	
6				
7	Taco Truck		Retained Earnings	
8	Fixed Assets		Owner's Equity	
9				
10	Total Assets		Total Liabilities & Equity	

Garcia Tacos' Financial Plan

Putting together all the research into the business, Garcia Tacos wants presents a complete business plan for their business, including financial projections about business in the future.

Break-Even Point

Carlos has fixed expenses of $938.15 per month. The unit cost for each taco is $2.15 and the selling price is $3.75. He needs to sell 586 tacos per month to break even.

Balance Sheet

	A	B	C	D
1	Assets		Liabilities and Equity	
2	Cash	$2,000.00	Accounts Payable	$50.00
3	Accounts Receivable	$300.00	Long-Term Liabilities	$48,000.00
4	Inventory	$700.00		
5	Current Assets	$3,000.00	Liabilities	$48,050.00
6				
7	Taco Truck	$60,000.00	Retained Earnings	$5,000.00
8	Fixed Assets	$60,000.00	Owner's Equity	$9,950.00
9				
10	Total Assets	$63,000.00	Total Liabilities & Equity	$63,000.00

Financial Projections

Carlos expects to attract more customers over time. In the next year he expects to sell 2,000 tacos each month. In the next 3 years, he plans to increase that to 3,500 tacos per month.

Section 7D: Homework

Part 1 - The Garcia Tacos' Financial Plan

Read Carlos' financial plan for his taco truck. Pretend you work for a bank and you decide which businesses will receive loans.

a. Based on the financial plan, would you lend money to his food truck? Why or why not?

b. What questions would you ask Carlos before lending him money?

Part 2 - Your Business

Write your own financial plan. Make sure to include your break-even point, balance sheet and financial projections.

Part 3 - Analyze a Classmate's Plan

Trade your financial plan with one of your classmates. Again, pretend you work for a bank and get to decide if this business will receive a loan or not.

a. Based on their financial plan, would you lend money to this company? Why or why not?

b. What questions would you ask the owner before lending them money?

Appendix A: Spreadsheet Basics

Columns and Rows

Columns

Columns are labeled with the letters of the alphabet and run vertically.

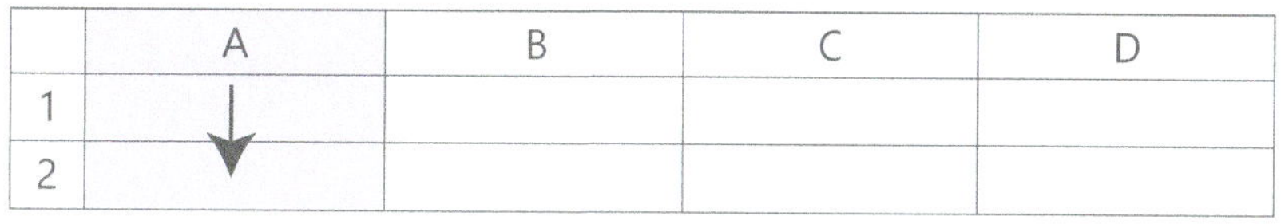

Rows

Rows are labeled with numbers and run horizontally.

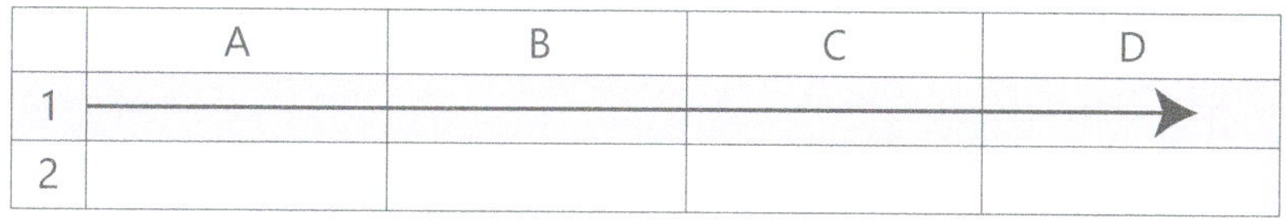

Cells

A cell is the intersection of a row and a column.

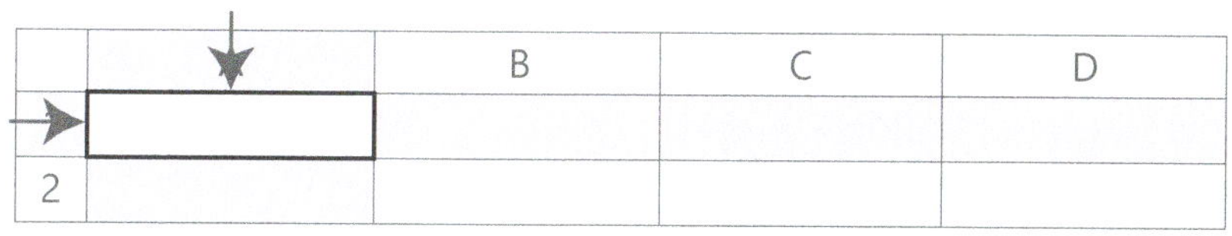

Selecting Cells

Select a Single Cell

To select a cell, click once on the cell. Be sure to click inside the cell, not on an edge. Once the cell is selected, you can type letters, numbers, and other characters in it.

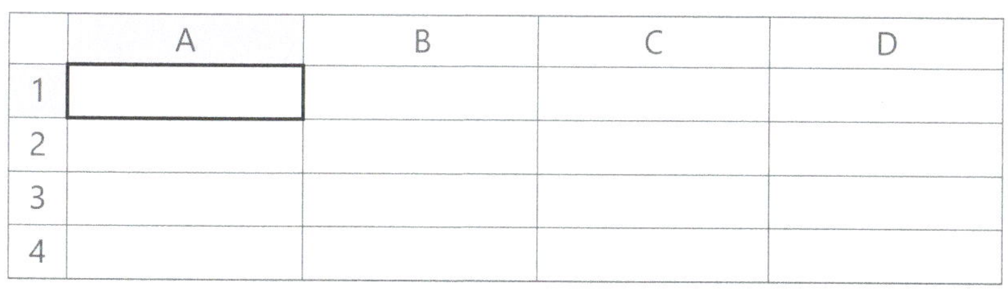

Select Multiple Cells

Click on the first cell (top left), hold and drag the mouse until you reach the last cell (bottom right). Then let go of the mouse.

Note: All of the cells you select will become highlighted except the first cell you clicked on.

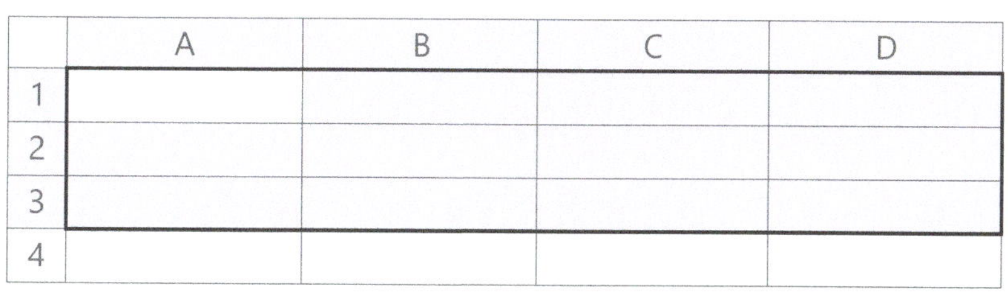

Naming a Cell

Select a Cell

To select a cell, click inside it.

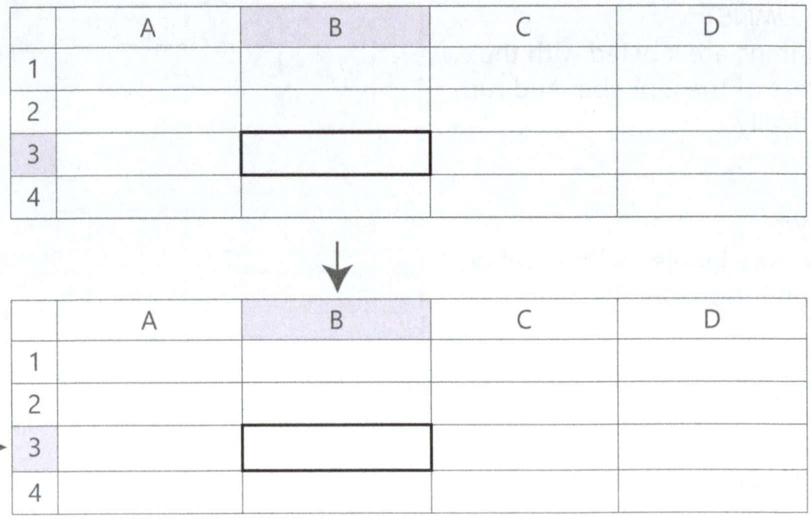

Cell Names

Every cell has a specific name. Once you select a cell, the column letter and row number become highlighted. This tells you the name of that cell. In this case, B and 3 are highlighted, so the cell name is B3.

Note: The letter always goes first and the number second.

Expanding a Cell

Increasing Row Height

Type the first word of your heading. Then press alt and enter on your keyboard. Type in the rest of your heading and press enter.

If you have a Mac, press option *and* enter.

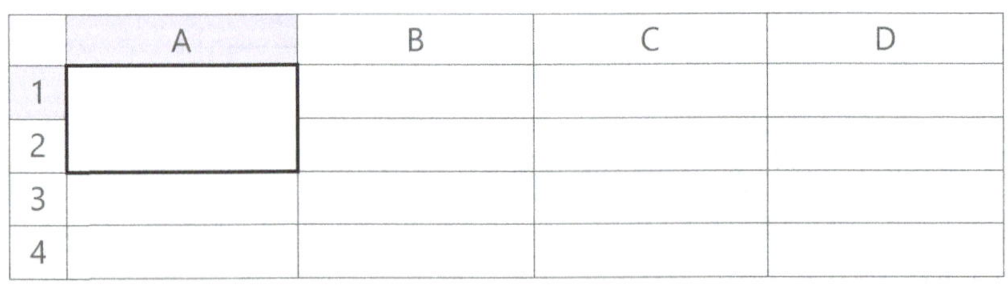

Cursors in a Spreadsheet

Selection Tool

To select a cell, click in the middle of it.

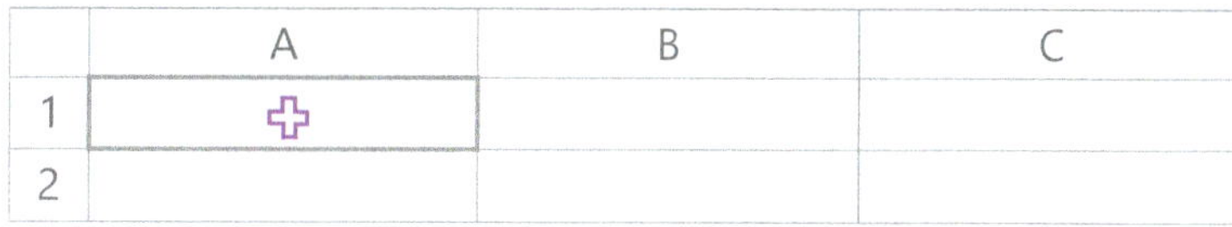

Move Tool

To move a cell to another location, click on the edge of it and drag it to the desired location.

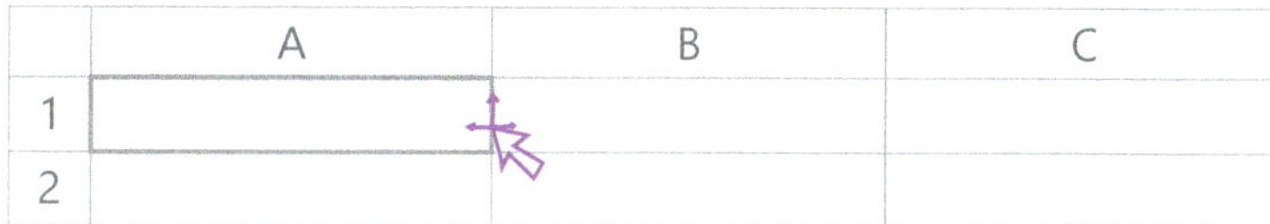

Fill Handle

To copy information and formulas into the rest of your spreadsheet, select the cell and then double-click on the bottom right-hand corner of the cell.

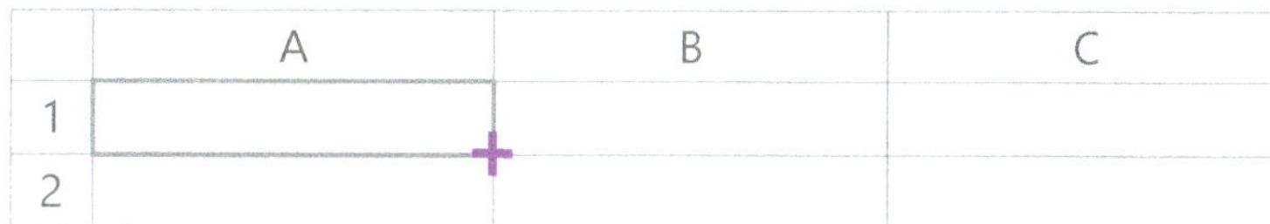

Column Selection

To select an entire column, click on the column letter.

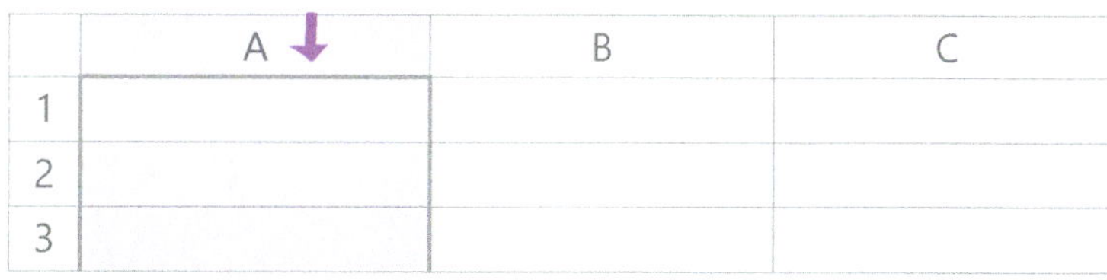

Column Width Tool

To change the width of your column, click, hold, and drag on the border between the column letters.

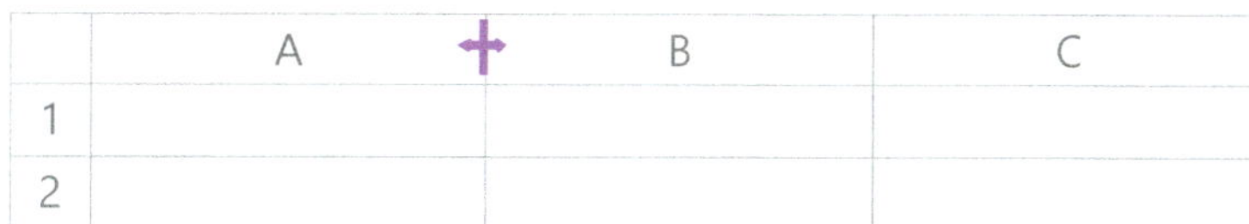

Row Selection Tool

To select an entire row, click on the row number.

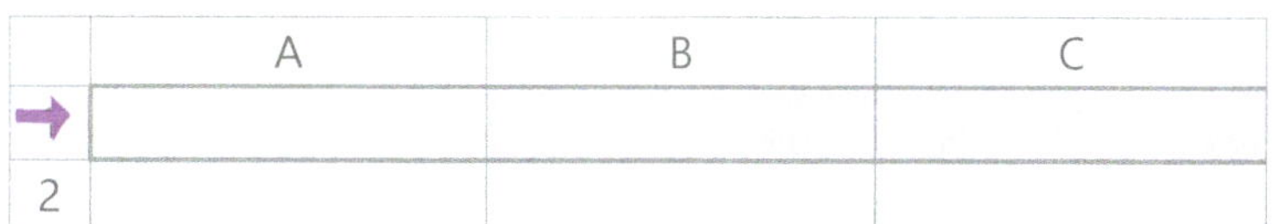

Row Height Tool

To change the height of a row, click, hold, and drag on the border between row numbers.

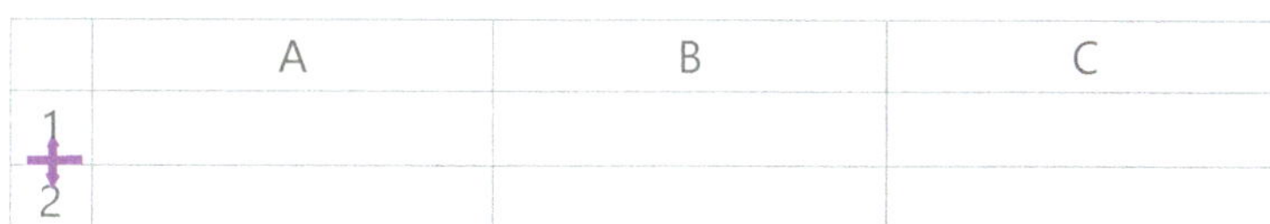

Appendix B: Essential Math Skills

Sign Rules

When Adding or Subtracting	When Multiplying or Dividing
If signs are the same, add the numbers and keep the same sign.	If signs are the same, the answer will be positive
3 + 4 = 7	3 (4) = 12
- 3 - 4 = - 7	-3 (-4) = 12
If signs are different, subtract the numbers and keep the larger number's sign.	If signs are different, the answer will be negative
3 - 4 = - 1	3 (-4) = -12
- 3 + 4 = 1	-3 (4) = -12

Solving Equations

Step 1: If there are like terms on the same side of the equals sign, combine them.

Step 2: If there are variables on both sides of the equals sign, cancel one of them by doing the opposite operation to both sides.

Step 3: If there are constants on both sides of the equals sign, cancel one of them by doing the opposite operation to both sides.

Step 4: If there is a number in front of the variable (coefficient), divide both sides by that number.

Percent Conversions

To turn a Percentage into a Decimal	To turn a Decimal into a Percentage
Divide the percentage by 100	Multiply the decimal by 100
75% ÷ 100 = 0.75	0.75 x 100 - 75%

Place Values

1	0	0,	0	0	0,	0	0	0	.	0	0	0	0
hundred-millions	ten-millions	millions	hundred-thousands	ten-thousands	thousands	hundreds	tens	ones		tenths	hundredths	thousandths	ten-thousandths

Rounding

Step 1: Identify the number in the place value you want to round to and underline it.

Step 2: Look at the number to the right of the underlined number. If that number is 5 or greater, add 1 to the underlined number and drop everything after it.

Round to the thousandths place:

15.73<u>6</u>82 = 15.73<u>7</u>

Step 3: If the number to the right is less than five, keep the underlined number the same and drop everything after it.

Round to the hundredths place:

11.8<u>2</u>4 = 11.8<u>2</u>

Order of Operations

Step 1: Perform any calculations that are inside parentheses.

Step 2: Evaluate any exponents.

Step 3: Do any multiplication or division, as they appear from left to right.

Step 4: Do any addition or subtraction, as they appear from left to right.

Appendix C: Glossary of Terms

Accumulation Phase
The period of time during which payments are made into an annuity account.

Amortization Schedule
A table that shows the progress in paying off a mortgage and details how much of each monthly payment goes toward the principal and how much goes toward interest.

Annual
Period of one year.

Annually
Occurring once a year.

Annuity
An account to which regular payments are made each month and that earns interest. At the end of the accumulation phase, the account makes regular payments to the recipient and is often used for retirement savings.

Annual Percentage Rate (APR)
Annual Percentage Rate (APR) is the percentage used to calculate the interest on money borrowed or invested.

APR
An abbreviation for Annual Percentage Rate.

Balance - Credit Card
The money owed on a credit card.

Bank Statement
A record showing all of the money deposited and withdrawn over a set period of time.

Break-Even Analysis
An analysis that shows the price a business must charge in order to recoup the cost of producing a product or providing a service.

Bronze Plan
A health insurance plan that offers the lowest premiums but also the highest deductibles. It is designed for people who do not have a history of medical conditions and are in good health.

Budget
A money management plan that tracks earnings and spending (usually monthly). It can be used to compare proposed (projected) spending to actual spending to show progress toward long-term financial goals and to aid in making informed decisions.

C

Car Insurance
Financial protection for the cost of repairs and medical expenses resulting from car accidents. Full coverage insurance covers one's own vehicle, while liability insurance covers the cost of repairs to others' vehicles. Coverage may also include financial protection in cases of theft or non-collision damage. Also referred to as auto insurance.

Cash Back - Credit Card
Some credit cards issue rebates based on qualifying purchases. These rebates, known as "cash back," are an incentive to use the credit card. Maintaining a balance (or owing) on a credit card may result in paying more interest than the cash back rebate. Paying off the full balance every month is the best way to take advantage of cash back rebates.

Compound Interest
Interest that is calculated periodically and then added to the principal.

Coefficient
The number component of a variable term, written in front of the variable and indicating multiplication. For example, "3x" means "three times the variable x."

Compound Period
The period of time before earned interest is added to the principal. Shorter periods indicate more frequent compounding.

Conservative Projections
When making a budget or opening a business, conservative projections are informed guesses (estimates) that involve little risk. Conservative projections do not underestimate expenses and do not overestimate revenues.

Constant
A constant is something that does not change. In mathematics, a constant is a number on its own (without a variable).

Co-pay
Co-pay refers to a fixed dollar amount paid for services as part of a health insurance plan. Costs vary based on the specifics of the health insurance plan.

Co-insurance
Co-insurance refers to a percentage of medical bills that must be paid by the insured person for services received as part of a health insurance plan. Percentages vary based on the specifics of the health insurance plan.

Costs
The amount of money spent on products and services.

Credit Card
A card that allows you to borrow money up to the card's credit limit to make purchases. Interest is charged on purchases unless the entire balance is paid off each month. APRs, minimum payments and penalties for late payments vary based on the terms of the card.

Credit Limit
A limit on the amount of money one can charge on your credit card, based on credit score and credit history.

Credit Score
A personal numerical score based on one's credit history and perceived creditworthiness. There are several credit reporting agencies, each with its own scoring system. Generally, higher credit scores correspond to lower APRs for loans and lower credit scores correspond to higher APRs.

Daily
Occurring 365 times a year.

Debt
Borrowed money that one agrees to repay with interest.

Deductible
The amount of money one must spend on medical care before the insurance plan begins to pay its percentage.

Demand
The desire of consumers for a good or service.

Deposit
Money, such as a paycheck or cash, put into a bank account.

Disposable Income
The money you have left over each month after paying for your fixed expenses and saving a percent of your income. Found by taking the total (take-home) income and subtracting the amount put into savings and total expenses.

Distribution Phase
The period of time, often beginning at the time of retirement, during which an account makes regular payments to the recipient of an annuity investment.

Down Payment
The amount paid up front (or down) as a percentage of the total cost when making a large purchase, as for a car or house. The remainder of the cost of the purchase is paid by the lender as a loan to the purchaser and must be paid off by him/her with interest.

Equation
A relationship of equality in which two expressions are equal and variables represent unknown quantities.

Expected Value
When dealing with a risk, such as when investing money, this looks at the chances of winning versus losing.

Expenses
The amount of money anticipated or actually spent on goods and services.

Expression
A collection of symbols (numbers, variables and operators) that express a quantity.

Feasibility
The chances of your business being able to earn more money than it spends.

Financial Goals
Personal goals that you want to achieve that will require money such as buying a house or going to college.

Fixed Costs
Costs that do not change based on frequency or volume.

Fixed Expenses
The amount of money you have to spend on your needs such as having a place to live, food to eat and transportation.

Frequency
The amount of times you spend money on something, save money or earn interest within a year.

Full Coverage Car Insurance
Protects yourself as well as the other driver in case a car accident happens.

Gas Mileage
The amount of miles you can travel on one gallon of gas, abbreviated as m.p.g.

Gold Plan
A health insurance plan that offers a higher premium with a lower deductible. It is designed for someone with a history of health problems who needs regular medication and treatment.

Health Insurance
An insurance plan that pays for doctor's visits, medication, medical emergencies and surgery.

Home Owner's Insurance
An insurance plan to protects your house from theft, damage, and natural disasters.

Inequalities
A relationship in which two expressions are unequal and variables represent unknown quantities.

Insurance
A plan you purchase to protect yourself or your property in the case of emergencies, accidents or other unexpected events.

Interest
In borrowing money, it is the charge, as a percentage, that you have to pay for the privilege of borrowing. When saving money, it is the money you earn for the financial institution's privilege of being able to loan out that money to others.

Introductory APR
Many credit cards offer 0% interest for the first few months you have the card. Then they increase the APR.

Investing
When you put money into a fund or account that will pay interest or bear a potential return. There is always a risk of losing money when investing.

IRA
Stands for Individual Retirement Account and is a retirement plan you can set up with your bank or other investment firm allowing you to save money and earn interest long-term. Upon retirement, the Distribution Phase begins, and you will receive monthly payments.

Liability Car Insurance
An insurance plan that covers only the other driver and his/her car in case of a car accident. It is the minimum insurance coverage permitted in most states.

Liberal Projections
When making a budget or opening a business, you will have to guess how much you will earn and spend in the future. Liberal projections are guesses that involve a lot of risk. Often it involves thinking you will earn more and have to spend less.

Life Insurance
An insurance plan that provides your family or a designated person money when you pass away.

Like Terms
Expressions containing the same variable and thus which can be combined.

Loan Repayment Schedule
A chart that shows how much principal and interest you pay each month while paying off a loan. It also shows the total amount of interest you will pay over the length of the loan.

M

Markup
Increase in price, often based on a percentage of the original price.

Minimum Payment
When paying off a credit card, it is the minimum amount you must pay without being penalized. Each credit card company is different, but many require that you repay 2% of your balance each month.

Moderate Projections
When making a budget or opening a business, you will have to guess how much you will earn and spend in the future. Moderate projections are guesses that involve a medium amount of risk.

Monthly
Something that happens 12 times a year.

Monthly Income
The amount of money you earn each month.

Monthly Payment
For borrowed money, this is the amount you must pay each month.

Monthly Savings
A percentage of your monthly income that goes into a savings account each month.

Mortgage
The name of a loan used to buy a house.

N

Needs
Refers to expenses, such as rent or food, that you cannot live without.

Number of Units Sold
A figure that represents how many of a particular item that has been sold.

O

Odds
Another word for probability. It means the chances of something happening or not happening.

Operating Costs
The expenses needed to keep a business running, such as rent, utilities, and employee salaries.

Original Price
The price of a good or service before it is marked up or down.

Out-of-Pocket Maximum
A limit to the amount of money you have to spend if you have insurance. Once you spend that amount of money, your insurance plan will pay for everything else covered for the rest of the year.

Percent
Out of 100.

Percent Discount
The reduction of a price based on a percentage of the original selling price.

Percent Markup
The increase of a price based on a percentage of the original price.

Pie Chart
A graph that is in the shape of a circle with slices to show how the parts of something relate to the whole amount. The whole pie chart is equal to 100%.

Platinum Plan
A health insurance plan that offers the highest premiums but the lowest deductibles. It is designed for people with a long history of health care needs or who are at a higher risk.

Premium
The amount of money paid to be covered under an insurance plan. It is usually paid monthly.

Preventative Care
Actions you can take to keep yourself healthy, such as diet and exercise. It can also refer to caring for your property, such as getting an oil change or washing your car. These actions can greatly reduce the cost of medical expenses and repairs to property. Preventative care in the form of annual physical exams by your doctor are covered by all Affordable Care Act plans.

Principal
The amount of money you borrow or invest before any interest is counted.

Prioritizing Goals
It is human nature to want many things. Prioritizing is the process of putting needs before wants, and then deciding which goals are the most important and worth pursuing.

Probability
The chance of something happening or not happening. The same as "odds."

Projected
When creating a budget or running a business, it is the money you think you will spend and earn in that month.

Prorate
Expenses often happen at different times of the year. Prorating them is finding the average amount you will spend each month.

Pros and Cons
The process of creating a list of the positive and negative sides of a situation to help you make better decisions.

Q

Quarterly
Happening four times a year.

Quality
Used to denote excellence in comparing one product to other products.

Quantity
Used to denote the amount or number of a product.

R

Renter's Insurance
An insurance plan that protects your material possessions in case of theft, damage or natural disasters.

Resale
The act of selling products previously bought.

Resale Price
The price at which products are sold, generally by a business that has bought the products wholesale.

Retirement
A period of time later in life when you stop working or only work part-time. Being able to afford this time in your life requires careful planning and long-term saving.

Rewards - Credit Cards
Many credit cards offer cash back, gift cards or frequent flier miles to encourage people to use their cards.

Risk
The possibility of losing money, getting into an accident, having a medical emergency or experience another unexpected life event that costs money.

Sales
The amount of money you make from customers who buy your products or pay for your services.

Sale Price
The price at which a product is sold, often at a lower price than previously advertised.

Selling Price
The amount of money something costs.

Semiannually
Something that happens twice a year.

Service
The performance of work for others, generally for a fee.

Silver Plan
A health insurance plan that offers low premiums and high deductibles. It is designed for someone who is in relatively good health and has few health care needs.

Simple Interest
When the amount of interest stays the same each year and is not compounded.

Simplify
To perform operations in order to write an expression with as few terms as possible.

Social Security
A retirement savings plan created by the government. During your working years you contribute a percentage of your income to Social Security, and when you retire you get a monthly check from the government to help pay for your retirement. Is is NEVER enough to pay all of your expenses.

Solve
The act of isolating a variable on one side of an equation in order to determine its value.

Start-Up Costs
The expenses needed to start a business. This includes business licenses, lawyer fees, equipment, etc.

Supply
The availability of goods or services.

T

Terms
Values represented by numbers, variables or a combination of numbers and variables separated by operational symbols, such as for addition, subtraction, multiplication ...

Time-Line of a Goal
The length of time needed to reach a financial goal.

Trade Discount
The reduction in price of goods or services below the retail price.

U

Unit
A single item.

Unit Costs
The cost of a single item.

V

Variable
A letter, such as "x," used to represent an unknown quantity.

Vision Insurance
An insurance plan that covers eye exams, glasses, contact lenses and medical procedures involving your eyes.

W

Wants
Expenses that provide fun, convenience and enjoyment but are not crucial for survival.

Weekly
Something that happens 52 times a year.

Withdraw
Anytime you spend from or take money out of your bank account.

Wholesale
The sale of goods and services, often at a price below retail, to businesses that resell the goods or services.

Wholesale Price
The price at which goods and services are bought directly from a supplier, generally lower than the retail price.

APPENDIX D: FORMULAS

1A LONG-TERM SAVINGS

Use this spreadsheet to find how much you could save over several years. You will need to know your monthly income, the percent you plan to save each month, and the total number of years.

	A	B	C	D
1	Monthly Income	% Monthly Savings	Yearly Savings	Long-Term Savings
2	TYPE IN THE INCOME	= A2 * THE PERCENT	= B2 * 12	= C2 * THE NUMBER OF YEARS

1B FREQUENCY OF EXPENSES

The frequency of an expense (how often it occurs) is an important part of creating your budget. Below are some commons frequencies.

ANNUALLY
1 time per year

QUARTERLY
4 times per year

WEEKLY
52 times per year

SEMIANNUALLY
2 times per year

MONTHLY
12 times per year

DAILY
365 times per year

1B PRORATE MONTHLY COSTS

Expenses occur at different times of the year, and some occur more frequently than others. Prorating will show you the average amount you spend each month. Use the frequency of expenses chart shown above.

	A	B	C	D	E
1	Expense	Frequency	Cost	Annual Cost	Monthly Cost
2	TYPE IN THE NAME OF THE EXPENSE	TYPE IN THE FREQUENCY	TYPE IN THE COST	= B2 * C2	= D2/12

1C DISPOSABLE INCOME

Most of your income will need to go toward paying for needs such as rent, food, and trasportation. What's left after savings and expesnes is disposable income.

	A	B	C	D
1	Monthly Income	% Monthly Savings	Fixed Expenses	Disposable Income
2	TYPE IN THE INCOME	= A2 * THE PERCENT	TYPE IN THE EXPENSES	= A2 - B2 - C2

1D BUDGET

A budget is a way to keep track of your expenses and income each month. It can help you make informed decisions and plan for long-term goals.

	A	B	C	D
1	Budget	Percent	Projected	Actual
2	Income		TYPE IN INCOME	TYPE IN ACUTAL INCOME
3	Savings	TYPE IN PERCENT OF SAVINGS	= B3 * C2	TYPE IN ACTUAL SAVINGS
4				
5	Expense		TYPE IN EXPENSE	TYPE IN ACTUAL SPENDING
6	Expense		TYPE IN EXPENSE	TYPE IN ACTUAL SPENDING
7	Expense		TYPE IN EXPENSE	TYPE IN ACTUAL SPENDING
8	Expense		TYPE IN EXPENSE	TYPE IN ACTUAL SPENDING
9	Expense		TYPE IN EXPENSE	TYPE IN ACTUAL SPENDING
10	Total Expenses		= SUM(C4:C9)	
11	Disposable Income		= C2 - C3 - C10	
12				
13	Financial Goal	TYPE IN PERCENT OF GOAL	= B13 * C11	TYPE IN ACTUAL SPENDING
14	Financial Goal	TYPE IN PERCENT OF GOAL	= B14 * C11	TYPE IN ACTUAL SPENDING
15	Financial Goal	TYPE IN PERCENT OF GOAL	= B15 * C11	TYPE IN ACTUAL SPENDING

2A SIMPLE INTEREST

Use this spreadsheet when the amount of interest stays the same each year.

	A	B	C	D
1	Year	Principal	APR	Interest
2	1	TYPE IN THE PRINCIPAL	TYPE IN THE APR	= B2 * C2
3	2	= B2	= C2	=B3 * C3

2A COMPOUND INTEREST

Use this spreadsheet when interest is compounded annually.

	A	B	C	D
1	Year	Principal	APR	Interest
2	1	TYPE IN THE PRINCIPAL	TYPE IN THE APR	= B2 * C2
3	2	= B2 + D2	= C2	=B3 * C3

2B COMPOUND INTEREST WITH PERIODS

Use this spreadsheet when interest is compounded several times per year.

	A	B	C	D	E
1	Period	Principal	APR	Periods per Year	Interest
2	1	TYPE IN THE PRINCIPAL	TYPE IN THE APR	TYPE IN THE PERIODS PER YEAR	= B2 * C2/D2
3	2	= B2 + E2	= C2	= D2	= B3 * C3/D3

2C MONTHLY PAYMENT (PMT)

When you get a loan, you will have to pay a fixed amount each month until the loan is paid off. You can use the PMT function in a spreadsheet to find your monthly payment.

	A	B	C
1	=PMT(INTEREST RATE/12,NUMBER OF YEARS*12,-PRINCIPAL)		
2			

2C LOAN REPAYMENT SCHEDULE

When you take out a loan, you make a monthly payment. Part of that payment goes toward interest and part goes toward paying off the loan principal. A loan repayment schedule will show you how much interest you pay each month.

	A	B	C	D	E	F
1	Month	Principal	APR	Monthly Payment	Amount Paid on Interest	Amount Paid on Principal
2	1	TYPE IN THE PRINCIPAL	TYPE IN THE APR	USE THE PMT FUNCTION	= B2 * C2/12	= D2 - E2
3	2	= B2 - F2	= C2	= D2	= B3 * C3/12	= D3 - E3

2D PAYING OFF A CREDIT CARD

Credit cards are different than loans because the amount you own can change over time. Also, your payment can change. Use this spreadsheet to see what happens when you just pay the minimum on your credit card.

	A	B	C	D	E	F
1	Month	Balance	APR	Minimum Payment	Amount Paid on Interest	Amount Paid on Balance
2	1	TYPE IN THE BALANCE	TYPE IN THE APR	= B2 * 2%	= B2 * C2/12	= D2 - E2
3	2	= B2 - F2	= C2	= B3 * 2%	= B3 * C3/12	= D3 - E3

3B ANNUITIES

Annuities are savings plans that earn interest. You pay a set amount each month. Over time, your amount of savings and the interest you earn on those savings adds up.

	A	B	C	D	E
1	Month	Balance	APR	Interest	Payment
2	1	0	TYPE IN THE APR	= B2 * C2/12	TYPE IN THE PAYMENT
3	2	= B2 + D2 + E2	= C2	= B3 * C3/12	= E2

3C AUTO & PROPERTY INSURANCE WHEN YOU MEET YOUR DEDUCTIBLE

When you have auto insurance, renters insurance, or homeowners insurance, you pay your deductible before the insurance company begins to pay for repairs. Use this spreadsheet if you have met your deductible.

	A	B	C	D	E
1	Cost of Repairs	Deductible	Annual Premium	What Insurance Pays	What You Pay
2	TYPE IN THE COST OF REPAIRS	TYPE IN THE DEDUCTIBLE	TYPE IN THE PREMIUM	= A2 - B2 + C2	= B2 + C2

3C AUTO & PROPERTY INSURANCE WHEN YOU DO NOT MEET YOUR DEDUCTIBLE

If the costs of repairs does not exceed your deductible, the insurance company will not cover the cost of repairs. Use this spreadsheet if you don't meet your deductible.

	A	B	C	D	E
1	Cost of Repairs	Deductible	Annual Premium	What Insurance Pays	What You Pay
2	TYPE IN THE COST OF REPAIRS	TYPE IN THE DEDUCTIBLE	TYPE IN THE PREMIUM	0	= A2 + C2

3D MEDICAL INSURANCE WHEN YOU MEET YOUR DEDUCTIBLE

When you have medical insurance, you need to pay your deductible before your insurance company pays for health care costs. Use this spreadsheet if you meet your deductible.

	A	B	C	D	E	F
1	Before Insurance	Premium	Deductible	%	Co-Pay	After Insurance
2	TYPE IN THE COST OF MEDICAL BILLS	TYPE IN THE PREMIUM	TYPE IN THE DEDUCTIBLE	TYPE IN THE PERCENT OF CO-PAY	=D2*(A2 - C2)	= B2 + C2 + E2

3D MEDICAL INSURANCE WHEN YOU DO NOT MEET YOUR DEDUCTIBLE

If you don't meet your deductible, the insurance company will not cover healthcare costs. Use this spreadsheet if you don't meet your deductible.

	A	B	C	D	E	F
1	Before Insurance	Premium	Deductible	%	Co-Pay	After Insurance
2	TYPE IN THE COST OF MEDICAL BILLS	TYPE IN THE PREMIUM	TYPE IN THE DEDUCTIBLE	TYPE IN THE PERCENT OF CO-PAY	0	= A2 + B2

4B AMORTIZATION SCHEDULE

When you buy a house, you make a fixed monthly payment each month. Part of this payment goes to pay interest and part goes to pay off the house. Use the amortization schedule to see how much interest you pay each month.

	A	B	C	D	E	F
1	Month	Principal	APR	Monthly Payment	Amount Paid on Interest	Amount Paid on Principal
2	1	TYPE IN THE PRINCIPAL	TYPE IN THE APR	USE THE PMT FUNCTION	= B2 * C2/12	= D2 - E2
3	2	= B2 - F2	= C2	= D2	= B3 * C3/12	= D3 - E3

5B BREAK-EVEN FORMULA

The break-even formula is used to find the minimum number of products or the minimum price you must charge so you break even. In order to make a profit you will have to charge more or sell more than the break-even point.

selling price*(number of units sold) = unit cost*(number of units sold) + fixed costs

5C SALES FORMULA

The sales formula is used when you are putting a product on sale. It can help you find the sale price or the original priced, depending on your needs.

original price - percent discount*(original price) = sale price

5D MARKUP FORMULA

The markup formula is used when a store purchases a product from a wholesale company and needs to mark up the price in order to make a profit.

wholesale price - percent markup*(wholesale price) = list price

5D Trade Discount Formula

The trade discount formula is used when a wholesale company wants to set the list price (the price customers pay) and gives stores a discount.

list price - percent discount*(list price) = wholesale price

6A The Balance Sheet

A balance sheet shows the relationship between what a company owns and what it owes.

	A	B	C	D	E
1	Assets			Liabilities and Equity	
2	Cash			Accounts Payable	
3	Accounts Receivable			Accrued Expenses	
4	Inventory			Current Portion of Debt	
5	Prepaid Expenses			Income Taxes Payable	
6	Current Assets	=SUM(B2:B5)		Current Liabilities	=SUM(E2:E5)
7					
8	Other Assets			Long-Term Liabilities	
9					
10	Fixed Assets at Cost			Capital Stock	
11	Accumulated Depreciation			Retained Earnings	
12	Net Fixed Assets	=SUM(B7:B11)		Shareholder's Equity	=SUM(E7:E11)
13					
14	Total Assets	=B6+B8+B12		Total Liabilities and Equity	=E6+E8+E12
15					

6A Balance Sheet Formula

The balance sheet is based on the following formula, where assests are everything the company owns, libilities are all the debt the company has, and equity is how much the company is worth.

assets = liabilities + equity

6B Gross Margin Formula

The gross margin is the profit on a product after expenses.

gross margin = revenue - cost of goods sold

6B THE INCOME STATEMENT

The income statement shows the relationship between the amount of revenue a company makes compared to its expenses.

	A	B
1	Revenue	
2	Cost of Goods Sold	
3	Gross Margin	=B1-B2
4	% of Revenue	=B3/B1
5	Operating Expenses	
6	% of Revenue	=B5/B1
7	Operating Income	=B1-B2-B5
8	% of Revenue	=B7/B1
9	Non-Operating Income and Expenses	
10	Net Income	=B7-B9
11	% of Revenue	=B10/B1
12		

6B OPERATING INCOME FORMULA

The operating income takes into account the expenses to make a product as well as how much it costs to keep the company open and pay employees.

operating income = gross margin - operating expenses

6B NET INCOME FORMULA

The net income formula shows profit after paying all expenses.

net income = operating income - non-operating expenses

6C TAXABLE INCOME FORMULA

When you earn money, you pay taxes on part of it. Use the taxable income formula to find the amount of money you will be taxed on.

taxable income = gross income - deductions - exemptions

6C FEDERAL INCOME TAXES: INDIVIDUALS

Taxable Income	Tax Bracket	Tax Formula
$0 to $9,225	10%	= 10%*(your taxable income)
$9,226 to $37,450	15%	= $922.50 + 15%*(your taxable income - $9,225)
$37,451 to $90,750	25%	= $5,156.25 + 25%*(your taxable income - $37,450)
$90,751 to $189,300	28%	= $18,481.25 + 28%*(your taxable income - $90,750)
$189,301 to $411,500	33%	= $46,075.25 + 33%*(your taxable income - $189,300)
$411,501 to $413,200	35%	= $119,401.25 + 35%*(your taxable income - $411,500)
Above $413,200	39.6%	= $119,996.25 + 39.6%*(your taxable income - $413,200)

6C FEDERAL INCOME TAXES: HEAD OF HOUSEHOLD

Taxable Income	Tax Bracket	Tax Formula
$0 to $13,150	10%	= 10%*(your taxable income)
$13,151 to $50,200	15%	= $1,135 + 15%*(your taxable income - $13,150)
$50,201 to $129,600	25%	= $6,872.50 + 25%*(your taxable income - $50,200)
$129,601 to $209,850	28%	= $26,772.50 + 28%*(your taxable income - $129,600)
$209,851 to $411,500	33%	= $49,192.50 + 33%*(your taxable income - $209,850)
$411,501 to $439,000	35%	= $115,737 + 35%*(your taxable income - $411,500)
Above $439,000	39.6%	= $125,362 + 39.6%*(your taxable income - $439,000)

6C FEDERAL INCOME TAXES: MARRIED FILING JOINTLY

Taxable Income	Tax Bracket	Tax Formula
$0 to $18,450	10%	= 10%*(your taxable income)
$18,451 to $74,900	15%	= $1,845 + 15%*(your taxable income - $18,450)
$74,901 to $151,200	25%	= $10,312.50 + 25%*(your taxable income - $74,900)
$151,201 to $230,450	28%	= $29,387.50 + 28%*(your taxable income - $151,200)
$230,451 to $411,500	33%	= $51,577.50 + 33%*(your taxable income - $230,450)
$411,501 to $464,850	35%	= $111,324 + 35%*(your taxable income - $411,500)
Above $464,850	39.6%	= $129,996.50 + 39.6%*(your taxable income - $464,850)

6C Federal Income Taxes: Married Filing Separately

Taxable Income	Tax Bracket	Tax Formula
$0 to $9,225	10%	= 10%*(your taxable income)
$9,226 to $37,450	15%	= $922.50 + 15%*(your taxable income - $9,225)
$37,451 to $75,600	25%	= $5,156.25 + 25%*(your taxable income - $37,450)
$75,601 to $115,225	28%	= $14,693.75 + 28%*(your taxable income - $75,600)
$115,226 to $205,750	33%	= $25,788.75 + 33%*(your taxable income - $115,225)
$205,751 to $232,425	35%	= $55,662 + 35%*(your taxable income - $205,750)
Above $232,425	39.6%	= $64,998.25 + 39.6%*(your taxable income - $232,425)

6C State Income Taxes: Individuals

Taxable Income	Tax Bracket	Tax Formula
$0 to $5,500	1.7%	= 1.7%*(your taxable income)
$5,501 to $11,000	3.2%	= $93.50 + 3.2%*(your taxable income - $5,500)
$11,001 to $16,000	4.7%	= $269.50 + 4.7%*(your taxable income - $11,000)
Above $16,000	4.9%	= $504.50 + 4.9%*(your taxable income - $16,000)

6C State Income Taxes: Head of Household or Married Filing Jointly

Taxable Income	Tax Bracket	Tax Formula
$0 to $8,000	1.7%	= 1.7%*(your taxable income)
$8,001 to $16,000	3.2%	= $136 + 3.2%*(your taxable income - $8,000)
$16,001 to $24,000	4.7%	= $392 + 4.7%*(your taxable income - $16,000)
Above $24,000	4.9%	= $768 + 4.9%*(your taxable income - $24,000)

6C State Income Taxes: Married Filing Separately

Taxable Income	Tax Bracket	Tax Formula
$0 to $4,000	1.7%	= 1.7%*(your taxable income)
$4,001 to $8,000	3.2%	= $68 + 3.2%*(your taxable income - $4,000)
$8,001 to $12,000	4.7%	= $196 + 4.7%*(your taxable income - $8,000)
Above $12,000	4.9%	= $384 + 4.9%*(your taxable income - $12,000)

ANSWER KEY

SECTION 1A:

1. Class Discussion
   A. Answers may vary
   B. Answers may vary
   C. Answers may vary

2. Now Do the Math

Coin	Value	Percent of a Dollar
Penny	$0.01	1%
Nickel	$0.05	5%
Dime	$0.10	10%
Quarter	$0.25	25%
Half-Dollar	$0.50	50%
Dollar	$1.00	100%

3. Now Do the Math

Name	Monthly Income	10% Savings
Sarah	$1,500.00	$150.00
Peter	$2,500.00	$250.00
Margaret	$1,175.00	$117.50
Gene	$3,245.00	$324.50

4. What Do You Think?
   A. Gene
   B. Margaret
   C. Their monthly income was different.

5. Now Do the Math in a Spreadsheet

	A	B	C	D
1	Income	10% Savings		
2	$5,800.00	=A2*10% $580.00		
3	$975.00	=A3*10% $97.50		
4	$1,350.55	=A4*10% $135.06		
5	$2,249.20	=A5*10% $224.92		

6. Now Do the Math
   A. $2,400
   B. $6,240
   C. $12,480

SECTION 1C

1. What Are Your Goals?
   A. Answers may vary

2. What Do You Think?
   A. Answers may vary

3. Now Do the Math
   A. The income of $30,000 with $15,000 in fixed expenses
   B. $450
   C. $176.40

4. Now Do the Math in a Spreadsheet
   A. Peter
   B.

	A	B	C	D	E
1	Name	Monthly Income	10% Monthly Savings	Fixed Expenses	Disposable Income
2	Peter	$3,360.00	=B2*10% $336.00	$1,500.00	=B2-C2-D2 $1,524.00
3	Nancy	$3,360.00	=B3*10% $336.00	$1,950.00	=B3-C3-D3 $1,074.00
4	Bill	$3,360.00	=B4*10% $336.00	$2,348.00	=B4-C4-D4 $676.00

5. What Do You Think?
   A. Peter
   B. Bill
   C. Decrease their fixed expenses

6. What Do You Think?
   A. Answers may vary

7. Now Do the Math in a Spreadsheet
   A. Answers may vary

8. Now Do the Math
   A. $53.50
   B. $237.50

9. What Do You Think?
   A. He has a higher disposable income

10. Now Do the Math
   A. 10 months
   B. 15 years

11. Now Do the Math With Your Goals
    A. Answers may vary
    B.

SECTION 1D

1. Now Do the Math in a Spreadsheet

	A	C	D
1	Monthly Budget	Projected	Actual
2	Income	$3,650.00	
3			
4	Monthly Savings	$365.00	
5			
6	Mortgage Payment	$1,250.00	
7	Groceries and Household	$575.00	
8	Health Insurance	$140.00	
9	Car Payment	$289.00	
10	Car Insurance	$82.00	
11	Gas	$120.00	
12	Phone Bill	$113.50	
13	Online Movie Subscription	$11.95	
14	Total Expenses	$2,581.45	
15			
16	Disposable Income	$703.55	
17	Retirement (50%)	$351.78	
18	Craft Supplies (40%)	$281.42	
19	Music and Concerts (10%)	$70.36	

2. Now Do the Math

Carlos' Income = $1,684.94
Susan's Income = $2,104.16
Savings = $378.91
Rent = $800.00
Phone = $75.00
Groceries & Household = $531.68
Daycare = $515.00
Gas = $129.64
Credit Card = $40.00
Student Loans = $224.41
Car Insurance = $105.00
Renter's Insurance = $14.00
Health Insurance = $125.00
Entertainment & Dining = $120.28
Car Payment = $120.00
Utilities = $45.00
Car Maintenance = $65.00
Dental Appointments = $20.00
Clothes = $12.99
Internet = $40.00

3. Now Do the Math in a Spreadsheet

	A	C	D
1	Monthly Budget	Projected	Actual
2	Income	$2,775.00	$2,775.00
3	Savings	$277.50	$277.50
4	Mortgage	$1,120.00	$1,120.00
5	Clothing	$30.00	$55.00
6	Groceries	$500.00	$397.50
7	Total Expenses	$2,110.00	
8	Disposable	$275.00	
9	Eating Out (30%)	$82.50	$78.18
10	Retirement (50%)	$137.50	$130.00
11	Vacation (20%)	$55.00	$55.00

4. What Do You Think?
   A. Clothing is over budget. Groceries, eating out and retirement are under budget.

SECTION 2A

1. What Do You Think?
   A. The rate is a percentage and the interest is a dollar amount.
   B. Answers may vary

2. Now Do the Math
   A. $700
   B. $1,000

3. Now Do the Math in a Spreadsheet

	A	B	C	D
1	Year	Principal	Rate	Interest
2	1	$15,500.00	3%	$465.00
3	2	$15,965.00	3%	$478.95
4	3	$16,443.95	3%	$493.32
5	4	$16,937.27	3%	$508.12
6	5	$17,445.39	3%	$523.36
7	6	$17,968.75	3%	$539.06
8	7	$18,507.81	3%	$555.23
9	8	$19,063.04	3%	$571.89
10				$4,134.94

4. What Do You Think?
   A. Double the principal = $8,269.87, Double the rate = $9,204.65,
   Double the time = $9,372.95
   B. Double the time

Section 2B

1. What Do You Think?
   A. Compound interest increases over time and the longer you wait, the more you will earn.
   B. Answers may vary

2. What Do You Think?
   A. Daily

3. Now Do the Math
   A. $5.02
   B. $0.09

4. Now Do the Math
   A. $300.00
   B. $303.75
   C. $305.67
   D. $306.97
   E. $307.48
   F. $307.60

5. What Do You Think?
   A. Compound Daily

Section 2C

1. What Do You Think?
   A. Answers may vary
   B. Answers may vary

2. Now Do the Math in a Spreadsheet

Name	Principal	Rate	Number of Years	Monthly Payment
Maria	$60,000	6.8%	20	$458.00
John	$40,000	6.8%	20	$305.34
Nancy	$20,000	6.8%	20	$152.67

3. What Do You Think?
   A. Higher principals produce higher monthly payments.
   B. $305.33
   C. Maria = 31 hours, John = 20 hours, Nancy = 10 hours
   D. Maria = 8 hours, John = 5 hours, Nancy = 3 hours

4. Now Do the Math

	A	B	C	D	E	F
1	Month	Principal	Rate	Monthly Payment	Amount Paid on Interest	Amount Paid on Principal
2	1	$35,000.00	4.5%	$362.73	$131.25	$231.48
3	2	$34,768.52	4.5%	$362.73	$130.38	$232.35
120	119	$721.41	4.5%	$362.73	$2.71	$360.03
121	120	$361.38	4.5%	$362.73	$1.36	$361.38
122					$8,528.13	

5. What Do You Think?
   A. The amount paid on principal increases over time.
   B. The amount paid on interest decreases over time.

SECTION 2D

1. What Do You Think?
   A. Answers may vary
   B. Answers may vary
   C. Answers may vary

2. What Do You Think?
   A. Answers may vary

3. Now Do the Math
   A. $40
   B. 50 months
   C. Answers may vary

4. Now Do the Math in a Spreadsheet
   A.

	A	B	C	D	E	F
1	Month	Balance	Rate	2% Minimum Payment	Amount Paid on Interest	Amount Paid on Balance
2	1	$1,500.00	18%	$30.00	$22.50	$7.50
3	2	$1,492.50	18%	$29.85	$22.39	$7.46
?	541	$100.13	18%	$2.00	$1.50	$0.50

B.

	A	B	C	D	E	F
1	Month	Balance	Rate	4% Minimum Payment	Amount Paid on Interest	Amount Paid on Balance
2	1	$1,500.00	18%	$60.00	$22.50	$37.50

3	2	$1,462.50	18%	$58.50	$21.94	$36.56
?	107	$102.47	18%	$4.10	$1.54	$2.56

5. What Do You Think?
    A. When you only pay the minimum payment on your credit card, most of your payment will go towards interest.
    B. By increasing the minimum payment to 4% of the balance, you will save 434 months or 36 years.

6. Now Do the Math
    A. Cash Back = $30, Interest = $28.17
    B. Cash Back = $24, Interest = $10.90
    C. Cash Back = $50, Interest = $78.75

7. What Do You Think?
    A. The interest was higher than the cash back reward.

SECTION 3A

1. What Do You Think?
    A. Answers may vary
    B. Answers may vary

2. Now Do the Math
    A. 0.17
    B. 0.08
    C. 0.5
    D. 0.25

3. Now Do the Math
    A. -$0.80
    B. +$281,000

4. What Do You Think?
    A. $10,950
    B. Answers may vary

SECTION 3B

1. Now Do the Math
    A. Answers may vary
    B. Answers may vary
    C. Answers may vary

2. What Do You Think?
    A. Answers may vary
    B. Answers may vary
    C. Answers may vary

3. Now Do the Math in a Spreadsheet

A. $72,000

B.

	A	B	C	D	E
1	Month	Balance	Rate	Interest	Payment
2	1	$0.00	5%	$0.00	$200.00
3	2	$200.00	5%	$0.83	$200.00
360	359	$164,675.74	5%	$686.15	$200.00
361	360	$165,561.89	5%	$689.84	$200.00

4. What Do You Think?
   A. $93,561.89

SECTION 3C

1. What Do You Think?
   A. Answers may vary
   B. Answers may vary
   C. Answers may vary

2. Now Do the Math in a Spreadsheet

A.

	A	B	C	D	E
1	Cost of Repairs	Deductible	Annual Premium	What Insurance Pays	What You Pay
2	$5458.00	$500.00	$1,275.00	$4,958.00	$1,775.00

B.

	A	B	C	D	E
1	Cost of Repairs	Deductible	Annual Premium	What Insurance Pays	What You Pay
2	$1,530.00	$1,000.00	$1,098.00	$530.00	$2,098.00

3. Now Do the Math in a Spreadsheet

A.

	A	B	C	D	E
1	Cost of Repairs	Deductible	Annual Premium	What Insurance Pays	What You Pay
2	$5,860.00	$500.00	$922.00	$5,360.00	$1,422.00

B.

	A	B	C	D	E
1	Cost of Repairs	Deductible	Annual Premium	What Insurance Pays	What You Pay
2	$315.00	$500.00	$922.00	$0.00	$1,237.00

4. What Do You Think?
   A. Karla benefited the most.
   B. Insurance starts paying off when you meet your deductible.

SECTION 3D

1. What Do You Think?
   A. Answers may vary

2. What Do You Think?
   A. Answers may vary
   B. Answers may vary

3. Now Do the Math in a Spreadsheet
   A. Answers may vary
   B.

Platinum Plan Annual Premium = \$2,760.00 Deductible = \$200.00 Co-Insurance = 10% Sarah Pays = \$3,066.00	Gold Plan Annual Premium = \$1,325.00 Deductible = \$850.00 Co-Insurance = 20% Sarah Pays = \$2,257.00
Silver Plan Annual Premium = \$1,210.00 Deductible = \$1,750.00 Co-Insurance = 30% Sarah Pays = \$2,470.00	Bronze Plan Annual Premium = \$944.00 Deductible = \$5,000.00 Co-Insurance = 50% Sarah Pays = \$2,204.00

4. What Do You Think?
   A. The Bronze plan is the best option for Sarah.

SECTION 4A

1. Now Do the Math
   A. \$462
   B. \$936

2. What Do You Think?
   A. \$1,398
   B. Answers may vary

3. Now Do the Math
   A. \$85.50
   B. \$1,040.25
   C. 24 bags
   D. \$268.79

4. What Do You Think?
   A. \$771.46
   B. Answers may vary

5. What Do You Think?
   A. The brown shoes were the most affordable over a 2 year period.

B. Answers may vary

6. What Do You Think?
    A. Answers may vary
    B. Answers may vary

SECTION 4B

1. Prioritizing
    A. Answers may vary

2. Now Do the Math
    A. The car will be worth $24,000 and will have lost $8,000 after 5 years.

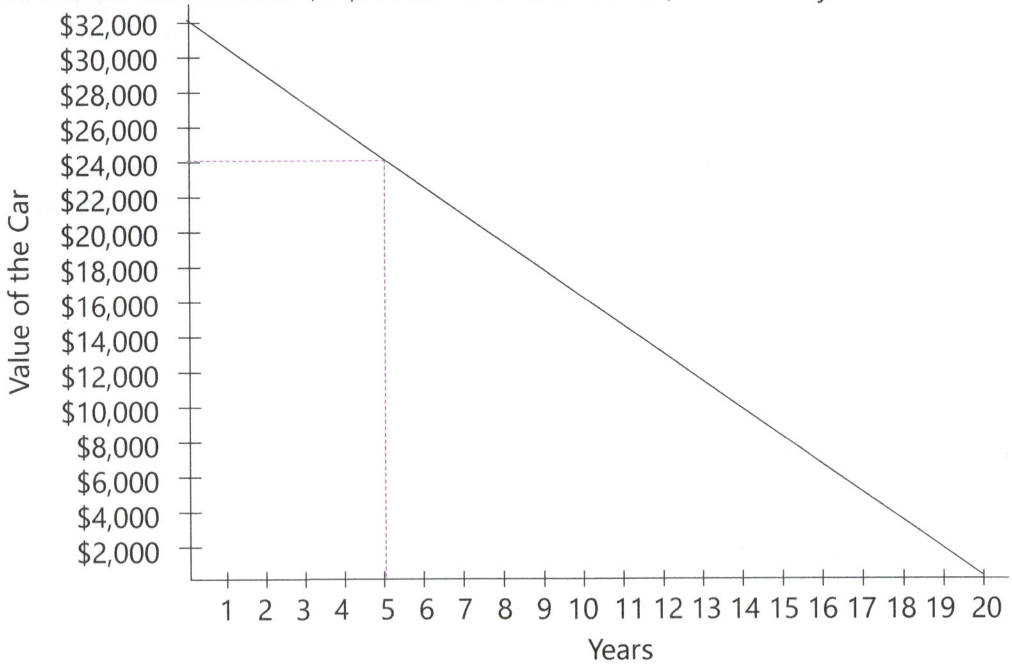

B. The car will be worth approximately $8,000 and will have lost close to $6,000 in value after 10 years.

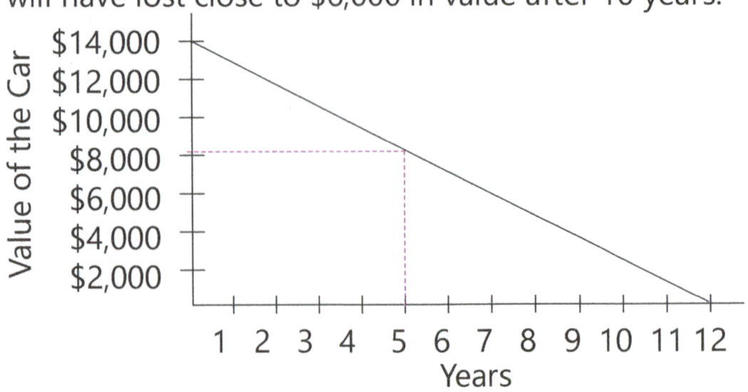

3. What Do You Think?
    A. Answers may vary
    B. Answers may vary

4. Now Do the Math
   A. $5,400
   B. 18 months

5. Now Do the Math
   A. 38 miles per gallon

6. Now Do the Math
   A. $42.69
   B. $104.36

7. What Do You Think?
   A. Answers may vary
   B. Answers may vary

SECTION 4C

1. What Do You Think?
   A. Answers may vary
   B. Answers may vary
   C. Answers may vary
   D. Answers may vary

2. Now Do the Math
   A. $1,623.21
   B. $2,514.94

3. What Do You Think?
   A. 15 years
   B. You have to pay a higher monthly payment in order to pay off the mortgage faster.

4. Now Do the Math
   A. Monthly payment = $1,987.26 Total Amount Paid = $715,414.14 Total cost of interest = $365,414.14
   B. Monthly payment = $1,670.95 Total Amount Paid = $601,543.27 Total cost of interest = $251,543.27
   C. Monthly payment = $2,859.79 Total Amount Paid = $514,762.58 Total cost of interest = $164,762.58

5. What Do You Think?
   A. The second house
   B. The third house
   C. The house with a shorter mortgage
   D. Answers may vary

6. What Do You Think?
   A. Month 1 = $1,750.00, month 12 = $1,730.35, month 60 = $1,630.79, month 120 = $1,467.65, month 360 = $10.44
   B. You pay more interest at the beginning of the mortgage, because the principal is higher. Once your principal goes down, you will pay less in interest each month.

Section 5A

1. Vocabulary Check
    - A. Constant
    - B. Variable
    - C. Variable
    - D. Constant

2. What Do You Think?
    - A. Answers may vary
    - B. Answers may vary

3. Now Do the Math
    - A. 16a - 10
    - B. 11y + 17
    - C. 15n + 9c + 5

4. Vocabulary Check
    - A. Expression
    - B. Equation
    - C. Equation
    - D. Expression

5. What Do You Think?
    - A. Answers may vary
    - B. Answers may vary

6. Now Do the Math
    - A. 10
    - B. 4
    - C. 7
    - D. 44
    - E. 11.50
    - F. 21
    - G. 18
    - H. 14

Section 5B

1. What Do You Think?
    - A. Answers may vary
    - B. Answers may vary
    - C. Answers may vary
    - D. Answers may vary

2. What Do You Think?
    - A. Answers may vary
    - B. Answers may vary
    - C. Answers may vary

3. What Do You Think?

A. Answers may vary
B. Answers may vary
C. Answers may vary

4. What Do You Think?
   A. Answers may vary
   B. Answers may vary
   C. Answers may vary

5. What Do You Think?
   A. Answers may vary
   B. Answers may vary
   C. Answers may vary

6. Now Do the Math
   A. $7.25
   B. Answers may vary
   C. 1,007 cups of coffee

Section 5C

1. What Do You Think?
   A. High supply with low demand

2. Now Do the Math
   A. $180
   B. $450
   C. $600

3. What Do You Think?
   A. $3.00 for 200 tacos

4. What Do You Think?
   A. $1,050

5. What Do You Think?
   A. The original price

6. Now Do the Math
   A. $32
   B. $1.90
   C. $299.25

7. Now Do the Math
   A. 25%
   B. 33%

8. Now Do the Math
   A. $22.50
   B. $97.60
   C. $347.54

SECTION 5D

1. What Do You Think?
   A. Answers may vary

2. What Do You Think?
   A. The list price

3. Now Do the Math
   A. $8.96
   B. $309.04
   C. $67.15

4. Now Do the Math
   A. $7.98
   B. $224.99

SECTION 6A

1. Now Do the Math
   A. $27,000
   B. $43,000
   C. $17,000

2. What Do You Think?
   A. Answers may vary

3. The Balance Sheet and Your Budget
   A. Answers may vary
   B. Answers may vary
   C. Answers may vary

4. Vocabulary Check
   A. Inventory
   B. Other Assets
   C. Prepaid Expenses
   D. Accumulated Depreciation
   E. Accounts Receivable
   F. Cash
   G. Fixed Assets at Cost
   H. Inventory
   I. Cash

5. Vocabulary Check
   A. Current Portion of Debt
   B. Income Taxes Payable
   C. Accrued Expenses
   D. Accounts Payable
   E. Long-Term Debt
   F. Long-Term Debt

6. Vocabulary Check
   A. Owner's Equity
   B. Retained Earnings

7. What Do You Think?
   A. Answers may vary

SECTION 6B

1. Now Do the Math
   A. $21,250
   B. $51,200
   C. $12,700
   D. $31,000

2. Now Do the Math

	A	B
1	Revenue	$5,480.00
2	Cost of Goods Sold	$750.00
3	Gross Margin	$4,730.00
4	% of Revenue	86%
5	Operating Expenses	$2,900.00
6	% of Revenue	53%
7	Operating Income	$1,830.00
8	% of Revenue	33%
9	Non-Operating Expenses	$1,400.00
10	Net Income	$430.00
11	% of Revenue	8%

SECTION 6C

1. What Do You Think?
   A. Answers may vary

2. Now Do the Math
   A. Payroll taxes = $66.17, pay after payroll taxes = $931.17
   B. Payroll taxes = $116.66, pay after payroll taxes = $1,408.34
   C. Payroll taxes = $358.33, pay after payroll taxes = $2,700.33

3. Now Do the Math
   A. $37,950

4. Now Do the Math
   A. $5,281.25

5. Now Do the Math
   A. $1,580.05

6. Now Do the Math

A. He will receive a refund of $757.50
B. He will owe $317.55

7. What Do You Think?
A. He paid a lower percentage.
B. 14%

SECTION 7A

1. Describe Your Company
A. Answers may vary
B. Answers may vary
C. Answers may vary
D. Answers may vary
E. Answers may vary
F. Answers may vary
G. Answers may vary

2. Complete a SWOT Analysis
A. Answers may vary
B. Answers may vary
C. Answers may vary
D. Answers may vary
E. Answers may vary
F. Answers may vary
G. Answers may vary
H. Answers may vary

3. How Do You Face Challenges?
A. Answers may vary
B. Answers may vary
C. Answers may vary
D. Answers may vary
E. Answers may vary
F. Answers may vary

SECTION 7B

1. Product/Service Description
A. Answers may vary
B. Answers may vary
C. Answers may vary
D. Answers may vary
E. Answers may vary
F. Answers may vary

2. Which Goals are SMART
A. None
B. Specific, Measurable, Achievable, Realistic, Timely
C. Specific, Measurable, Timely

3. Employee Chart
    - A. Answers may vary

SECTION 7C

1. What Do You Think?
    - A. Answers may vary
    - B. Answers may vary

2. What Do You Think?
    - A. Answers may vary
    - B. Answers may vary
    - C. Answers may vary
    - D. Answers may vary

3. Now Your Turn
    - A. Answers may vary

4. Create a Marketing Plan
    - A. Answers may vary
    - B. Answers may vary
    - C. Answers may vary

5. What Do You Think?
    - A. Answers may vary
    - B. Answers may vary

SECTION 7D

1. What Do You Think?
    - A. Answers may vary
    - B. Answers may vary

2. What Do You Think?
    - A. Answers may vary
    - B. Answers may vary

3. What Do You Think?
    - A. Answers may vary
    - B. Answers may vary

4. Your Break-Even Point
    - A. Answers may vary
    - B. Answers may vary
    - C. Answers may vary
    - D. Answers may vary

5. Your Balance Sheet
    - A. Answers may vary

CPSIA information can be obtained at www.ICGtesting.com
Printed in the USA
LVOW01s1109120815

449831LV00010B/160/P